PETO'S REGISTER OF
GREAT WESTERN
RAILWAY
LOCOMOTIVES

Edited by Martin Smith

Workaday Manor - 7805 BROOME MANOR at Reading, 1950.

VOLUME TWO
Manor 4-6-0s

IRWELL
PRESS

Contents

Acknowledgements

We are deeply indebted to all those who provided advice and
assistance during the preparation of this book. They are:
Messrs. Eric Youldon and Bryan Wilson, who undertook a
considerable amount of research on our behalf, and Maurice
Dart, Ron Hacker, Chris Hawkins, Peter Herring, John
Hodge, Alan Lathey, Gerry Parkins, R.C.Riley, George Reeve
and Michele Smith. Sincere thanks to you all.
Bill Peto, London
Martin Smith, Coleford, Somerset

First Published in the United Kingdom by
IRWELL PRESS 1996
P.O.Box 1260, Caernarfon, Gwynedd, LL55 3ZD
Printed in Huddersfield by The Amadeus Press

Foreword

7824 IFORD MANOR heads 6925 HACKNESS HALL on Rattery, 1954.

This book - the second of what is hoped will be a lengthy series - owes itself to Bill Peto's researches. Bill is one of the best respected authorities on the Great Western Railway, and combines his role as the Historical Research Officer of the Great Western Society with a genuine enthusiasm for all things GWR. Over many years he has amassed a vast amount of detailed information about GWR locomotives, most of it from Swindon records and other official sources, and has gradually collated the material in the form of the *Peto Registers*.

Although the registers are derived mainly from primary reference sources, it should be emphasised that, in the case of some locomotive classes which survived after 1963 - including the Manors - official records were not always maintained as impeccably as might be desired. Consequently, in order to build a complete and, it is hoped, wholly reliable, picture of the Manors' activities, it has been necessary to cross-reference official documents with tried and tested secondary sources. By combining and cross-referencing material from various sources, it has been possible to build a comprehensive picture of the engines' allocations, works visits, repairs, boiler and tender changes and so on - right through to the very end of their lives. This book devotes considerable space to the duties undertaken by the engines - information gleaned largely from contemporary magazines, in particular the *Railway Observer*, but, where appropriate, we have conducted additional research to confirm or enlarge on certain events.

Our aim - bold, conceited, or just plain idealistic - is that this and other books in the series will be the most comprehensive works on their respective subjects. While every care has been taken to ensure as great a degree of accuracy as possible in this book, the authors readily acknowledge that they are far from infallible - witness the *Addenda and Corrigenda*. While the authors have explored a huge variety of avenues in order to present as thorough a picture as possible, there are certain topics about which further details were simply unavailable. But all is not lost. As this book is part of an on-going series, we are fortunate in that additional information can be presented and errors corrected in a subsequent volume. With those aims in mind, we would welcome further information or, where appropriate, confirmation (or otherwise!) of matters raised in the text.

The official portrait - No.7800 TORQUAY MANOR ex-works at Swindon in 1938. PHOTOGRAPH: BY ARRANGEMENT JOHN TATCHELL

Chapter One
The Background

The Manor class 4-6-0s were intended to fulfil a specific requirement, as opposed to being just an up-to-date addition to the GWR fleet of mixed traffic types. To understand the background to their introduction in 1938, we actually need to go back to 1911, when the GWR introduced one of its most successful locomotive types ever. This was the 43XX class mixed traffic 2-6-0, of which 322 were eventually built to the original design with a further twenty, with various improvements but an increase in weight, constructed in 1932. The 43XXs were not only very well designed and constructed, but they were also extremely versatile; the engines built to the original design - i.e. *excluding* the 1932 examples - had a maximum axleweight of 18tons 4cwt (later reduced to 17 tons 13cwt) which enabled them to work on 'Blue' routes (see page 6). The 43XXs were capable of handling almost any job they were given. One well-known story - apocryphal, perhaps - relates that on one occasion when Charles Collett was travelling on the highly prestigious 'Cheltenham Flyer', he blinked in disbelief when the 'Flyer' was overtaken on a parallel track by a passenger train hauled by a 43XX.

Despite the success of the 43XXs, in some quarters it was considered that the basic idea could be developed to greater effect. The Running Department pressed for a locomotive based on a 43XX but with a Standard No.1 boiler for greater power and a longer wheelbase and leading bogie for improved stability; however, one problem was that such a locomotive would have a heavier axleweight and, consequently, would not qualify for 'Blue' route availability. The Locomotive Superintendent, George Jackson Churchward, favoured, instead, the eight-coupled format, his eventual response being the introduction, in 1919, of the 47XX class 2-8-0s. As things turned out, the Standard No.1 boiler fitted to the prototype 47XX was found to be inadequate for the locomotive`s needs, and so the engine was subsequently rebuilt with a much larger boiler, raising the axleweight ironically,

to the highest so far seen on the GWR. Churchward was succeeded in 1922 by Charles Collett who also accepted that there was a requirement for larger mixed traffic locomotives. Collett addressed the situation in 1924 when he rebuilt Saint class 4-6-0 No.2925 SAINT MARTIN with 6ft 0in coupled wheels in place of 6ft 8½in. The rebuilt locomotive became the forerunner of the Hall class, and between 1928 and 1950 no less than 329 locomotives were built to basically similar specifications. The unwitting prototype, No.2925, was subsequently renumbered 4900. The Halls were extremely successful, but they did not circumvent the problem of route availability as their maximum

Nameplate of No.7808. PHOTOGRAPH: IAN S. CARR

axleweight of 18tons 19cwt placed them in the 'Red' category.

By the mid-1930s, the problem of motive power for 'Blue' routes had become a little more pressing, mainly because the earlier 43XX 2-6-0s were, by then, a little past the first flush of youth. Somewhat perversely, though, the continuing construction of new 2-6-0s (until 1925) had provided the GWR with more of the engines than the Traffic Department actually required. The GWR announced its solution - to the problem and the perversity - in 1936. The matter was to be resolved by withdrawing the older 43XXs and incorporating some of the parts - mainly wheels and motion - in ten new Grange class 4-6-0s (the relevant lot number eventually covered eighty Granges) and ten new Manor class 4-6-0s. The Granges were to be similar to the Halls but with 5ft 8in coupled wheels - the reduction in axleweight was a mere one hundredweight, and this didn't lift the Granges

out of the 'Red' category - but the Manors were to be fitted with smaller, lighter boilers, which would reduce their axleweight to within the limits of the 'Blue' category.

The first Granges were completed later in 1936, but work on the Manors did not commence immediately. The delay was partly because an effective stopgap had been found to the shortage of engines suitable for lighter routes. The stopgap took the form of reconditioned Bulldog class 4-4-0s - twenty-nine of these veteran double framed engines had been fitted with 'Duke' type boilers, which reduced their axleweight from 'blue' to 'yellow' status, thereby making them suitable for lighter routes such as those of the Cambrian system in Wales. (The original intention, incidentally, had been to recondition forty Bulldogs).

Digressing slightly, it should be mentioned that, during the 1930s, Swindon seemed to have what has been politely described as a 'make do and mend' policy. Not only were the 43XXs 'converted' to Granges and Manors, and Bulldogs and Dukes reconditioned into hybrids, but some 42XX 2-8-0Ts were converted to 2-8-2Ts and some 51XX 2-6-2Ts into 81XXs. Also, it could be argued that the 'new' 48XX (later 14XX) 0-4-2Ts and the 2251 class 0-6-0s weren't much more than reincarnations of older designs. There were various reasons for this - the inevitable bottom line being a quest for economy - but after the impressive designs of the Churchward era it was a time of comparative stagnation at Swindon.

Returning to the matter in hand, the emergence of the reconditioned 4-4-0s in 1936 meant that the requirement for lightweight 4-6-0s was less urgent. On the subject of the reconditioned 4-4-0s, enthusiasts usually referred to them as 'Earls' while enginemen referred to 'New 32s'; in later years they were known by some enthusiasts as 'Dukedogs' (as they incorporated some parts from the Duke and Bulldog class locos), but it seems the sobriquet was actually dreamed up by a certain publisher for a trainspotting readership. Whatever the

One of the first batch of Manors was No.7810 DRAYCOTT MANOR. It is seen in its original condition leaving Twyford with a Trowbridge-Paddington train sometime in 1946. As 7810 was allocated to Banbury throughout that year it is tempting (despite the engine's less than immaculate condition) to suggest that this working might have been a running-in turn after a 'general' at Swindon. PHOTOGRAPH: MAURICE EARLEY

origins of the term 'Dukedog', it was wholly unofficial.

Work on the Manors was put in hand in 1937, and the initial order was apparently for twenty instead of just ten, as had been announced earlier. As we shall see later, a further twenty Manors were ordered in 1939, but one might ask whether the additional twenty hadn't actually been under consideration from the outset. This query is based on the names given to the first twenty engines - ignoring the first, No.7800 TORQUAY MANOR, the name sequence was roughly alphabetical, starting with ANTHONY (No.7801) and finishing with HINTON (No.7819). If the GWR intended that the class should comprise no more than twenty engines, would the name sequence for those engines (No.7800 excepted) really have run only from 'A' to 'H'? It is one of those wonderfully pointless debates.

The total weight of the Manors was a little over five tons less than that of the Granges - 68tons 18cwt compared to 74 tons - but apart from frames which were shorter at the rear by some 15ins and the use of a lightweight running plate, almost all of the weight saving was achieved by incorporating a smaller boiler and firebox. The boiler, designated Standard No.14, had been

specially designed for the Manors, with weight saving a prime consideration. Many other features were identical to those of the Granges - 5ft 8in diameter driving wheels (a long favoured Swindon dimension for mixed traffic locomotives) contained in a wheelbase of 27ft 1in, the same combined castings for cylinders, steamchest and saddle, and the same heavy motion. Although the Grange cylinder castings were used for the Manors, the latter were bored to 18in diameter instead of 18½in.

The leading dimensions of the Manors, as given by the GWR, were:

Cylinders: (2) 18" diameter by 30" stroke
Boiler: Barrel 12' 6"; diameter outside 4' 7⅝" and 5' 3"; pitch 8' 4"
Firebox: Length outside 8' 8⅛"
Tubes: Fire - 158 x 2"; flue - 12 x 5⅛"; element 72 x 1"
Heating surfaces: Tubes - 1285.5sqft; firebox 140sqft; superheater 190sqft (later altered). Total 1615.5sqft
Grate area: 22.1sqft
Boiler pressure: 225lb
Wheels: Coupled 5' 8"; bogie 3' 0"
Wheelbase (engine): 7'0" + 5'4" + 7'0" + 7'9"; total 27'1"
Weights (full): bogie - 18t 10c
leading - 17t 5c

driving - 17t 1c
trailing - 16t 2c
Total engine - 68t 18c
Tender - 40t 0c
Tender capacities: 7 tons, 3,500gall
Tractive effort (@ 85%): 27,340lb
Power Classification: 'D' (later classified '5MT' by BR)

Usually, a new type of locomotive received considerable attention in the railway press, but a statement in *The Locomotive* of 15 March 1938 was disappointingly matter of fact: *'Twenty of a new class are now being constructed at Swindon Works to the designs of Mr C.B.Collett, chief mechanical engineer. They are of the 4-6-0 general utility type and will be used on express passenger and freight train services....These engines are slightly smaller than the "Grange" class....'*

The report continued: *'The first of the class, No.7800 TORQUAY MANOR, has been put into service to work the Banbury-Swansea portion of the through service from Newcastle to South Wales* (but was that last statement totally accurate, or was it railway company PR? We shall see.....). *It is expected that the next nine locomotives of the class will be turned out from Swindon Works within the course of the next few weeks, and the remainder of the class by the end of the summer".*

The April issue of *The Railway Magazine* added that the Banbury-Swansea trains ran: '*.....over the Banbury-Stow-on-the-Wold-Cheltenham branch* (sic), *on which nothing larger than a 2-6-0 of the "4321" class* (these were the second batch of 43XXs, which had slightly increased weights) *has previously been permitted to work.....While the new 4-6-0s are some 3¹/₂tons heavier than the 2-6-0s, the provision of a bogie has enabled a more even distribution of weight over the axles*'.

In some quarters, it was anticipated that the Manors would permit an acceleration of schedules or an increase in loadings on the Banbury-Cheltenham section. However, the official GWR line was that the new locomotives were intended to work to existing schedules and with existing loadings, although an all-round increase in efficiency was expected. Those who had expected to see any earth-shattering performances from the Manors were, in fact, very disappointed as, from the outset, the locomotives gained a reputation as rather poor steamers. It is possible that, had it not been for the outbreak of war in 1939, one of the class might have been taken into Swindon Works for evaluation at the test plant, but this had to wait until BR times.

There was a school of thought that, if one regarded a Manor simply as a Grange with a smaller boiler, an inferior steaming capability should have been anticipated by the design team. It has since been opined - admittedly, with the benefit of hindsight - that if the Manors had been designed with a shorter, more compact chassis, it might have been possible to utilise a larger boiler while retaining an axleweight within the limitations of 'Blue' routes. However, we shall probably never know whether an adequately balanced engine could have been accommodated on a shorter chassis. An alternative opinion is that the Manors were hampered by Swindon's enthusiasm for the use of standard components - "standardisation carried too far", it has been suggested. That opinion is certainly valid, but it prompts another question. If the Manors had to incorporate an abundance of new design features and specially built components, would they have been considered a cost-effective proposition? In other words, would they have been built at all? Without wishing to prolong the debate unnecessarily, one might draw a parallel with Gresley's V4 2-6-2s for the LNER - excellent engines, superbly constructed, and acceptable on over 75% of LNER routes. But at what price? In straight financial terms, Gresley's V4s cost some £7,900 each, whereas the GWR Manors (though with the benefit of incorporating existing parts) cost only £5,015 apiece. Furthermore, non-standard features made the 2-6-2s expensive to maintain - perhaps the bottom line in this argument is that the non-standard Gresley V4s were withdrawn as early as 1957. Returning to the subject in hand, the Manors' mediocre steaming was later blamed on the draughting arrangement, but it was not until the 1950s that the problem was resolved - more of which anon.

Mention was made earlier of the GWR's proposal to incorporate parts of withdrawn 43XX 2-6-0s in Grange and Manor class 4-6-0s. This was indeed done, although there are no records showing exactly what proportion of each Mogul was recycled. There are various opinions about this - some sources state that in most cases little more than wheels and motion were reused, another that approximately 50% of each Mogul was reused, while a former GWR footplateman considers that about the only parts *not* to be reused were the boilers and side sheets. It is even unclear whether the 43XXs' frames were reused - after all, the old frames would be likely to require repairs before too long, and the provision of new frames would have been a better long-term proposition. As far as we are aware there is no surviving documentation which can provide the definitive answer to this matter, and so we shall probably never know the full story. Although a record of 'recycled' 43XXs was kept by the GWR (and is

No.7818 GRANVILLE MANOR, only a few months old, on 6 May 1939 at Tyseley. The early Mogul pattern wheel centres can be clearly seen. PHOTOGRAPH: R.C. RILEY COLLECTION

Whereas some sheds used their Manors mainly for passenger duties, others - particularly those in the West Midlands or the Border Counties - used theirs as all-round mixed traffic engines. Oswestry's No.7809 CHILDREY MANOR hauls an up ballast train between Tyseley and Acocks Green on 6 June 1962. PHOTOGRAPH: MICHAEL MENSING

given in page 7), the list was little more than a book-keeping exercise which, if taken only superficially, can be extremely misleading.

We can quote one specific example which illustrates how misleading such records can be. As mentioned earlier, the 'Earl' 4-4-0s were built using parts from Bulldog 4-4-0s, and when the Bluebell Railway dismantled the only preserved representative, No.3217, for repair, the engine's true pedigree was revealed. Official records stated that this engine had been rebuilt using parts from No.3258 THE LIZARD, but the Bluebell engineers found nothing at all from No.3258. Instead, many parts bore evidence of having come from No.3282 CHEPSTOW CASTLE which, according to the official records, had been incorporated in No.3216. Don't say that we didn't issue a warning!

The original proposal was to renew *all* the 43XXs as either Granges or Manors, but that was one of many proposals shelved during World War II, never to be resuscitated. With the benefit of hindsight, one might ask whether that proposal had considered the problems of turning the larger engines at the end of various secondary routes - the turntables at many of the locations where the 4-6-0s would have been required to work simply couldn't accommodate anything larger than a 2-6-0 or 4-4-0 and, furthermore, at

some of those places extension bars had to be used even for those types.

At the outbreak of war eighty Granges and twenty Manors had been built - all containing, nominally at least, parts of withdrawn 43XXs - but that is as far as the programme ever reached. In 1939 an order was placed for another twenty Manors as replacements for a similar number of 43XXs. The proposed names for the new engines more or less picked up the alphabetical sequence with the letter 'H'. They were:

7820	HENLEY MANOR
7821	HUGHENDEN MANOR
7822	HUNTLEY MANOR
7823	IFTON MANOR
7824	KENFIG MANOR
7825	LECKWITH MANOR
7826	LIDDINGTON MANOR
7827	MEMBURY MANOR
7828	MARDEN MANOR
7829	NEWNHAM MANOR
7830	NORTON MANOR
7831	OGWELL MANOR
7832	PIMLEY MANOR
7833	RAMSBURY MANOR
7834	RODLEY MANOR
7835	STANDEN MANOR
7836	SUTTON MANOR
7837	THORNTON MANOR
7838	WIDFORD MANOR
7839	WILCOTE MANOR

The order for those twenty was subsequently cancelled due to the outbreak of war and when peace was restored the order was not reinstated. Further-

more, as mentioned earlier, the proposal to rebuild *all* of the 43XXs as either Manors or Granges also fell by the wayside. From the turntable point of view, this might be considered a blessing in disguise.

However, an additional ten Manors, Nos.7820-7829, were constructed by BR in November and December 1950. It might be thought that, as a continuation of an existing class, their names would follow the near-alphabetical sequence of their predecessors, but things didn't work exactly like that. As discussed earlier, the name sequence of the original twenty engines finished with the letter 'H' (HINTON MANOR - No.7819), but the list of names given to the ten new engines started with the letter 'D' (DINMORE MANOR, No.7820, and DITCHEAT MANOR, No.7821). A likely explanation is provided by a GWR ledger - in 1937 the Lords of Dinmore and Ditcheat Manors had written to the GWR requesting that locomotives be named after their properties, and the GWR had agreed. British Railways was, presumably, carrying out these wishes, albeit thirteen years on. Despite the foregoing, we can find no similar reason to explain why No.7822 was named FOXCOTE MANOR, thus interrupting the alphabetical sequence. As a last word on the topic, it is interesting to note that of the names proposed for the twenty Manors ordered in 1939, only one - RAMSBURY MANOR - was actually used for the 1950 engines.

It has often been stated that the ten new Manors of 1950 were built specially for service on the Cambrian system, but their initial allocations do not substantiate that statement. As will be seen from the registers, three went to Oswestry, two to Croes Newydd, two to Chester, one to Cheltenham and two to Neath. The new engines cost £8,189 apiece compared to the £5,015 of each of the pre-war examples. The sharp hike in price might have been due to the fact that the BR-built engines did not incorporate parts of 43XXs, but all prices had risen greatly since pre-war days. In 1953 Swindon requested permission to construct a further ten Manors (Nos.7830-7839) primarily for the Cambrian section, but the British Railways Board refused and, instead, allotted a small batch of Standard 4MT (75XXX) 4-6-0s to that section.

The ten new Manors of 1950, Nos.7820-7829, were built to the same specifications as their pre-war counterparts. That raised a few eyebrows on two counts. Firstly, the original engines were widely regarded as very mediocre steamers, but no effort had been made to rectify this for the new engines. The lack of action was almost certainly due to the hiatus that had been caused by the war - any plans to take one of the original engines into Swindon Works for evaluation on the test plant had had to be shelved, and in the late 1940s and early 1950s there was still much work outstanding on other projects. There simply hadn't been the opportunity to investigate what was wrong with the original design. There was another surprise caused by the design of the post-war Manors. In 1944, Frederick Hawksworth (who had succeeded Charles Collett in 1941) had introduced several new features on his Modified Halls, and although these were also to be found on the County 4-6-0s of 1945, the ten new Manors did not incorporate the new design features. On the Modified Halls and Counties these were subtle, but they represented a huge swing away from design practices which had been established decades earlier by George Churchward for locomotives with two outside cylinders. They included full plate frames (instead of plate frames for the coupled wheels and a bar frame extension), and individual cylinder castings and a separate smokebox saddle (instead of cylinder, steamchest and half saddle cast as one unit).

So - why didn't the Manors which were built in 1950 incorporate the new features which had been developed by Hawksworth? There appears to be three possible explanations - perhaps a revision of the original Manor design was considered unwarranted for only ten extra engines, or maybe the Hawksworth modifications had, by then, shown no real advantage. Alternatively, the internal politics of the era might have held sway. By 1950 new BR 'Standard' designs were emerging, and in the interim the British Railways Board would sanction only existing designs - a revised version of the Manors would not have been regarded as an existing design. Whatever the case, Hawksworth had by then retired, and so he was unable to influence any decisions. Consequently, Britain did not see what might have been designated 'Modified Manors'.

The Manors went on to gain a considerable following among enthusiasts. They had unmistakable Swindon lines, albeit on a slightly smaller scale, and were seen on some routes where no other GWR 4-6-0s had previously penetrated. Conversely, they appeared only infrequently at other locations and, for much of their lives, it was unusual to see one in London. Instead, they established strongholds in the West Country and on the Cambrian, and it is, perhaps, the latter area with which the class is most strongly associated. Indeed, twenty were allocated - at one time or another - to sheds servicing the Cambrian system, and every single one would have traversed Cambrian metals at some stage in their

One of the BR-built engines, No.7823 HOOK NORTON MANOR, piloting a Hall, comes off the Royal Albert Bridge with an up train on an unspecified date in 1958. The Manors were closely associated with Devon and Cornwall from the late 1940s until the late 1950s. PHOTOGRAPH: MAURICE EARLEY

In the BR era, the Manors were regularly used on pilot duties on the South Devon banks. This is No.7812 ERLESTOKE MANOR piloting No.7028 CADBURY CASTLE near Hemerdon signal box with the up 'Cornish Riviera' on Sunday 6 September 1959. PHOTOGRAPH: DEREK CROSS

lives. Many saw out their days on the Shrewsbury-Aberystwyth route and a number were actually withdrawn from Shrewsbury shed. Nevertheless, despite the strong Celtic connection, only one - No.7826 - actually spent its entire life allocated to Welsh sheds. For what it is worth, No.7826's Welsh connection was still in evidence at the very end, as it was eventually cut up in Wales.

The Manors were the last class of GWR 4-6-0s to remain intact, the first withdrawal being that of No.7809 in April 1963. By the start of 1964 the other twenty-nine still remained (see page 7), but as from the end of that year no repairs were undertaken. Inevitably, this took its toll on the general condition of the surviving engines. For the record, the last to undergo heavy repairs was No.7802 (in Swindon Works 17.6.64 to 28.8.64), while the last to undergo *any* sort of repair was No.7803, which had a light casual at Swindon between 31.7.64 and 21.10.64. At the beginning of 1965 no less than nineteen Manors were still in BR stock, but that year was to be the last for the class. The final two representatives, Nos.7808 and 7829 of Gloucester, were withdrawn from BR service in December.

Somewhat ironically, no less than nineteen Manors ended their days

in London Midland Region stock. This was a result of regional boundary changes in which five WR sheds - and their locomotives - passed to LMR control at the end of 1962. But wherever the Manors ended their days, it is heartening to note that nine of the class - almost *one third* - were eventually saved for preservation.

It is traditional to comment on the mileages achieved by locomotive classes, but it is impossible to give precise figures for the Manors as the recording of mileages ceased on 28 December 1963. At this date, the highest and lowest mileages accredited to the GWR-built Manors were: No.7807 (949,807) and No.7813 (704,558). The figures for the BR-built examples were: No.7827 (468,993) and No.7829 (394,695). Taking into account the locomotives' subsequent life-spans and duties, it is possible to estimate the highest and lowest lifetime mileages. Our calculations are: **GWR-built engines**: Highest - probably No.7819 (approx. 980,000) followed by No.7807 (approx. 970,000). Lowest - probably No.7813 (approx. 740,000). **BR-built engines:** Highest - Nos.7822 or 7827 (approx. 520,000). Lowest - probably No.7829 (approx. 420,000).

'COLOUR CODING'

In July 1905 the GWR introduced a

system of colour codes to denote which types of locomotives were permitted on which routes; from *circa* 1919 a locomotive's classification was shown in the form of a coloured circle on the cabside. The system was based on axle weights, but it should be pointed out that that it was not adhered to rigidly. The 43XX class 2-6-0s provide evidence of the flexibility of the system - as will be seen below, routes categorised 'Blue' could nominally accept locos with axleweights of up to 17tons 12cwt, but the 43XXs, which were 'Blue' engines, had a maximum axleweight of 17tons 13cwt - i.e. one hundredweight over the prescribed limit. Also, in 1950 the 57XX class 0-6-0PTs were re-categorised from 'Blue' to 'Yellow', although the engines had not had one ounce pared from their axleweights. The categories were as follows:

Route colour	Max. axle load
Uncoloured	14 tons 0cwt
Yellow	16 tons 0cwt
Blue	17tons 12cwt
Red	All others except 'King' class
Double Red	'King Class'

There were also the intermediate categories of 'Dotted Blue' and 'Dotted Red' (introduced *circa* 1913), although these were shown only on official maps and *not* on the cabsides. 'Blue' engines were permitted on 'Dotted Blue' routes, and 'Red' engines on 'Dotted Red' routes, but were subject to speed limits of 25mph and 20mph respectively. The August 1938 issue of the *GWR Magazine* explained how the company`s network was categorised at that time:

Route colour	Total miles	%
Uncoloured	495	13%
Yellow	695	18%
Dotted Blue	150	4%
Blue	320	9%
Dotted Red	295	8%
Red	1,280	34%
Double Red	522	14%

WITHDRAWN 43XX 2-6-0s INCORPORATED IN THE MANORS

As emphasised in the text, this list was for book-keeping purposes only. It is included here only for the sake of completeness.

Manor	built	2-6-0	wdn
7800	1/38	8363	9/37
7801	1/38	4322	9/37
7802	1/38	4321	9/37
7803	1/38	4316	9/37
7804	2/38	4343	10/37
7805	3/38	8301	10/37
7806	3/38	4389	10/37
7807	3/38	4382	1/38
7808	3/38	4369	2/38
7809	3/38	4379	2/38
7810	4/38	4307	3/38
7811	12/38	4312	3/38
7812	1/39	4325	4/38
7813	1/39	4319	5/38
7814	1/39	4342	5/38
7815	1/39	4360	5/38
7816	1/39	4399	5/38
7817	1/39	4302	6/38
7818	1/39	4349	6/38
7819	2/39	4355	6/38

DECLINING NUMBERS IN SERVICE. DATES REFER TO THE END OF THE 'RAILWAY MONTH'

Month	Total	Month	Total
3/63	30	8/64	25
4/63	29	9/64	24
5/63	29	10/64	23
6/63	29	11/64	20
7/63	29	12/64	19
8/63	29	1/65	18
9/63	29	2/65	18
10/63	29	3/65	18
11/63	29	4/65	16
12/63	29	5/65	15
1/64	29	6/65	15
2/64	29	7/65	13
3/64	29	8/65	13
4/64	29	9/65	11
5/64	28	10/65	9
6/64	27	11/65	2
7/64	26	12/65	0

MANOR 4-6-0s - PASSENGER TRAIN LOADING RESTRICTIONS

Weights in tons. Loadings for other classes shown for comparison.
N.B: Although loading restrictions were issued for numerous branch lines and secondary routes, many such lines were never actually traversed by the Manors. For that reason, a number of restrictions which were given in WTTs are not listed here.

M=Manors
H/G=Halls/Granges

	M	H/G
Paddington-Bath-Bristol	420	420
Bristol-Taunton	420	420
Taunton-Bristol	420	450
Bristol-Bath-Swindon	392	420
Bristol-Filton Jct (through)	364	392
Filton Jct-Badminton	420	455
Badminton-Swindon	455	485
Swindon-Paddington	455	485
Paddington-Pilning HL	420	420
Pilning-Severn Tunnel Jct	406	420
Severn Tunnel Jct-Cardiff	420	420
Cardiff-Neath	406	420
Neath-Swansea	364	392
Swansea-Cockett	252	280
Cockett-Carmarthen	420	420
Carmarthen-Fishguard	364	392
Fishguard-Manorowen	266	280
Manorowen-Whitland	336	364
Whitland-Carmarthen	336	370
Carmarthen-Gowerton North	360	395
Gowerton North-Cockett	266	280
Cockett-Neath	392	427
Neath-Cardiff	406	420

Another BR-built example, No.7827 LYDHAM MANOR, with a typical working on a customary route - a local train on the Cambrian main line. The date is 4 June 1964, and the location is Talerddig. PHOTOGRAPH: DEREK CROSS

'Cambrian Coast' close-up - and the later style of headboard. No.7821 DITCHEAT MANOR at Shrewsbury on 11 June 1963. PHOTOGRAPH: B.J. ASHWORTH

Westbury-Yeovil	392	420
Yeovil-Yetminster	400	420
Yetminster-Evershot	232	260
Evershot-Weymouth	392	420
Weymouth-Dorchester	260	288
Dorchester-Chippenham	392	420
Weymouth-Portland	254	-
Portland-Weymouth	276	-
Westbury-Warminster	312	336
Warminster-Salisbury	384	408
Salisbury-Portsmouth	364	-
Portsmouth-Netley-Salisbury	364	-
Salisbury-Warminster	360	384
Warminster-Salisbury	420	420
Cheltenham-Cirencester W	320	-
Cirencester W - Swindon T	320	-
Swindon T - Savernake LL	336	-
Savernake LL -Andover Jct	314	-
Andover Jct-Southampton	420	-
Southampton-Savernake LL	392	-
Savernake LL - Swindon T	320	-
Swindon T - Swindon Jct	420	-
Swindon Jct-Cirencester W	392	-
Cirencester W - Cheltenham	336	-
Ludgershall-Tidworth	392	-
Tidworth-Ludgershall	392	-
Taunton-Wellington	420	420
Wellington-Whiteball	394	420
Whiteball-Newton Abbot	420	420
Newton Abbot-Brent	252	288
Brent-Plymouth	364	392
Plymouth-Penzance	350	385
Penzance-Plymouth	350	385
Plymouth-Hemerdon	252	288
Hemerdon-Newton Abbot	288	315
Newton Abbot-Exeter	420	450
Exeter-Taunton	420	450
Newton Abbot-Paignton	394	420
Paignton-Kingswear	300	340
Kingswear-Paignton	320	340
Paignton-Torquay	364	420
Torquay-Newton Abbot	300	340
Taunton-Barnstaple	280	-
Barnstaple-Taunton	280	-
Taunton-Minehead	360	-
Minehead-Taunton	310	-
Durston-Yeovil	308	-
Yeovil-Durston	308	-
Par-Newquay	180	190
Newquay-Par		
Cheltenham-Notgrove	252	-
Notgrove-Kingham	336	-
Kingham-Banbury	336	-
Banbury-Kingham	336	-
Kingham-Bourton	336	-
Bourton-Notgrove	252	-
Notgrove-Cheltenham	336	-
Grange Court-Hereford	308	336
Hereford-Grange Court	308	336
Filton-Cheltenham	420	420
Swindon-Cheltenham	420	420
Cheltenham-Stratford	420	420
Stratford-Birmingham	308	336
Birmingham-Cheltenham	420	420
Cheltenham-Swindon	420	420
Cheltenham-Filton	420	-
Bristol-Fishponds	352	380
Fishponds-Yate	420	420
Yate-Bristol	420	420
Filton Junct-Avonmouth	420	420
Avonmouth-Filton Junct	392	420
Stapleton Rd-Clifton Down	330	353
Clifton Down-Avonmouth	392	420

Cardiff-Severn Tunnel Jct	420	455	Hereford-Shrewsbury	406	420
Severn Tunnel Jct-Patchway	406	420	Shrewsbury-Pontypool Road	406	420
Patchway-Badminton	420	455	Pontypool Road-S.T.Junct	420	420
			S.T.Junct-Bristol	406	420
Pyle-Porthcawl	406	-			
Porthcawl-Pyle (through)	406	-	Hereford-Ledbury	364	392
			Ledbury-Colwall	336	364
Swansea-Felin Fran	320	360	Colwall-Worcester	420	420
Felin Fran-Swansea	280	325	Worcester-Stourbridge Jct	364	392
			Stourbridge Jct-Birmingham	232	280
Carmarthen-Pencader	240	-	Birmingham-Stourbridge Jct	392	420
Pencader-Aberystwyth	215	-	Stourbridge Jct-Gt Malvern	364	392
Aberystwyth-Strata Florida	200	-	Gt Malvern-Ledbury	336	392
Strata Florida-Carmarthen	240	-	Ledbury-Hereford	364	392
Whitland-Templeton	252	288	Reading-Castle Cary	392	420
Templeton-Pembroke Dock	288	300	Castle Cary-Taunton	420	420
Pembroke Dock-Tenby	288	300	Taunton-Castle Cary	450	450
Tenby-Narberth	252	288	Castle Cary-Savernake	392	420
Narberth-Whitland	288	300	Savernake-Reading	455	485
Johnston-Milford Haven	364	420	Patney-Holt Jct	330	352
Milford Haven-Johnston	336	340	Holt Jct-Bathampton	420	420
			Bathampton-Holt Jct	392	420
Clarbeston Road-Neyland	364	392	Holt Jct-Seend	312	336
Neyland-Whitland	336	364	Seend-Devizes	264	286
			Devizes-Patney	330	352
Filton-Pontypool Road	406	420			
Pontypool Road-Hereford	364	392	Chippenham-Westbury	392	420

Avonmouth-Clifton Down	308	330
Clifton Down-Stapleton Rd	420	420
Bristol-Mells Rd-Frome	260	-
Frome-Mells Rd	238	-
Mells Rd-Bristol	260	-
Yatton-Wells	330	-
Wells-Shepton Mallet	220	-
Shepton Mallet-Cranmore	264	-
Cranmore-Witham	420	-
Witham-Cranmore	220	-
Cranmore-Wells	364	-
Wells-Yatton	330	-
Gloucester-Severn Tunnel J	420	420
Severn Tunnel J-Gloucester	420	420
Paddington-Leamington	392	420
Leamington-Wolverhampton	336	392
Wolverhampton-Shrewsbury	420	420
Shrewsbury-Ruabon	308	336
Ruabon-Birkenhead	420	420
Birkenhead-Chester	420	420
Chester-Wrexham	308	336
Wrexham-Ruabon	392	420
Ruabon-Wellington	364	392
Wellington-Wolverhampton	350	378
Wolverhampton-Birmingham	336	392
Birmingham-Leamington	392	420
Leamington-Paddington	364	420
Ruabon-Dolgelly	280	-
Dolgelly-Barmouth	392	-
Barmouth-Dolgelly	392	-
Dolgelly-Llanuwchllyn	252	-
Llanuwchllyn-Ruabon	280	-
Whitchurch-Oswestry	308	-
Oswestry-Welshpool	392	-
(Shrewsbury-Welshpool	364	-)
Welshpool-Moat Lane Jct	392	-
Moat Lane Jct-Talerddig	315	-
Talerddig-Borth	420	-
Borth-Aberystwyth	315	-
Aberystwyth-Borth	364	-
Borth-Machynlleth	420	-
Machynlleth-Talerddig	288	-
Talerddig-Welshpool	392	-
Welshpool-Oswestry	392	-
Oswestry-Whitchurch	364	-
Dovey Jct-Barmouth Jct	336	-
Barmouth Jct-Barmouth	392	-
Barmouth-P'deudraeth	336	-
P'deudraeth-Criccieth	288	-
Criccieth-Pwllheli	392	-
Pwllheli-Afon Wen	392	-
Afon Wen-P'deudraeth	288	-
P'deudraeth-Barmouth	364	-
Barmouth-Barmouth Jct	392	-
Barmouth Jct-Dovey Jct	288	-
Hartlebury-Shrewsbury	392	420
Shrewsbury-Hartlebury	392	420
Oxford-Worcester	420	420
Worcester-Moreton	364	392
Moreton-Oxford	420	420
Princes Risboro'-Oxford	308	336
Oxford-Princes Risboro'	336	364
Princes Risboro'-Aylesbury	280	-
Aylesbury-Princes Risboro'	252	-
Maidenhead-Wycombe	308	-
Wycombe-Maidenhead	336	-
Reading-Basingstoke	364	392
Basingstoke-Reading	364	392
Didcot-Winchester	364	-
Winchester-Didcot	364	-

A splendid photograph of No.7818 GRANVILLE MANOR on shed at Tyseley, some time in 1956. PHOTOGRAPH: T.E. WILLIAMS

NAMES

TORQUAY MANOR (7800): Initially, the name allotted to the first of the new Manor class engines was ANTHONY MANOR, but that name was bestowed upon No.7801 instead. The change of mind was due to a request from Sir Francis Leyland-Barratt, the Member of Parliament for Torquay who was also a well known railway artist and modeller. When Sir Francis heard of the GWR's plans to build a new class of locomotives and name them after manor houses, he wrote to the company saying that, as his paintings and models had given the GWR a consider-able amount of publicity, he would be grateful if, firstly, he could be loaned the drawings for the Manors so that he could build a model (this was done) and, secondly, that one of the new engines could be named after his residence which (he said) was named Torquay Manor. The house was, in fact, named Torwood Manor, but Sir Francis wanted to publicise his constituency. Torwood Manor was actually on high ground above Torquay and so, in purely geographical terms, the facts were being mildly manipulated, rather than brutally bent.

After World War II, Torwood Manor was purchased by the United

States Government and presented to the United Kingdom as a home for the blind. The US Government's action was a show of appreciation for the kindness shown to US servicemen while in this country - the people of South Devon, particularly around Start Bay, knew a little more than most about certain problems faced by the American forces during the war. Torwood House was still a home for the blind in the early 1990s.

ANTHONY MANOR (7801): This engine was to have been named ASHLEY MANOR (near Box in Wiltshire), but that name was not used. Anthony Manor is correctly known as Place Manor, and stands at St.Anthony-in-Roseland, near the entrance of Falmouth Harbour. The name 'Roseland', incidentally, derives from the Cornish word 'ros', meaning heath. The house was built in 1840, and is now in use as a hotel.

BRADLEY MANOR (7802): Bradley Manor is a relatively small 15th Century manor house situated two miles west of Newton Abbot. It is now under National Trust administration, and boasts the Jacobean screen which was once at a church in Ashburton.

BARCOTE MANOR (7803): It was originally intended to name this engine BOSTON MANOR, but that name was not used, possibly because there was a Boston Manor station on the Metropolitan Line near the GWR's own branch to Brentford. Railway companies, particularly the GWR, were very wary about naming locomotives after places they served as some members of the travelling public actually confused locomotive names for destination labels. Indeed, in the late 1920s the GWR removed all engine names which coincided with the names of stations. No.7803 was named, instead, after Barcote Manor, a holding which appeared in the Domesday Book and is situated eight miles south-west of Oxford. The late change of name for No.7803 probably accounts for the departure from strict alphabetical sequence for Nos.7801-7819.

BAYDON MANOR (7804): Although this name is also out of strict alphabetical sequence, there is no evidence that a different name had been previously allotted. Baydon Manor stands 6 miles or so north-east of Marlborough.

BROOME MANOR (7805): Broome Manor is to the east of Swindon.

COCKINGTON MANOR (7806): The building which the GWR had in mind was Cockington Court, near Torquay. That said, there was a Cockington Manor in the Domesday Book - it yielded a rent of 159 sheep and 42 goats. As for the actual building, it was sold in 1933 and became part of a rural crafts centre.

COMPTON MANOR (7807): This building, near Paignton in Devon, is more usually - albeit incorrectly - referred to as Compton Castle. Remarkably, in August 1937 - i.e. just seven months before No.7807 was built - the GWR named Castle class No.5047 COMPTON CASTLE. Two locomotives named after the same building? It certainly seems so! As for the building itself, it had its origins in the 14th century, but much of what can be seen today is Tudor with 20th century restoration and reconstruction.

COOKHAM MANOR (7808): Cookham Manor isn't the name of a building, but the name of an estate. A manor is actually a freehold estate which, up to medieval times, was granted by a sovereign to one of his/her nobles (although there were certain 'help yourself' nobles, such as Jack Horner who took a fancy to Mells Manor in Somerset - but that's another story). If the noble built a house on the estate it was usually named after the manor, but there were many cases where a house was not built on the estate. Such a case was Cookham Manor, near the Berkshire village of Cookham - the estate, which includes the open common land of Winter Hill and Pinkneys Green, has never had a manor house built upon it. Since 1934 the estate has been owned by the National Trust who, as the current 'Lord(s) of the Manor', are entitled to hunt deer in Windsor Great Park on seven occasions each year. There is a manor house at Odney, near Cookham, but that is Lullebrook Manor.

CHILDREY MANOR (7809): Another out-of-sequence name, Childrey Manor (which was listed in the Domesday Book) lies three miles west of Wantage in Oxfordshire.

DRAYCOTT MANOR (7810): There is a manor estate (but with no house) of Draycott near Abingdon in Oxfordshire, while the village of Draycott to the west of Wells has neither estate nor house. The 'real' Draycot Manor - note the spelling with only one 't' - is the estate which is four miles north-west of Chippenham.

DUNLEY MANOR (7811): Dunley Manor stands four miles north of Whitchurch in Hampshire (between Basingstoke and Andover). On present day maps the railway line shown running through Whitchurch is the ex-Southern Railway (!) West of England main line, but until the 1960s there was, of course, also the GWR's Didcot, Newbury & Southampton line, which had its own station at Whitchurch.

ERLESTOKE MANOR (7812): The estate (and house) was originally known as Earl Stoke Manor. Situated six miles south-west of Devizes in Wiltshire, the house was built in 1786-91 for the then-owner Joshua Smith. The house has now been demolished and only the magnificent gate posts remain. Ironically, the community of Erlestoke is better known today for its prison.

FRESHFORD MANOR (7813): Freshford Manor is four miles to the south-east of Bath and one mile or so west of Bradford-on-Avon. The estate was listed in the Domesday Book as being 'on the Avon Canal'. Freshford is not far from Farleigh Hungerford Castle, after which Castle class No.5027 was loosely named.

FRINGFORD MANOR (7814): Fringford Manor stands near the Oxfordshire village of Fringford, a little to the northeast of Bicester. There is also a Fringford Hall, but before you look, this name was not applied to a GWR 'Hall'.

FRITWELL MANOR (7815): About four miles to the west of Fringford (see above) is the village of Fritwell, which was listed in the Domesday Book. In more recent times, Fritwell Manor was the home of the Morton family, who acquired one of the engine nameplates in the 1960s. The estate was sold in 1972, and the engine nameplate was included in the sale.

FRILSHAM MANOR (7816): Frilsham Manor is five miles north-east of Newbury in Berkshire. The village church is dedicated to St.Frideswide, a Saxon princess who founded a convent in the nearby forest.

GARSINGTON MANOR (7817): Garsington Manor is situated four miles south-east of Oxford.

GRANVILLE MANOR (7818): This is another GWR mis-spelling. The estate, which is near the village of Haddenham in Buckinghamshire, is actually spelt Grenville Manor.

HINTON MANOR (7819): Hinton Manor is seven miles to the west of Abingdon in Oxfordshire.

DINMORE MANOR (7820): The manor house, which dates from the fourteenth century, is a private residence eight miles north of Hereford. One of No.7820's nameplates is on display at

On 16 December 1965 - only a few weeks after its official withdrawal from active duty - No.7816 (devoid of its FRILSHAM MANOR nameplates) languishes at the rear of Horton Road shed at Gloucester. Note the GWR lettering on the tender. PHOTOGRAPH: P.J. LYNCH

the house. The community of Dinmore had a station on the Hereford-Shrewsbury line.

DITCHEAT MANOR (7821): On 9 July 1936, the owner of Ditcheat Manor, four miles to the north of Castle Cary in Somerset, wrote to the GWR suggesting that one of the proposed Manor class locomotives be named after his residence. The GWR promised to do so, but over fourteen years were to elapse before the promise was honoured - by British Railways. (The list of proposed names for the unbuilt batch of 1939, Nos.7820-7839, did not include the name of Ditcheat Manor.)

FOXCOTE MANOR (7822): The Foxcote Manor after which the locomotive was named stands one mile south of Andoversford in Gloucestershire.

HOOK NORTON MANOR (7823): The village of Hook Norton is some eight miles south-west of Banbury and was once served by the Banbury-Cheltenham line - the very line which was intended to be worked by the Manors in

1938. The manor house stands in Netting Street. It was recorded in the Domesday Book as having two mills, and was noted as being the site of a Danish massacre.

IFORD MANOR (7824): On 19 February 1937 Major J.M.Peto (a not unfamiliar surname!) wrote to the GWR requesting that a Manor class engine could be named after his home one mile south-east of Bradford-on-Avon. The promise was kept - by British Railways - in 1950.

LECHLADE MANOR (7825): Lechlade Manor is in the town of the same name on the Oxfordshire/Gloucestershire border. At the time of writing it is in use as a convent.

LONGWORTH MANOR (7826): Longworth Manor is in the Abingdon area, to the south-west of Oxford.

LYDHAM MANOR (7827): Lydham Manor, another holding which appeared in the Domesday Book, is a little to the north of Bishop's Castle in Shropshire

(some six miles north-west of Craven Arms). The little Bishop's Castle Railway - one of life's ever-impecunious independents - linked the community of its title to Craven Arms station.

ODNEY MANOR (7828): Here we have another little slip-up from the GWR. There has never been a property - estate or house - called Odney Manor. There is a manor house at the village of Odney, near Cookham in Berkshire, but that house is - and always has been - called Lullebrook Manor. (See also No.7808).

RAMSBURY MANOR (7829): Ramsbury Manor stands two miles north-west of Hungerford in Berkshire in what was once an important town with its own cathedral. Nowadays, though, Ramsbury is a large village, albeit an important centre for the horse racing industry. The manor house - part of which was laid out by the son-in-law of Inigo Jones - was where, in earlier times, Oliver Cromwell had laid his plans for the subjugation of Ireland. The house was sold in the late 1980s.

Chapter Two

Details and Modifications

During their relatively brief lives, the Manors were subjected to few changes. Indeed, apart from the modifications to the interior of their smokeboxes and the fitting of new chimneys, the alterations involved little more than changes of livery.

Liveries

The first twenty Manors were originally finished in standard GWR middle-chrome green, but *without* lining. They had the customary brass and copper fittings and embellishments, albeit without the brass beading on the front corners of the side sheets. The tenders were inscribed with a circular totem formed by the letters 'GWR', popularly known as the 'shirt button' emblem, which had been introduced in 1934. During World War II the Manors received unlined black (applied to all GWR locomotives except Castles and Kings) primarily as an economy measure; after the war green, still without lining, was reinstated. A further post-war change - although not applied to all of the class - was that the tenders were inscribed with the letters 'G' and

Still awaiting repainting in BR unlined black, No.7815 FRITWELL MANOR sports GWR green at Cheltenham on 2 October 1949. PHOTOGRAPH: W.A. POTTER

The original livery of the pre-war Manors was unlined green, as on No.7801 ANTHONY MANOR. Note the 'GWR' roundel - the so-called 'shirt button' emblem - on the tender. PHOTOGRAPH: R.C. RILEY COLLECTION

BR unlined black on No.7811 DUNLEY MANOR, fresh from a heavy general, at Swindon on 21 June 1955. PHOTOGRAPH: BRIAN MORRISON

'W', separated by the company's coat of arms.

None of the GWR-built Manors was inscribed with the 'W' prefix of the early BR period. The prefix system was used by BR to denote a locomotive's pre-Nationalisation origins - 'W' for GWR, 'E' for LNER, 'M' for LMS, and 'S' for Southern - prior to the application of the new BR numbers, but the vast majority of locomotives went straight from their pre-1948 number to their BR number, without ever carrying a prefix. On the Western Region, the prefixes were hardly used at all. The consensus at Swindon Works was that, as the ex-GWR locomotives were to retain their old numbers in the BR era, and as the numberplates themselves were readily distinguishable from those of ex-LNER, LMSR and SR locos, a 'W' prefix was somewhat superfluous.

There was also the not inconsiderable matter of Swindon pride.....

After Nationalisation, all but one of the original Manors (Nos.7800-7819) ultimately received BR unlined black as they passed through the shops. The exception was No.7804, which in July 1948 was painted green (unlined), principally for regular pilot duties with the 'Cornish Riviera' between Newton Abbot and Plymouth.

The ten additional Manors built in 1950, Nos.7820-7829, were all turned out in the new BR mixed traffic livery of lined black, cryptically referred to as 'Riddles Revenge' - a pointed reference to railway company politics of a quarter of a century earlier. To explain briefly, the CME of British Railways was Robert Riddles who, prior to the grouping in 1923, had been a loyal London & North Western employee. In the mid-1920s the LMSR seemed hell-bent on dispensing with as much LNWR tradition as possible and adopting, as far as apparently practical, ex-Midland practices instead. One of the LMSR's moves was to use ex-Midland red as its standard livery and, somewhat predictably, this did not amuse the ex-LNWR faction who, of course, considered their old livery of lined black to be far superior. The lined black adopted by Robert Riddles for BR wasn't absolutely identical to the old LNWR livery, but it was close enough for some observers to suggest that he had, after all that time, at last gained revenge on behalf of the LNWR. According to some,

Nos.7820-7829 were turned out in lined black. No.7821 DITCHEAT MANOR was photographed at Southall in December 1953. PHOTOGRAPH: R.C. RILEY COLLECTION

Riddles was also content to score against the GWR, as many years earlier his application to become an apprentice at Swindon had been turned down.

For a while, some locomotives repainted in BR black - lined or unlined - were given a red background to their name and number plates. Unfortunately, we do not have a list of which Manors were thus treated, but we believe the number was small. The red background was not successful - it faded very quickly, and went back to black. Starting in 1953, Nos.7820-7829 lost their lined black liveries in favour of unlined black as they passed through the shops (see summary), but from July 1956 lined BR green was applied. The first of the class to receive its green livery was No.7828, the last being No.7819 which was repainted early in 1960.

The engines built by BR, Nos.7820-7829, were fitted with smokebox numberplates from new, and by November 1951 all but one of the GWR-built examples had been similarly equipped. The exception was No.7812, which didn't receive its smokebox numberplate until 1952.

For a short period after Nationalisation, the standard inscription on locomotive tenders were the words BRITISH RAILWAYS in full. In 1949 that gave way to the 'lion and wheel' emblem (irreverently referred to as the 'ferret and dartboard' emblem) which, in March 1957, was succeeded by the second style of BR crest. No.7828, incidentally, had the fenders on its tender lined out in January 1957 - believed to be the first such lining of a low-sided tender. Perhaps the most intriguing variety of later years was evidenced by No.7816 - there is a photograph of the engine at Gloucester in 1965 showing

Top. Another example of 'Riddles Revenge' - the BR lined black livery - with the BR emblem of the period. No.7828 ODNEY MANOR passes Canton shed at Cardiff with an up freight on 15 May 1952. Note also the red-backed name and number plates. PHOTOGRAPH: R.C. RILEY

Middle. A clearer view of the red-background name and number plates - No.7809 CHILDREY MANOR at Swindon on 6 April 1952. The engine had just undergone a heavy general and was about to return to its home shed of Laira. PHOTOGRAPH: LES ELSEY

Bottom. The final livery worn by the Manors was lined green, the first of the class to receive it being No.7828 ODNEY MANOR, in July 1956. Judging by the old style BR emblem, this picture was taken very shortly after the new livery had been applied. PHOTOGRAPH: T. MIDDLEMASS/PAUL CHANCELLOR COLLECTION

T E N D E R S

N.B: In the 'built for' column, loco numbers in brackets are those carried post-1912.

Tender	Locos	Built	Lot	Built for
1824	7800	1911	A82	3824 COUNTY OF CORNWALL
1878	7800, 7813	1912	A86	2948 STACKPOLE COURT
1879	7800, 7815, 7822	1912	A86	2949 STANFORD COURT
1758	7800	1908	A77	4013 KNIGHT OF ST.PATRICK
1876	7801	1912	A86	2946 LANGFORD COURT
1938	7801	1914	A91	4052 PRINCESS BEATRICE
1773	7801	1908	A78	4108 (4156) GARDENIA
1936	7802, 7816, 7817	1914	A91	4050 PRINCESS ALICE
1725	7803	1907	A74	4001 DOG STAR
1764	7803	1908	A77	4019 KNIGHT TEMPLAR
1740	7803, 7815	1907	A75	2916 SAINT BERNARD
1780	7803	1908	A78	4115 (4163) MARIGOLD
1708	7803	1906	A73	3814 COUNTY OF CHESHIRE (later renamed COUNTY OF CHESTER)
1699	7803, 7823	1906	A72	3805 COUNTY KERRY
1656	7803, 7823	1906	A69	3702 (3412) (later named JOHN G.GRIFFITHS)
1632	7804	1905	A65	181 (2981) IVANHOE
1792	7804, 7823	1910	A79	4037 QUEEN PHILIPPA
2230	7804, 7815	1922	A107	4061 GLASTONBURY ABBEY
1560	7804, 7810, 7822	1903	A55	98 (later named VANGUARD, then renamed ERNEST CUNARD, later renumbered 2998)
1837	7805, 7812	1911	A83	2937 CLEVEDON COURT
1662	7806	1906	A69	3708 (3418) SIR ARTHUR YORKE
1703	7806	1906	A72	3809 COUNTY WEXFORD
1917	7808, 7815	1913	A89	4043 PRINCE HENRY
2232	7809	1922	A107	4063 BATH ABBEY
1782	7810	1908	A78	4117 (4165) NARCISSUS
1935	7810, 7817	1914	A91	4049 PRINCESS MAUD
1831	7811, 7825, 7829	1911	A83	2931 ARLINGTON COURT
1941	7811	1914	A92	4056 PRINCESS MARGARET
1785	7813	1908	A78	4120 (4168) STEPHANOTIS
2233	7813, 7818	1922	A107	4064 READING ABBEY
1748	7814	1907	A75	2924 SAINT HELENA
1743	7814	1907	A75	2919 SAINT CECILIA (later renamed SAINT CUTHBERT)
1919	7814	1913	A89	4045 PRINCE JOHN
1873	7815, 7817	1912	A86	2943 HAMPTON COURT
1911	7815	1913	A89	2951 TAWSTOCK COURT
1933	7816, 7823, 7826	1914	A91	4047 PRINCESS LOUISE
1657	7816	1906	A69	3703 (3413) (later named JAMES MASON)
1778	7816	1908	A78	4113 (4161) HYACINTHE
1777	7817	1908	A78	4112 (4160) CARNATION
1674	7818	1906	A70	3720 (3430) (later named INCHCAPE)
1871	7819	1912	A86	2941 EASTON COURT
1762	7819	1908	A77	4017 KNIGHT OF THE BLACK EAGLE (later renamed KNIGHT OF LIEGE)
1683	7819	1906	A70	3729 (3439) WESTON-SUPER-MARE
1793	7819	1911	A79	4038 QUEEN BERENGARIA
1794	7819	1911	A79	4039 QUEEN MATILDA
1750	7820	1907	A75	2926 SAINT NICHOLAS
1696	7820	1906	A72	3802 COUNTY CLARE
1784	7820, 7821	1908	A78	4119 (4167) PRIMROSE
1761	7820	1908	A77	4016 KNIGHT OF THE GOLDEN FLEECE (later renamed THE SOMERSET LIGHT INFANTRY [PRINCE ALBERT'S])
1749	7821	1907	A75	2925 SAINT MARTIN
1838	7823	1911	A83	2938 CORSHAM COURT
1698	7824	1906	A72	3804 COUNTY DUBLIN
1638	7826	1905	A65	2987 (later named ROBERTSON, then renamed BRIDE OF LAMMERMOOR)
1781	7827, 7829	1908	A78	4116 (4164) MIGNONETTE
1827	7829	1912	A82	3827 COUNTY OF GLOUCESTER

Taking one of those tenders at random, No.1638 was built in 1905 and finished its days in 1965 paired with Manor No.7826. The tender had cost £483 to construct and so, ignoring inflation, its depreciation during its sixty year life worked out at around £8 per annum (or just over 2p per day). Not bad value!

it paired with a tender lettered 'GWR' - a style dating to the early post-war period!

Tenders

As related earlier, it was the intention from the outset that the Manors would incorporate parts from withdrawn 43XX 2-6-0s. With this 'economy' aspect in mind, it was, perhaps, inevitable that money would not be spent on constructing brand new tenders. Most of those used by the Manors - even the ones built in BR days - had been constructed *circa* 1910-1915. They were standard Churchward tenders which held 3,500 gallons of water and 7 tons of coal; they weighed 18tons 5cwt empty and 40tons full, and had a wheelbase of 7ft 6in + 7ft 6in.

Three of the Manors were paired for a time with a 4,000 gallon Churchward tender which had been built in 1903 specially for the first real Churchward 4-6-0 - No.98, later named VANGUARD, then renamed ERNEST CUNARD, and later renumbered 2998. The tender, No.1560, was extensively rebuilt by Collett, with new frames and Collett-pattern continuous fenders; it weighed 19tons 5cwt empty and 43tons 3cwt full, running with Manor No.7804 from March 1960 to July 1963, and then briefly with No.7822 before being paired with No.7810 where, it seems, it remained until withdrawal in 1964.

Another variation involved what were known as the 'intermediate pattern' tenders - a Collett revision of the Churchward design - of which ten were constructed (as Lot A112) in 1925 and 1926. Two existing Churchward tenders - Nos.2210 and 2222 - were also eventually modified, to similar specifications. The 'intermediate pattern' tenders had higher sides than the standard Churchward tenders and were fitted with full-length fenders. Six of the 'intermediate' tenders ran with ten different Manors at one time or another; they also saw service with Castles, Stars, Saints, 28XXs, 43XXs and 2251s. A further departure from the norm appears to have involved No.7808, which is known to have been paired with a Collett 4,000-gallon tender in the summer of 1964. This change is not noted in the official records, which might suggest that it was for only a very short period.

The pedigree of many of the Manor tenders is interesting, as several had originally been built for well-known named engines. A complete list of tenders used by the Manors is given in the registers; those with interesting origins are listed in Table 2:1:

Cabs

The first twenty Manors - i.e. the pre-war examples - had their cab side win-

dows removed during the war, the resultant gaps being filled by steel plates. This was also applied to other engines - the principal intention was to reduce the effects of bomb blast, but it was also of some efficacy as a black-out measure, in that it reduced firebox glare. The cab windows were replaced between 1945 and 1948 as the engines passed through the works.

The cab layout of the Manors adhered to the GWR principle of right-hand drive. It is believed that principle had originally been adopted (in the 1800s) merely to follow the lead set by contemporary road vehicles - i.e. when keeping to the left of a road, a driving position on the right gives a clearer view of what lies ahead. In railway practice, however, the situation was usually reversed as on most railways, signals and so on were on the left-hand side of the track. In the days of cab-less locomotives, a driver would have had a fairly unimpeded view (smoke permitting!) all around, but when full cabs started to appear, the observation of signals was sometimes slightly better from the left-hand side of the footplate. That said, any former GWR footplateman worth his salt will argue that the company positioned its signals so carefully that, even at bends, it was seldom necessary for a driver to cross the footplate to look at them.

Nevertheless, in pre-grouping days about half of the railway companies in Britain used right-hand drive - it was widely considered that, especially in a cramped cab, a right-handed

Top. No.7827 LYDHAM MANOR displays its newly applied lined green livery - complete with the second style of BR emblem on the tender - at Swindon Works on 20 September 1959. PHOTOGRAPH: W.A. POTTER

Middle. The Manors spent most of their lives paired with standard Churchward 3,500 gallon tenders, such as this one with No.7809 CHILDREY MANOR, at Canton in 1961. PHOTOGRAPH: J. HODGE

Bottom. A different view of Churchward 3,500 gallon tenders - the engine nearer the camera is No.7811 DUNLEY MANOR, the farther one is 0-6-0 No.3209, and both are paired with similar tenders. Although we are endeavouring to emphasise the type of tenders, a few words about this actual working are in order - on Sunday 30 August 1959 No.7811 and No.3209 worked an excursion from Birmingham and Wolverhampton to Barmouth and Aberystwyth. The train was divided at Dovey Junction, No.7811 proceeding with the Aberystwyth portion and No.3209 with the Barmouth portion. This is the return trip preparing to leave Dovey Junction - No.3209, having brought the Barmouth portion back, joins up with No.7811. PHOTOGRAPH: MICHAEL MENSING

fireman had more room in which to work without getting in the way of the driver (or incurring the driver's wrath, perhaps). Whatever the case, after the grouping the LMSR, LNER and Southern standardised on left-hand drive for most new engines, but the GWR, individualistic to the last, stuck with right-hand drive. In BR days, incidentally, all new 'Standard' locomotives were left-hand drive - this did not please the ex-GWR men who had to work with them.

Automatic Train Control

ATC, also referred to as audible signalling apparatus (but *not* on the GWR!), was routinely fitted to all GWR main line locomotives. Despite the fact that ATC was not exclusive to the Manors, it seems appropriate to expand on the subject at an early point in this series of books. The first experiments with ATC were conducted as far back as January 1906 on the Fairford branch. A ramp, formed by an insulated steel bar, was laid centrally between the rails, and a spring contact shoe was fitted underneath the test locomotive so that, when the engine passed over the ramp, the shoe came into contact with it. The ramp was installed near to a distant signal, and if the signal were 'all clear' the ramp was electrified so that the current passing via the shoe rang a bell in the engine cab. If the signal were at 'caution' (or if there were a failure), the ramp remained electrically dead and the raising of the shoe caused a warning to be sounded in the cab. The experiments were so successful that, in De-

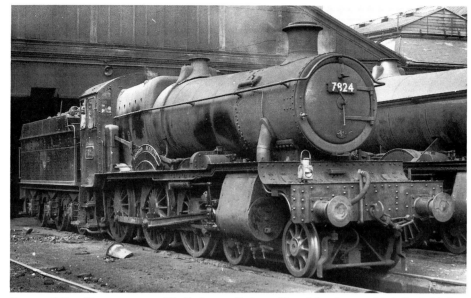

Some of the Manors ran with 'intermediate pattern' tenders, which had higher sides and full-length fenders. One such pairing, which lasted from 1958 to 1961, involved No.7824 IFORD MANOR and intermediate tender No.2380. This picture was taken at Swindon at an unspecified date in 1960. PHOTOGRAPH: BRYAN WILSON COLLECTION

cember of that year, further trials were conducted along the entire length of the Fairford branch, but this time with the visible distant signals removed. Only suitably fitted locomotives were used.

ATC was hailed as a major safety feature - drivers could not fail to be aware of a coming distant signal, even in the foggiest weather. Convinced of the usefulness of the system, the GWR applied it to the main line between Reading and Slough in November 1908, and in 1910 it was extended to Paddington. In this instance, the

visible signals were retained because only a few GWR locomotives were fitted with the necessary equipment.

The system was gradually refined. Possibly the most important modification was that the raising of the shoe under the locomotive by an electrically dead ramp (i.e. when the signal was at 'Caution') also opened a valve which admitted air to the vacuum brake pipes, thereby applying the engine and train brakes. In 1929 the GWR made a start on equipping all its main and some secondary lines, and by Septem-

Two different types of tenders meet fleetingly at Gloucester Central on 13 August 1964 - full marks to the photographer for having the awareness to grab this picture. On the left is No.7815 FRITWELL MANOR with a standard tender (on the 7.0am to Hereford), and on the right No.7814 FRINGFORD MANOR with an intermediate tender (on the 7.10am to Cardiff). PHOTOGRAPH: B.J. ASHWORTH

An unusual tender pairing was that of No.7808 (here devoid of nameplates) with a Collett 4,000 gallon tender. The ensemble is seen passing Newtown (Cardiff) on 9 August 1965. As explained in the text, from 1963 onwards the recording of details such as tender changes was far from thorough, and the pairing of No.7808 with this tender is one which eluded the registers. PHOTOGRAPH: MICHAEL HALE

ber 1931 the whole of the GWR main lines between Paddington, Wolverhampton, Swansea and Plymouth (a total of 2,130 miles of track) and 2,500 locomotives had already been equipped at a total cost of some £250,000. By 1939 ATC was installed throughout the entire GWR main line network.

New Boilers

A total of 22 boilers was built for the first twenty Manors and the two 'spares', Nos.6420 and 6421, were first used in 1943, when they were fitted to Nos.7802 and 7808 respectively. One spare boiler (No.6432) was provided for the Manors built in 1950, although it appears that the spare might not actually have been constructed until 1953 or 1954. Whatever the case, it was first used on No.7805, from January 1954. The provision of spare boilers was, of course, routine, as it took longer to overhaul a boiler than it did a locomotive - having a reconditioned boiler on standby helped to cut down the time spent at the works. During the GWR period boilers were usually changed after 70 to 80,000 miles, but after Nationalisation that figure was often exceeded, and was occasionally doubled. Although boiler changes were - in theory - scheduled well in advance, an engine

Another 'late in the day' tender pairing which went undocumented was that of No.7814 FRINGFORD MANOR with a Collett 3,500 gallon intermediate. The location is Ross-on-Wye (obviously!), the train the 2.47pm (SO) Gloucester-Hereford, 8 August 1964. PHOTOGRAPH: HUGH BALLANTYNE

For the last year or so of its life, No.7816 FRILSHAM MANOR was famously paired with a tender still inscribed 'GWR'. It was photographed - nameless - at Gloucester shed on 5 August 1965. See also page 11. **PHOTOGRAPH: BRYAN WILSON**

destined for a boiler change was not permitted to enter the jurisdiction of Swindon Works until a replacement boiler was available.

The Manors had their superheater elements shortened on two occasions. On the first occasion this reduced the heating surface to 182.3sqft, and on the second occasion to 160sqft, but they were then restored to the in-termediate length, although the revised heating surface was officially given as 182.43sqft. There was a further change in the late 1950s when 56 x 1¹/₄" elements were substituted, giving a heating surface of 138.24sqft.

The Manors were alone among GWR 4-6-0 types in not having four-cone (also known as 'Torpedo') ejectors. This was clearly evidenced by the ab-sence of the pipe which ran from the right-hand side of the firebox, along the length of the boiler barrel, and entered the smokebox beneath the chimney. The single-cone ejector was a potential trap for the unwary driver, as is explained by former driver Ron Hacker whose reminiscences are featured later in this book.

No.7818 GRANVILLE MANOR was the guinea pig for smokebox and draughting experiments, which led to the adoption of a different style of chimney. Following the experiments, the engine retained the capuchon on its chimney for a while. This picture was taken at Swindon on 6 April 1952. **PHOTOGRAPH: LES ELSEY**

Chimneys and Draughting

Initially, the Manors were criticised by some for being fairly mediocre steamers, but most enginemen considered that even an indifferent Manor was usually a better bet than a 43XX Mogul. Indeed, one former driver told us that "...with a larger capacity boiler, there was usually something in hand when working a Manor, but the Moguls had to be right on form - in tip-top condition". Nevertheless, it was considered that something had to be done to improve the steaming of the 4-6-0s.

During the early 1950s various tests, particularly concerning steaming rates and draughting, were conducted on the stationary plant (referred to as the 'home trainer') at Swindon Works, under the direction of Sam (S.O.) Ell. The tests prompted various improvements to different locomotives, perhaps the best known being the highly effective revision of the draughting arrangements of King No.6001 KING EDWARD VII (see Volume One of *Peto's Register*). Less well publicised were the modifications made to Manor No.7818 in 1952 - these involved alterations to the blast pipe (to reduce the diameter of the jumper ring), modifications to the firebars, an increase in the air space through the grate, and the fitting of a narrow stovepipe chimney (with an orifice some 25% less than before). The locomotive was subsequently tested at Swindon alongside a Standard 4MT 4-6-0 - it was '....found to be fitted with numerous recording devices....', according to a contemporary magazine report.

Following the tests, the all-round verdict was that No.7818's steaming had been greatly improved and so the other Manors were similarly treated. The modification was designated W/SW/L/41 (dated 17 February 1953), and a progress report in March 1954 noted that ten engines - Nos.7800, 7802, 7803, 7808, 7809, 7823, 7824, 7826, 7827 and 7829 - had so far been modified with successful results. The modifications were made standard on 21 July 1954, and were subsequently applied to the remaining Manors. As part of the process, a new design of chimney was developed for the class. The new style chimney was narrower and lacked a deflector (capuchon); it had a flared copper cap and a flared base, which could be - and sometimes was - mistaken for an overall 'concave' profile. A close study of various photographs will reveal that there were slight differences between some of the new chimneys - they were manufactured individually as and when required.

The original style of chimney - complete with capuchon - is evident on No.7813 FRESHFORD MANOR, approaching Starcross with a down stopper some time in the early 1950s. PHOTOGRAPH: R.K. BLENCOWE

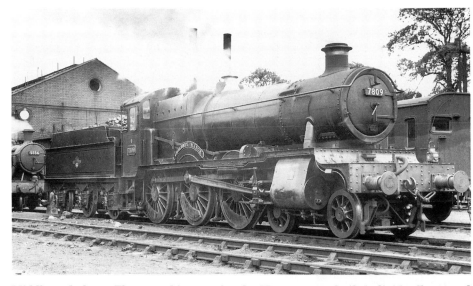

Middle and above. The new chimneys for the Manors were built individually as and when required, and this resulted in slight variations. Although subtle, two different styles can be clearly seen here - the familiar 'concave' profile of the chimney of No.7803 BARCOTE MANOR (at Welshpool with the 3.45pm Shrewsbury-Aberystwyth on 10 August 1956), and the straighter lines of No.7809 CHILDREY MANOR (at Westbury shed, 11 May 1958). PHOTOGRAPHS: BRIAN MORRISON; W.A. POTTER

Chapter Three

At Work - the GWR period

Where allocations and transfers are discussed, we quote either precise dates (if known) or 'four weeks ending' dates. In the case of the latter, we have standardised by quoting the month at the end of the relevant four-week period - for example, four weeks ending 20.4.46 is quoted as April 1946. Similarly, four weeks ending 1.4.39 is quoted as April 1939, although the allocation/transfer in question almost certainly occurred during the previous month.

As with any other new class of locomotive, the early activities of the Manors were duly reported in the contemporary railway press. For example, on 29 January 1938 No.7800 was noted at Gloucester, having brought in a train from Swindon, while in mid-February No.7801 was 'observed at Reading'. It was subsequently reported that No.7801 was regularly working the Bristol-Trowbridge-Newbury-Paddington route, 'arriving at Paddington about 2.55pm' and returning the same evening on a fast goods. No.7802 was noted on Birmingham-Leamington locals on 5 February, and subsequently on a through goods train from Birmingham to South Wales. It was reported that No.7803 had been hauling a fish train bound for Neyland - nothing too remarkable as the engine was allocated to Neyland - but in mid-February it was allegedly observed at Reading. If that latter report was correct, the sight of a Neyland engine so far east was not common at all. No.7804 was observed working from Swindon on 10 February, and later that year, on 13 August, was noted at Plymouth, having worked in from Bristol with a thirteen-coach Sheffield-Plymouth express.

As related earlier, one of the intended duties for the Manors was the Banbury-Cheltenham-South Wales route. It was not long before the engines were seen on that route, although contemporary reports indicate that they were almost exclusively on goods duties at first. In March 1938 No.7800, recently transferred to Banbury after a brief stint at Stafford Road, was reported to be one of the two engines in regular charge of the 3.10am ex-Banbury to Cardiff goods ("not much more than a pick-up until it reached Gloucester", we have been informed), returning from Cardiff at 12.45am the following day. Another turn regularly undertaken by No.7800 was the 10.55am Banbury-Bilston goods, returning with the 2.15am goods ex-Cannock Road Junction (Wolverhampton). The goods emphasis was such that, according to one observer, by the middle of March No.7800 had worked only one passenger train from Banbury - the 2.30pm to Leamington on 7 March.

Of the Manors delivered in March 1938, Nos.7805 and 7806 (both of Shrewsbury) soon took up a regular residency, working the 2.55pm Dorrington-Marylebone (Rossmore Road) milk on alternate days. Later that year, No.7806 was reported as the most common engine on that turn. The Manors - and other GWR locomotives engaged on that duty - worked only to and from Banbury (arr. 5.30pm), where the milk tanks were handed over to/from the LNER. Earlier - on 22 March - No.7806 had been observed at Salisbury, presumably on a running-in turn before being despatched to Shrewsbury. No.7808, allocated to Old Oak, was reported taking turns with No.7802 of St. Philip's Marsh on the 2.45pm Paddington-Bristol (via Devizes). The former

Although two Manors were allocated from new to Old Oak both were transferred away before the war, and from then on the class was not often seen in London. The only date for this photograph of No.7804 BAYDON MANOR on a Paddington-bound train at Ealing Broadway is 'circa 1939'. PHOTOGRAPH: R.C. RILEY COLLECTION

Photographs of the 'Ports-to-Ports Express' in South Wales are rare indeed, but we have tracked down this picture of No.7811 DUNLEY MANOR passing Barry Sidings Signal Box with the down train at an unspecified date in 1939. PHOTOGRAPH: J.G. HUBBACK/COURTESY JOHN HODGE

engine was later noted on the 4.35pm Paddington-Reading local.

On 5 June 1938 (Whit Sunday) No.7800 took over an excursion train from Nottingham at Banbury and worked it right through to Portsmouth via Eastleigh. This was the first time a Manor had appeared at Portsmouth, and was possibly the first appearance of the class on 'foreign' metals. On 12 December 1938 No.7808 was noted at the Southern Railway stronghold of Guildford, where it was undergoing plat-

form clearance tests. After the outbreak of war in September 1939 Manors appeared regularly at Guildford with workings between Reading and Redhill, while in the BR era the sight of a Manor on that route was far from unusual.

Returning to 1938, more new territory was broken when a Manor ventured on to ex-Cambrian metals. The first trial of a Manor on the Cambrian section - where the class later established a firm hold and a firm following - seems to have been on 31 October

when No.7805 worked into Barmouth with the engineers' saloon attached, having undergone clearance tests along the line from Ruabon. (It should be pointed out that, prior to the Grouping in 1923, the section between Ruabon and Dolgelly station had been GWR property, the Cambrian Railway not actually commencing until a point 30ch west of Dolgelly station). The trial with No.7805 in October 1938, incidentally, followed on the heels of two sets of tests to check the strength of Barmouth Bridge. The first set of tests involved a pair of pannier tanks coupled together, and the second a 39XX class 2-6-2T coupled to a 43XX 2-6-0. On each occasion the deflection of the bridge timbers was monitored very carefully and, somewhat ironically, the only weakness found was not in Barmouth Bridge itself, but in Tunnel Viaduct, just to the north of the bridge.

Although many of the Manors' early activities came under scrutiny in the railway press, there are a couple of aspects which remain a mystery. One aspect concerns the initial allocation of No.7800 - the official Swindon allocation registers clearly show that the engine was sent to Stafford Road when new in February 1938. We have found no reference whatsoever to any activities undertaken by No.7800 while at Stafford Road, and that might be considered unusual given that it was the first of a new class. Assuming that the entry in the registers is correct (and we emphasise that it is unmistakable!) it might have been that

The 'Ports-to-Ports' again - this time it is No.7810 DRAYCOTT MANOR with the down train at Porthkerry Park in 1939. PHOTOGRAPH: J.G. HUBBACK/ COURTESY JOHN HODGE

No.7810 DRAYCOTT MANOR at Landore on 28 May 1939. Landore only ever had one Manor of its own - and that was for just one month in 1956. However, they were allocated to South Wales sheds from the outset, and were no strangers to Landore. That said, at the time this picture was taken No.7810 was a Banbury engine, and it is assumed to have worked in with the 'Ports-to-Ports'. PHOTOGRAPH: R.C. RILEY COLLECTION

as Stafford Road was the divisional motive power headquarters, it had No.7800 simply to give it a 'once over' prior to it being put into traffic at one of the sheds in the division. Whatever the true facts, it's stay at Stafford Road was very brief as it is shown as being transferred to Banbury during the four-week period ending 5 March 1938. It was a vaguely similar story with Nos.7810 and 7811 - the registers show

their initial allocation as 'Wolverhampton' which, presumably, implied the *district* rather than the actual depot.

When all twenty Manors were in service - 13 February 1939 - the distribution was as follows:
Banbury: 7800, 7810, 7811
Bath Road: 7801, 7804, 7812
St.Philip's Marsh: 7802,
Neyland: 7803, 7807, 7816
Shrewsbury: 7805, 7806

Old Oak Common: 7808
Westbury: 7809, 7814
Oxley: 7813
Gloucester: 7815 (possibly not allocated until 3/1939)
Croes Newydd: 7817
Worcester: 7818
Carmarthen: 7819
We will now look at the engines' duties from those - and other - sheds.

Banbury
The duties of the first Banbury based Manor, No.7800, are a little unclear. As related earlier, one of the principal reasons for allocating Manors to Banbury was to work the Banbury-Swansea leg of the Newcastle-Swansea through trains - the 'Ports-to-Ports Express' - but as we have seen, No.7800 appears to have spent most of its early period at Banbury on goods duties. It is uncertain how much use was made of No.7800 on the 'Ports-to-Ports' in 1938, but any early appearances on those workings would almost certainly have been alongside the 43XX 2-6-0s, which had enjoyed a monopoly for some fifteen years.

The 'Ports-to-Ports Express' - an unofficial title incidentally - had been introduced in May 1906, initially operating between Newcastle and Barry. One purpose was to provide a means of transport for seamen who were changing vessels, and before the grouping the service was extended to Swansea while, in LNER days, a through coach to/from Hull via Goole was added. Thus, the ports of Newcas-

Oswestry shed, 10 May 1947, and No.7807 COMPTON MANOR.

No.7817 GARSINGTON MANOR was allocated from new to Croes Newydd, partly for working between Ruabon and Barmouth. It is seen at the latter point in June 1946. Note the blanked-off cab window - a wartime precaution. PHOTOGRAPH: W.A. POTTER

tle, Middlesbrough, Hull, Goole, Cardiff, Penarth, Barry and Swansea were ultimately served by the same train. The route was interesting - on the Banbury-Cheltenham section it was the only regular train not to stop at Kingham, at Cheltenham it stopped only at Cheltenham South & Leckhampton and, until after the grouping, the Barry-Swansea part of the journey was undertaken on Barry Railway metals as far as Bridgend. By the late 1930s - i.e. the era of the Manors - the southbound 'Ports-to-Ports' was scheduled to leave Newcastle at

9.30am, arriving at Swansea at 8.45pm, while the northbound working left Swansea at 8.15am and arrived at Newcastle at 6.15pm. The train was usually formed of seven or more carriages - GWR and LNER stock being used on alternate days - which, with the hilly Banbury-Cheltenham section forming just one part of the 161-mile trip, wasn't the easiest of workings. Indeed, trains of more than eight carriages required assistance on that section if schedules were to be maintained. The 'Ports-to-Ports' was suspended with the outbreak of World War II, and when rein-

stated in October 1946 it was rerouted via Swindon and Oxford, usually with a Landore-based Castle in charge. The service was suspended during the coal crisis in 1947, and was not reintroduced until 1949; it ceased altogether in the winter of 1952/53, by which time it was operating only on Fridays and Saturdays.

Returning to the subject of the Manors themselves, despite the vagueness surrounding the early activities of No.7800 at Banbury, it is a little more certain that, with the arrival of Nos.7810 and 7811 in December 1938, the shed's Manors were at last employed regularly on the Newcastle-Swansea trains - tending to monopolise them, in fact. The older one, No.7800, was mainly employed on the 3.10am Banbury-Cardiff goods, returning with the 12.45am ex-Cardiff, or ironstone trains to Bilston, returning with empties. By March 1940 Banbury's stud of Manors had been boosted to five with the transfer of No.7805 and No.7806 from Shrewsbury, but the tradition of undertaking more goods than passenger duties continued. Nevertheless, No.7806 was noted, somewhat unusually, on the 6.20pm Paddington-Slough in March 1940, although its return home from Slough was in a more customary manner - with a Wolverhampton goods.

During the war, Banbury's Manors were sometimes seen a little farther afield than was usual in peacetime. For example, on 26 April 1940 Nos.7800, 7805 and 7806 were all observed at Southampton; No.7805 was there again on 4 October 1941, while No.7810 was noted at Eastleigh on 13

As a class, the Manors maintained a lengthy association with Aberystwyth. Oswestry No.7819 HINTON MANOR waits there on 20 August 1949 - 'GWR' lettering on tender. PHOTOGRAPH: J. SUTTON/PAUL CHANCELLOR COLLECTION

July 1943. These workings were, apparently, via the Didcot and Newbury line. At various times in 1942 Nos.7800, 7810 and 7811 all worked to Southampton via the Midland & South Western Junction route. (The MSWJ line is discussed at slightly greater length in the section dealing with Gloucester shed). It can be assumed that other Manors worked unnoticed via the Didcot and Newbury line and also the MSWJ line to Southampton after spring 1943 (following the upgrading of the DN&S from 'Yellow' to 'Blue' *circa* April of that year), but we will probably never know the full picture as the reporting of railway activities was, of course, not an urgent priority during hostilities.

In the opposite direction, a different wartime working for a Banbury Manor involved No.7806 which, in June 1942, became the first of the class to work an ordinary train throughout on the recently upgraded Oswestry-Aberystwyth section. (No.7817 of Croes Newydd had traversed the line in December 1940, but only under test conditions). It is believed that the Banbury Manors were not infrequent visitors to the Cambrian section during the war - one such sighting was No.7811, on shed at Aberystwyth on 11 May 1943.

After the war - in July 1946 - No.7810 was noted on the Banbury diagram which took in the 8.38am Banbury-Paddington passenger, assisting the 1.45pm Paddington-Stourbridge Junction as far as Oxford, and the 5.12pm Morris Cowley-Banbury workmen's train.

At least one - and possibly more - of Banbury's Manors ventured into Cornwall. The engine history sheets show that, in August and September 1947, No.7800 was repaired at St.Blazey shed in Cornwall. At first, it was tempting to suggest that 'St.Blazey' on the history sheet was an erroneous entry for Stourbridge - after all, it was not unknown for the GWR shed codes (StB or SBZ for St.Blazey and STB for Stourbridge) to be confused - but the relevant entry actually spells 'St.Blazey' in full. The matter seems to have been resolved by Mr.Maurice Dart, the well respected Cornish railway historian. Mr.Dart informs us that he personally observed several Banbury engines at Plymouth at various times during the 1945-48 period - most were 2-6-0s, but No.7811 was noted at Plymouth North Road on many occasions during the summer of 1946. Mr.Dart considers that some of those engines almost certainly penetrated through to Cornwall, and if Banbury Moguls (and possibly No.7811) worked through to Cornwall, one might well assume that No.7800 did likewise in 1947. Mr.Dart suggests that No.7800 might have been working through to Newquay on one of the summer Saturday trains when it developed the fault which required attention at St.Blazey. Another hypothesis suggested by Mr.Dart is that No.7800 might have routinely turned up at Newton Abbot shed after working through to Paignton or Kingswear, and due to traffic requirements the engine had to be sent out as pilot to a train bound for Cornwall. Given that sheds 'borrowed' engines which had arrived for coaling etc., the latter hypothesis is perfectly feasible.

Bristol

Nos.7801, 7804 and 7812 were allocated from new to Bath Road, while No.7802 moved to St.Philip's Marsh (from Old Oak Common) in May 1938. There was some early interchange between the two Bristol sheds - No.7802 moved to Bath Road in April 1939, but that engine *and* the other three made the reverse trip in late 1939/early 1940. To add to the confusion, No.7812 returned to Bath Road in February 1940. The reason for the exchanges of Manors between the two Bristol sheds is unclear but, for what it is worth, Bath Road usually looked after passenger engines while St.Philip's usually accommodated goods and mixed traffic locomotives. (Until the mid-1920s, incidentally, the allocations for the two sheds were officially given as one, under the combined heading of 'Bristol'). As will be seen from the registers, while Nos.7801, 7802 and 7804 (and, later, No.7812) were allocated to Bath Road they had regular spells outstationed at Weston-Super-Mare for the stoppers and semi-fasts originating there. The Bristol contingent of Manors was boosted in 1940 when Nos.7809 and 7814 were transferred to Bath Road from Westbury.

Bath Road Manors were used on virtually every type of train, both goods and passenger. A regular return

Manors worked to Aberystwyth, not only from the east, but also from the south. The Carmarthen-Aberystwyth line was a regular haunt right through to 1965. On 1 August 1960 No.7803 BARCOTE MANOR approaches Aberystwyth with the 10.35am ex-Carmarthen. PHOTOGRAPH: MICHAEL MENSING

Although Oswestry Manors were used mainly on the Cambrian Section, they were certainly no strangers to England. In this instance, No.7819 HINTON MANOR arrives at Solihull with the 2.15pm Birmingham (Snow Hill)-Leamington Spa on 5 May 1957. The engine appears to retain its chimney capuchon. PHOTOGRAPH: MICHAEL MENSING

working from London was the 8.05pm Paddington Goods-Kingsland Road (Bristol) routed via Newbury (where it stopped for examination) and Devizes where it took on water. The train was invariably well loaded, and required considerable effort from the fireman, particularly on the climb over Savernake and from Patney to Devizes. In the other direction, Bristol Manors working to South Wales often returned with a heavy coal train bound for the West of England. In contrast, a five coach load to Weymouth (8.5am from Bristol) and return was considered by Bristol men a relatively undemanding day out - an 'office hours' job.

Another fairly regular duty for the Bath Road Manors was the 9.35am Temple Meads-Paddington, returning with the 2.45pm Paddington-Temple Meads via Newbury and Devizes. The Bristol Manors were also frequently used on the 'west to north' mails on Saturday nights/Sunday mornings during the winter. These trains were usually very well loaded - often 25 vehicles, including coaches and parcels vans - and during weekdays were rostered for a Castle or a Star (or, later, a County) via the Severn Tunnel. However, during the winter months the tunnel - invariably referred to by enginemen as 'The Hole' - was closed on Saturday nights and all day Sunday

for permanent way work, and so GWR trains to and from the north were routed, instead, via Gloucester and Ross-on-Wye. This precluded the use of Castles or Stars, and the Manors were the most suitable - and most popular - alternatives. Prior to the introduction of the Manors the 43XX 2-6-0s had worked the Saturday night/Sunday morning 'west to north' trains, and if the 43XX was not in peak condition, the crew were usually in for a very rough trip with the heavy load.

As for 'non standard' duties undertaken by Bristol-based Manors, on 16 June 1940 No.7809 worked double-headed with Grange No.6823 on a Bertram Mills circus special to Worcester. On another occasion No.7809 (again) was observed heading the 1.20pm Taunton-Bristol-Paddington, while on 10 February 1942 No.7802 appeared at Southampton with the 12.45pm from Didcot. On 31 July 1942 No.7802 was seen at Ludgershall, probably with a troop train. Of the Bristol-based Manors, No.7814 proved to have a bit of a jinx in 1946/47 when it was stopped three times in the space of nine months - once at Southall, once at Hereford and once at Taunton. If nothing else, those stoppages reveal further details about where the Bristol engines worked.

Old Oak Common (referred to in the registers as 'Paddington')

Two Manors were allocated from new to Old Oak - Nos.7802 and 7808. The former was transferred to St.Phillp's Marsh after only three months, but the latter remained in London until March 1939 when it was transferred to Gloucester. No other representatives of the class were ever allocated to Old Oak. It has been suggested that one reason for their absence from Old Oak was almost certainly their reputation as poor steamers - the argument is that if the engines had been held in high regard, 'big sheds' such as Old Oak (or Stafford Road) would certainly have held on to them. However, if one studies the duties undertaken by Old Oak, it can be seen that the shed actually had little need for engines such as Manors. Come to that, Old Oak had little requirement for 43XX Moguls either - from the late 1940s, the 43XXs were almost entirely absent from the Old Oak allocation lists, and that was certainly *not* due to their mediocrity.

Apart from the duties already mentioned - Paddington-Bristol semifasts via Devizes and, occasionally, Paddington-Reading locals - the Old Oak locomotives' duties seem to be largely unrecorded. For some years, the class continued to appear in the capital with some regularity, usually on excursion, relief or other special workings; a number of such Manor-hauled workings originated in the Bristol Division, and so a Manor at Paddington would usually be from Bath Road or St.Phillp's Marsh. In later years, the sighting of a Manor in London was something of a treat for the locals.

Neyland

Neyland received three of the first twenty Manors, Nos.7803, 7807 and 7816. They were employed principally on the fish trains from Milford Haven to Gloucester, returning with empties, but in 1942/43 No.7807 was a fairly regular performer on the munitions trains between Llanelly and Saltney via the recently upgraded Cambrian line (Aberystwyth-Oswestry). Even farther afield, on 20 September 1941 No.7807 was noted at Basingstoke. No.7807 departed from Neyland for Oswestry in 1943 and No.7803 went to Aberystwyth in 1946, leaving only No.7816, which remained at Neyland until October 1952.

Shrewsbury

Shrewsbury's early allocation of Manors was fairly short-lived, Nos.7805 and 7806 transferring to Banbury in November 1939 and March 1940 respectively. As already mentioned, principal duty of the two locomotives at Shrewsbury was the 2.55pm (later rescheduled for 2.50pm) milk train from the Independent Milk Supplies depot at Dorrington - the train was GWR-hauled to Banbury, from where the LNER took over for the rest of the journey to Marylebone. Although the Manors forged a strong association with Shrewsbury and the old Cambrian sec-

tion during the BR era (more of which anon), in GWR days their activities westwards were hampered by the classification of the Shrewsbury-Welshpool section as 'Dotted Blue' - this meant that 'blue' engines such as the Manors were subjected to a strict speed limit.

Westbury

The shed received two new Manors, Nos.7809 and 7814. Among their regular duties were milk trains to West Ealing (probably the 6.45am ex-Westbury), and stopping trains to Bristol and Weymouth. No.7809 is shown as outstationed at Salisbury for a few weeks in September/October 1938 - Salisbury, incidentally, had had its own identity (coded SAL) until 1932, when it became a sub-shed of Westbury. The two Manors remained at Westbury only until 1940, when they were transferred to Bath Road. It is unlikely that tears were shed at Westbury when the Manors departed, as they had not been very popular.

Oxley

No.7813 was sent new to Oxley, where it remained until transfer to Newton Abbot in 1948. Like most of its Midlands-based fellows, it was used more on goods than passenger duties. One interesting working was observed on 9 September 1940, when No.7813 was seen with a goods train near Gresty Lane (Crewe) - unless it had worked in from Whitchurch via the LMS line, one must assume that it worked to Crewe via the Wellington-Market Drayton-Nantwich route. The interesting aspect here is that, only the previous year (1939), the working instructions had

stipulated that the Manors were prohibited from the Wellington-Crewe line. We are not sure when the prohibition was lifted, but by the early 1950s (if not before) the Manors were actually allotted loading limits for the route (420 tons from Wellington to Crewe and 392 tons in the opposite direction). In 1939, incidentally, the Manors were one of eight types prohibited from the Wellington-Crewe line - despite the stricture, Castles and Stars *were* permitted on that route. This apparent perversity is presumably explained by limited clearances at platforms - the four-cylinder Castles and Stars, having respective cylinder diameters of 16in and $14^1/4$in, were actually a few inches narrower over the cylinders than the Manors, which had 18in diameter cylinders.

As for passenger workings undertaken by Oxley's No.7813, it was noted with the 6.20pm Paddington-Slough passenger working in March 1940, although it worked home from Slough with a Wolverhampton goods. (A similar pair of workings was undertaken that same month by No.7806 of Banbury). On 4 September 1942 it was observed on the 9.10am Reading-Portsmouth through passenger train.

Gloucester

In March 1939 Gloucester received two Manors - brand new No.7815, and No.7808, transferred from Old Oak. Their principal duty was in conjunction with Neyland-based Manors on the Milford Haven-Gloucester fish trains, returning with empties, but they appeared quite often on goods workings to Bristol via the LMS line. In February 1940 representatives of the class (*not* Gloucester engines) were tried to and from Cheltenham, working the 9.30am ex-Gloucester and the 11.35am return; the engines used were No.7812 of Bristol and No.7819 of Carmarthen.

It is clear that Gloucester's Manors were also used on the Hereford line at a fairly early stage; No.7815 for instance was in collision with LMS (ex-L&Y) 0-6-0 No.12103 on the down platform line at Hereford (Barrs Court) station on 12 February 1944. The Manor was damaged and the Hereford pilot had to work the train (the 8.15pm Hereford-Gloucester) instead.

Gloucester received another Manor in May 1944 when No.7818 was transferred from Worcester, and on 7 August of that year was observed piloting on-loan LNER B12 No.8554 on an ambulance train. A fascinating motive power combination - but one which eluded photographers. Gloucester's stud of Manors reverted to just two in 1946 when No.7808 left for Oswestry. Nos.7815 and 7818 remained until 1952, although they had regular spells

No.7808 COOKHAM MANOR approaches Ash Junction with the 11.35am Redhill-Reading on 16 April 1964. PHOTOGRAPH: P.J. LYNCH

A diary kept by a railwayman during World War II reveals some of the routine activities undertaken by the Manors in the West Midlands. These are the workings he observed:		
Loco and shed	**date**	**seen at/with**
7816 (Neyland)	20.7.40	Stourbridge - goods train
7811 (Banbury)	22.7.40	Stourbridge
7818 (Worcester)	29.8.40	Worcester
7813 (Oxley)	9.9.40	Nr.Gresty Lane - goods train
7801 (SPM)	16.2.41	Kidderminster Yard
7807 (Neyland)	2.7.41	Kidderminster - up goods
7805 (Banbury)	6.7.41	Kidderminster - up goods
7818 (Worcester)	6.7.41	Kidderminster - up goods
7818 (Worcester)	16.7.41	Kidderminster - down Birmingham passenger
7800 (Banbury)	27.8.41	Hockley, Birmingham - light engine
7818 (Worcester)	10.11.41	Kidderminster shed
7806 (Banbury)	26.9.42	Honeybourne - down goods
7805 (Banbury)	10.10.42	Bearley Junction South - down goods
7818 (Worcester)	21.10.42	Worcester shed
7818 (Worcester)	23.12.42	Wylds Lane, nr.Worcester - light engine (up)
7817 (C.Newydd)	24.4.43	Bersham, nr.Chirk - light engine (down)
7800 (Banbury)	15.2.43	Stratford-upon-Avon - passenger train
7801 (SPM)	9.6.43	Evesham - stores train to Long Marston
7818 (Worcester)	10.6.43	Evesham - light engine (down)
7807 (Oswestry)	25.6.43	Oswestry shed
7816 (Neyland)	10.7.43	Evesham - up passenger
7818 (Worcester)	29.7.43	Evesham - up goods
7818 (Worcester)	31.7.43	Worcester - engine and van (up)
7818 (Worcester)	2.8.43	Laverton, Evesham - down goods
7807 (Aberystwyth)	2.8.43	Whitchurch

out-stationed at Cheltenham. It had been a sub-shed of Gloucester since 1932, and as such its former coding of CHEL had ceased to be applied to locomotives. Nevertheless, the official party line seems to have been overlooked in May 1944 when, during a 'general' at Swindon, No.7818 had the long-since defunct code of CHEL inscribed on its buffer beam. The engine carried this inscription until at least 1947.

The Gloucester Manors were at Cheltenham primarily for working on the Midland & South Western Junction line via Swindon and Ludgershall to Andover and Southampton, a route known to railwaymen as 'The Smack'. The section beyond Red Post Junction (near Andover) was on SR metals. The Manors were passed to work via Eastleigh or Millbrook. The first recorded allocation of one to Cheltenham was that of No.7818 in May 1944, but the first Manors had traversed the MSWJ line southwards from Cheltenham some six years previously. Following clearance tests, in 1938 one of the class, apparently ex-works from Swindon, had been used on the 10.29am Cheltenham-Southampton Terminus, returning with the 4.36pm ex-Southampton. At the Terminus, the turntable was not large enough to accommodate a Manor and so (as with larger Southern Railway locomotives) turning was done on the Terminus-Tunnel Junction-Northam Junction triangle. In 1939, No.7815 (of Gloucester) and No.7818 (then of Worcester) were both observed on the MSWJ line at different times.

The use of Manors on the MSWJ line had been made possible by

a programme of bridge strengthening, which had been completed in 1932; previously the Duke class 4-4-0s had been the largest engines in regular use on what had been a 'yellow' route, but the upgrading of the line had been deemed necessary for the improved working of the sometimes intense military traffic. Predictably, there was a considerable amount of military traffic on the MSWJ during World War II, and although Manors were not infrequent participants, it was often those based at Banbury which appeared, working through via Honeybourne and Cheltenham. Among the Banbury Manors noted on the MSWJ line during the war were Nos.7800, 7810 and 7811 (all in 1942); Bristol's No.7802 was also observed on the line in that year.

Croes Newydd

As mentioned earlier, on 31 October 1938 Shrewsbury's No.7805 underwent clearance tests between Ruabon and Barmouth. This was the prelude to the regular use of Manors on that route, and for that purpose No.7817 was allocated from new to Croes Newydd shed at Wrexham. Indeed, from the outset No.7817 had frequent outings on Chester-Barmouth passenger workings, either returning the same day or spending the night at Penmaenpool. However, No.7817 was evidently not confined to the Barmouth route as it is also known to have worked through to Birkenhead, while on 6 January 1942 it was observed on a Reading-Portsmouth through train - possibly a troop special. The engine was also noted with an up local at Paddington on 19 December 1946, but that was almost certainly an ex-works run-

ning in turn. A word of caution here - the official repair sheets state that No.7817 left Swindon Works for Croes Newydd on 14 December, but the engine's appearance at Paddington five days later indicates that the 'book' and 'actual' dates of the return home were slightly adrift.

In December 1940, No.7817 was used on clearance tests between Oswestry and Aberystwyth - a couple of decades later and the Manors were positively synonymous with that line. Apart from a brief stay at Shrewsbury in 1958, No.7817 remained allocated to Croes Newydd until February 1961 - almost 22 years at one shed.

Worcester

Worcester had one brand-new Manor, No.7818, which was transferred to Cheltenham in May 1944. It was regularly observed on goods workings at Kidderminster and Evesham, but it is also known to have had outings on the MSWJ line southwards from Cheltenham; for example, it was noted heading a troop train on 6 August 1939 - thirteen coaches, two vans and a flat wagon, and operated from Malvern to Ludgershall via Honeybourne and Cheltenham. It is believed that, between 1940 and 1944 - i.e. while still allocated to Worcester - No.7818 was used regularly on the MSWJ line to Ludgershall and Southampton. The engine was also noted at Reading in August 1941.

Carmarthen

The last of the pre-war Manors, No.7819, was allocated from new to Carmarthen. It was used mainly on passenger trains to and from Swansea, Pembroke Dock and Neyland. To the north, the Carmarthen-Aberystwyth route was upgraded to 'Blue' status on 2 May 1939 and, more importantly, the Aberystwyth-Oswestry section was re-categorised 'Blue' in 1942. This enabled Manors to be used on the munitions trains between Llanelly and Saltney via Aberystwyth, but it appears that the Manors which were normally employed were those from Neyland and, later, Oswestry. As far as passenger workings go, it seems that Manors weren't used with any sort of regularity on the Carmarthen-Aberystwyth route until 1953. That said, a contemporary magazine reported the sighting of No.7819 at Lampeter in the spring of 1941, although there is no indication as to the nature of the working. No.7819 was transferred to Oswestry in 1943.

Oswestry

Initially, the desire to use Manors on the Oswestry-Aberystwyth route (the old Cambrian main line) was a consequence of the wartime air raids. When the raids commenced it became common practice to divert vital traffic, wherever possible, via secondary and minor (i.e. less vulnerable) lines, but although the Oswestry-Aberystwyth line was considered to be one of the less vulnerable routes, it was hampered by punitive restrictions as to the types of engines which could be used. The restrictions effectively dictated that the largest engines permitted were less-than-modern 4-4-0s, and these were far from ideal for working the heavier trains. But the seemingly obvious solution - that of using more powerful engines such as the Manors - wasn't that simple. One of the problems was that of tight clearances at intermediate platforms, but as related earlier, in December 1940 Croes Newydd's No.7817 undertook clearance tests between Oswestry and Aberystwyth. The other problem was that most of the Oswestry-Aberystwyth line was categorised as 'Yellow', and so nothing heavier than the customary 4-4-0s was officially permitted.

The problem of the 'Yellow' route categorisation of the Oswestry-Aberystwyth line was circumvented - rather than wholly solved - by reclassifying the line as 'Blue'. Although the GWR Civil Engineer had been prepared to upgrade the line in 1938, it is believed that the first actual test run of a Manor was in December 1940. Following the upgrading and the subsequent tests with a Manor, the daily munitions trains (in both directions) between Llanelly and Saltney were diverted via Aberystwyth (dep. Aberystwyth 6.55pm). On the munitions jobs the Manors were used in conjunction with Aberdare 2-6-0s, the first Manor to be noted on one of these workings being No.7806 of Banbury in June 1942.

It was, however, 1943 before a Manor was first allocated to Oswestry shed. This was No.7807, transferred from Neyland during the four-week period ending 1 March. In July of that year it was joined by No.7819, latterly of Carmarthen. Initially, the engines' most regular duties were the morning mail in the down direction, returning with the midday Aberystwyth-Whitchurch, and the 10.00am Whitchurch-Aberystwyth, returning with the up mail in the evening. Later in 1943 it was reported in the contemporary railway press that: '....Manor class 4-6-0s are now working regularly on the Cambrian line'. Apart from the aforementioned duties (and the munitions trains), the Manors also undertook various passenger workings on the Cambrian route during the war. Oswestry's first resident Manor, No.7807, was noted on several such passenger workings, apparently to the satisfaction of at least one passenger - it is said that after arriving at Aberystwyth with the 3.5pm ex-Oswestry on 24 April 1943 he made a 'presenta-tion' to the crew as it was the first 'on time' arrival he could remember. Sorry, but we cannot verify that oft-repeated tale!

Two other Manors, Nos.7802 and 7808, were transferred to Oswestry in April 1946, although the former soon moved to Aberystwyth. It was usual to find one of Oswestry's representatives outstationed at the LNWR shed at Whitchurch; the practice of outstationing engines at that 'foreign' depot had originated in Cambrian Railways days and lasted right through GWR days and into the BR era, principally for the Whitchurch-Aberystwyth services. Another instance of outstationing involved the sub-shed at Moat Lane, which had No.7819 for a short while in February and March 1947.

The Manors were ultimately very successful on the Cambrian section, but the Oswestry allocation remained at a mere three (with only two others at Aberystwyth) until after Nationalisation. The pre-1948 scarcity of Manors in the area was due mainly to the comprehensive rebuilding, in 1936-1939, of twenty-nine Bulldog 4-4-0s, many of which were subsequently drafted to the Cambrian section; the 4-4-0s, with their 'Yellow' route availability, could be used on routes denied to the Manors. But, as we shall see, it was a rather different story in the BR era, when the Manors became synonymous with the area.

On 1 January 1965 - the last day of steam haulage on the Redhill-Reading route - No.7829 RAMSBURY MANOR approaches Reading with the 11.35am ex-Redhill. PHOTOGRAPH: P.J. LYNCH

Aberystwyth

In April 1946, Aberystwyth received No.7802 from St.Philip's Marsh and No.7803 from Neyland. It appears that they performed the majority of their work on the Oswestry route, although the earlier upgrading of the Aberystwyth-Carmarthen line to 'Blue' status permitted them to work southwards as well. By the time they arrived at Aberystwyth it was a sub-shed of Machynlleth - prior to the shed code reorganisation of 1932 Aberystwyth had been regarded as a main shed in its own right, coded ABH.

The 'parent' and 'sub' relationship of Machynlleth and Aberystwyth sheds was not reflected by the allocation of the Manors. Usually, one might expect that a parent shed would need the best engines, but in this instance the Manors had no reason to go 'on shed' at Machynlleth - their daily duties started and finished at Aberystwyth. In fact, it is believed that the first Manors to use Machynlleth shed didn't do so until 1944 - the year after their debut on the Cambrian main line. This 'first' involved Nos.7807 and 7819 (both of Oswestry) which, after finishing their usual duties at Aberystwyth, ran light to Machynlleth to be prepared for a pair of troop train workings from Machynlleth to 'somewhere on the South Coast'. The troop trains actually originated at Tonfanau, but were hauled from there to Machynlleth by 'two small engines' (probably 4-4-0s) as the coast line was then out of bounds to the Manors.

A final word on the relationship between Machynlleth and Aberystwyth - No.7802 was the first Manor to be inscribed with the MCH shed code but was not officially allocated to that shed until 1963.......

Leamington

Leamington was a late addition to the list of sheds which had Manors prior to 1948. In February 1947 No.7810 was transferred to Leamington from Banbury, but its stay was not particularly lengthy, as it moved to Shrewsbury late in 1950. While at Leamington, No.7810 undertook occasional passenger duties to Birmingham and Stratford-on-Avon, but on the whole it had more outings with goods than passenger trains - a familiar situation with most of the Manors based at sheds in the West Midlands. It also occasionally served as the Leamington station pilot.

Devon and Cornwall

Although no Manors were allocated to sheds in Devon or Cornwall until after Nationalisation, that didn't prevent representatives from penetrating into the west in GWR days. On summer Saturdays, in particular, 'foreign' Manors were far from infrequent visitors on the main holiday routes in Devon - Paignton and Kingswear, and through to Plymouth. It seems to have been a slightly different matter in Cornwall, for prior to 1948 appearances west of the Tamar seem not to have been too frequent and, perhaps inevitably, some

such forays were noted in the contemporary railway press. For example, No.7802 of St.Philip's Marsh was observed at Truro on 12 February 1940 (was this the first time a Manor had ventured so far west?), while later that same year - on 6 September - No.7804 (another SPM engine) was noted at Par, and on 26 October No.7802 (again) was seen at St.Austell.

Mr.Maurice Dart personally observed Cheltenham's No.7818 piloting Castle No.4082 on a Royal train heading for Wearde (near Saltash) on 1 February 1947. Later that month, No.7808 of Oswestry was observed at Plymouth - the first sighting of an Oswestry engine at Plymouth, it is believed, for over twenty years. In October 1947 No.7818 reappeared in Devon with a Royal train during a tour of the West Country, this time working in conjunction with Castle No.5069. On the night of 28/29 October the two engines and the train were stabled about a mile or so along the Ashburton branch in South Devon, proceeding to St.Austell in the morning. As mentioned earlier, No.7800 of Banbury is recorded as being under repair at St.Blazey in August/ September 1947. The Manors were to become very familiar sights in the South-west, especially on the Newton Abbot-Plymouth section, but not until 1948.

The next chapter will take up the story on 1 January 1948 - the day when British Railways formally came into existence.

Gloucester Manors were frequently used on the Hereford line, a duty which lasted until the end of their days. No.7815 FRITWELL MANOR pulls into Weston-under-Penyard station - a somewhat minimalist affair, with its platform built from old sleepers - with a Hereford-Gloucester train in August 1964. Although the engine was transferred from Carmarthen to Gloucester in June of that year, the 87G shedplate of Carmarthen is still affixed. PHOTOGRAPH: ANDREW MUCKLEY

Chapter Four

At Work - the BR Period

Where allocations and transfers are discussed, we quote either precise dates (if known) or 'four
weeks ending' dates. In the case of the latter, we have standardised by quoting the month at the end of the relevant four-week period - for example, four weeks ending 9.8.52 is quoted as August 1952. Similarly, four weeks ending 1.11.52 is quoted as November 1952, although the allocation/transfer in question almost certainly occurred during the previous month.

At the time of Nationalisation - 1 January 1948 - the Manors were allocated thus:
Banbury: 7800, 7805, 7806, 7811
St.Philip's Marsh: 7801, 7804
Aberystwyth: 7802, 7803
Oswestry: 7807, 7808,
Bath Road: 7809, 7812, 7814
Leamington: 7810
Oxley: 7813
Gloucester: 7815
Neyland: 7816
Croes Newydd: 7817 (on 1/1/48 was at Chester awaiting repair)
Cheltenham: 7818
Whitchurch LMR: 7819

Ten additional Manors, Nos.7820-7829, were completed at the end of 1950, although the last two were not allocated until the following February. Before being dispatched to their permanent homes the new engines undertook the customary round of running-in turns; among those reported in the contemporary railway press were Nos.7820 and 7824 on Didcot-Oxford locals. Of the new engines, Nos.7828 and 7829 were observed on Wolverhampton-Paddington expresses in April, although those were not running-in turns, for they had by then been allocated to Neath (q.v.). When all the new engines were finally in service in March 1951 the allocation of the entire class was:
Banbury: 7800, 7811
Laira: 7801, 7804, 7809, 7814
Aberystwyth: 7802, 7803 (7802 actually at Stafford Rd Works)
Newton Abbot: 7805, 7812, 7813
St.Blazey: 7806
Oswestry: 7807, 7819, 7820, 7821, 7822
Whitchurch: 7808
Shrewsbury: 7810
Cheltenham: 7815, 7818, 7824
Neyland: 7816

Croes Newydd: 7817, 7825, 7826
Chester: 7823, 7827
Neath: 7828, 7829

We will now look at each depot's Manors in turn. For ease of reference the shed codes are noted - the switch from GWR to BR codes was made in 1950, while the regional boundary alterations of January 1963 are evidenced by the change (not actually executed until September of that year) from the '84' and '89' area codes of the Western Region to the '2' and '6' of the London Midland. For simplicity, the sheds are listed in the order of the familiar numerical system - i.e. '81' group sheds, then '82' sheds and so on.

Reading (coded RDG, then 81D)
The first Manor to be allocated to Reading was No.7814, transferred from Laira in August 1955. Despite rumours that No.7815 was also set to make the move from Laira to Reading, that engine went, instead, to Worcester. During its relatively brief stay at Reading, No.7814 was used mainly on secondary passenger and goods turns, but it occasion-

For many years, Reading and Didcot engines appeared fairly frequently on the SR route between Reading and Redhill. This is Reading's No.7808 COOKHAM MANOR, entering Guildford with the 11.35am Redhill-Reading on 10 March 1964. On the extreme right is USA 0-6-0T No.30064 which, like No.7808, is now preserved. PHOTOGRAPH: P.J. LYNCH

Reading No.7817 GARSINGTON MANOR approaches Reigate on a cold January day in 1963. PHOTOGRAPH: R.K. BLENCOWE

ally had outings on faster passenger workings. One such occasion was Sunday 17 September 1955 - the last day of that year's summer timetable - when it hauled the 1.10pm Paddington-Wolverhampton, which stopped only at Banbury, Leamington and Birmingham.

No.7814 was transferred away in June 1956, and it was 1962 before any more Manors were allocated to Reading. The newcomers were Nos.7808 and 7813 from Tyseley and Nos.7816 and 7817 from Stourbridge, and it was reported in the contemporary railway press that the latter pair were principally employed on up line pilot duties. It should be emphasised that the term 'pilot engines' did not necessarily imply station shunting - on the GWR (and, after it, the WR) the term 'up line pilots' was used for the designated *standby* engines for up trains. A trifle misleading, perhaps, but on the old GWR certain aspects of individuality tended to linger! One random example of the pilot work undertaken by Reading's Manors was that of No.7817 assisting a 'Hymek' diesel on an up express on 31 August 1963.

Whatever their duties, Reading's Manors were usually kept in very good external condition at least. By early 1963 (if not before), Nos.7808 and 7817 had been found reasonably regular work on the SR route between Reading and Redhill, both engines being noted at different times on the 6.51am ex-Read-ing, returning with the 10.50am ex-Redhill. By the end of 1963 the Redhill passenger turns were usually worked by Hymek diesels, but Reading's Manors were not completely ousted from that duty. In August 1964, however, the Redhill duty was allotted to Didcot shed (which reverted to steam haulage, usually employing 2-6-0s), and the four Manors which remained at Reading, being virtually redundant, were transferred away. Although a Manor continued to appear occasionally on the Redhill passenger trains, it was usually one of Didcot's.

As a brief final word on the subject of Reading's Manors on the Southern Region, it is known that one of the engines worked to Ashford in the early 1960s - unfortunately, we have no details save for the fact that it was sent home with less than polite thanks.

As Reading, and also nearby Didcot, had an allocation of Manors in the early and mid-1960s, it might be thought that they worked regularly into London. That, however, was certainly not the case. Indeed, the sighting of a Manor at Paddington invariably warranted an enthusiastic mention in the railway magazines of the day.

A summary of the Reading Manors follows. The figures in brackets (which appear throughout this chapter) are the running totals of Manors at the shed on the dates quoted - for example, in the following list, after the transfers of 5/64 there were five Manors at Reading.

8/55: 7814 ex-Laira (1)
6/56: 7814 to Newton Abbot (-)
8/62: 7816, 7817 ex-Stourbridge (2)
9/62: 7808 ex-Tyseley (3)
10/62: 7813 ex-Tyseley (via Swindon Works) (4)
12/63: 7825 ex-Neyland (5)
5/64: 7829 ex-Llanelly; 7825 withdrawn (5)
6/64: 7817 withdrawn (4)
8/64: 7808, 7813, 7816, 7829 to Swindon (-)

Didcot (coded DID, then 81E)
Didcot only ever accommodated four Manors, and all arrived rather late in the day due to the rapidly dwindling scope for steam traction elsewhere. Nevertheless, Didcot had one significant diagram for the Manors - 2.50am goods Washwood Heath-Reading, 7.0am passenger Reading-Basingstoke (train continued with another loco to Southampton), and the 9.45am goods from Basingstoke to Reading West Junction. As mentioned earlier, in August 1964 Didcot took over the daily through trip to and from Redhill; although this duty was usually entrusted to 2-6-0s it was not unknown for a Manor to be used. The Reading-Redhill workings, which had regularly taken GWR/WR locomotives into SR territory, were given over to diesel traction as from 1 January 1965. However, this did

not prevent Didcot's Manors from penetrating the SR system, one instance being No.7816's trip to Eastleigh with a special van train on 5 March 1965. It enjoyed another foray on 20 May with a parcels train to Micheldever. At that time, incidentally, its tender was still lettered 'GWR'.

In 1965 Didcot occasionally - and briefly - supplied a Manor for the Wrexham van trains, a duty newly acquired by Southall. Although the registers show that Nos.7816 and 7829 were transferred to Didcot during the four weeks ending 7 November 1964, it is clear that No.7829 - at least - actually made the move in October. This is evidenced by observations of the engine on the Reading-Redhill passenger services (6.50am ex-Reading, 11.35am ex-Redhill) on several occasions in October 1964. Didcot shed closed in June 1965, and its three remaining Manors were transferred to Gloucester for the rest of their brief existence.

To summarise:
11/64: 7816, 7829 ex-Swindon (2)
3/65: 7813 ex-Gloucester (3)
5/65: 7814 ex-Gloucester; 7813 withdrawn (3)
7/65: 7814, 7816, 7829 to Gloucester (-)

Bristol sheds (Bath Road - BRD, then 82A; St.Philip's Marsh - SPM, then 82B) The Bristol sheds retained their allo-

cations of Manors for only a few months after Nationalisation, all five engines transferring to Newton Abbot and Laira by mid-June 1948. The Swindon allocation registers indicate that No.7808 had a very brief spell at St.Philip's Marsh in December 1953/ January 1954 - there is no suggestion that it was a case of a stoppage for repair, and so we assume it to have been a 'proper' transfer.

During the opening part of 1948, the duties of Bristol's Manors were, inevitably, very similar to those of the pre-BR era (see previous chapter). Apart from the brief stay of No.7808 at St.Philip's Marsh, during the 1950s Manors were seen only infrequently in the city. There was, however, a minor swansong in the early and mid-1960s, usually involving members of the class which were, at the time, allocated to Gloucester and Swindon (q.v.).

Taking the two Bristol sheds together, the transfers were:
5/48: 7801, 7804 from St. Philip's Marsh to Laira; 7814 from Bath Road to Laira; 7812 from Bath Road to Newton Abbot (1)
6/48: 7809 from Bath Road to Laira (-)
12/53: 7808 ex-Oswestry (1)
1/54: 7808 to Gloucester (-)

Swindon (coded SDN, then 82C) Swindon was another shed which received its first permanent allocation of Manors very late in the day, due to the

rapidly changing motive power situation of the period. Manors had, of course, worked from Swindon virtually from the moment the first of the class had entered traffic, but for some 25 years most such workings had been running-in turns after works visits. There was no intriguing reason why Manors were absent from the Swindon complement for so long - it was simply that the shed had few duties which required engines of that type.

Four Manors arrived in August 1964, displaced from Reading. In the autumn of 1964 No.7816 - paired with a tender inscribed with the letters GWR - was regularly used on one of Swindon's three remaining diagrams. This was the 7.50am Highworth Junction-Oxley goods, returning from Wolverhampton in the late afternoon with the 11.25am ex-Saltney-Stoke Gifford goods. The other diagrams of that period included Swindon-Bristol and Swindon-Gloucester locals. Swindon's Manors were occasionally seen on unlikely workings - for example, on 29 August 1964 No.7816 was noted at the head of the 11.25am Barmouth-Birmingham (Snow Hill), and on that same day No.7829 was observed at Salisbury taking over the 8.48am ex-New Milton to Swansea train.

Swindon shed closed in October 1964 and its four Manors subsequently found new homes yet again, two going to Gloucester and two to Didcot. The

Stranger at the gate..... No.7808 COOKHAM MANOR waits at Reading (Southern), having brought in a train from Redhill. PHOTOGRAPH: B.J. ASHWORTH

During the GWR era, Bristol-based Manors worked to Weymouth reasonably regularly. Although they reappeared at Weymouth in the late 1950s and 1960s, it was usually representatives from Gloucester. This is Gloucester's No.7808 COOKHAM MANOR - in rather lacklustre condition - at Yeovil Pen Mill. The train, it is assumed, is returning from Weymouth to Bristol, and the year might well be 1958; the clue is the presence of 0-4-2T No.1467 temporarily berthed in the bay with the local Yeovil Town shuttle. PHOTOGRAPH: R.C. RILEY COLLECTION

official dates of the transfers were recorded during the four-week period ending 7 November, and so the registers and summary show the date as November 1964.

Swindon's allocation of Manors can be summarised thus:
8/64: 7808, 7813, 7816, 7829 ex-Reading (4)
11/64: 7808, 7813 to Gloucester; 7816, 7829 to Didcot (-)

Newton Abbot (coded NA, then 83A)
For a couple of years or so prior to Nationalisation, the distribution of the Manors had remained fairly constant. That, however, changed significantly in the spring of 1948 when two of the class were transferred to Newton Abbot and four to Laira. Among their intended duties was piloting on the South Devon banks. This usually had to be undertaken by locomotives with a front bogie; in earlier days Bulldog 4-4-0s had been widely used but by the late 1940s Hall, Grange and occasionally even Castles performed much of that work.

Piloting was an everyday part of railway activities in South Devon, the banks between Newton Abbot and Plymouth having presented an operational problem ever since the railway had opened through to Plymouth in 1848.

It had originally been intended to use atmospheric traction on the Exeter-Plymouth line, and in anticipation of this the railway had been built with little concern over the steepness of the gradients. However, the atmospheric system proved to be a complete disaster and so, at a very late stage, locomotive traction had to be adopted instead. Matters were soon compounded. Plymouth grew in importance as a passenger port, and the ocean liner trains from Millbay Docks at Plymouth assumed an extremely high public profile, with little leeway for the difficult nature of the route in South Devon. The GWR invariably put its newest and best passenger locomotives to work on the Plymouth route, but south of Newton Abbot the assistance of a pilot engine was a routine requirement for heavy trains. From May 1948, the Manors were widely used on such duties.

With a Manor attached as a pilot between Newton Abbot and Plymouth, heavier trains could be taken over the South Devon banks. The maximum permitted loads between Newton Abbot and Plymouth were: **King:** 360 tons; **Castle:** 315 tons; **Manor:** 252 tons; **King + Manor:** 612 tons; **Castle + Manor:** 567 tons. In practice, the usual maximum taken by a piloted King or Castle was fifteen coaches - some

550 tons. The best known regular working through South Devon was undoubtedly the 'Cornish Riviera'; during the summer (in the early 1950s, at least) it usually comprised thirteen coaches, but from mid-October ten was the norm. Nevertheless, pilots - usually Manors or Halls - were normally used for even the ten-coach winter period 'Riviera'. In November 1951, incidentally, the 'Riviera' comprised only nine coaches - stated to be '....a record low for modern times....' - but that was partly due to the train being diverted, because of engineering works, via Melksham. Occasionally, even the nine-coach 'Riviera' was piloted (usually by a Manor or a Hall) in South Devon.

As will be seen from the summary (below) and the registers, in May 1948 Newton Abbot received No.7812 from Bath Road and No.7813 from Oxley. These - and subsequent arrivals - were used, not only for pilot work to and from Plymouth, but also local passenger and goods, principally to and from Plymouth, Kingswear and Exeter. The goods workings on the Kingswear line - in the mid- and late-1950s, at least - included coal trains from Kingswear to Torquay Gas Works and returning the empties to Kingswear. At the other end of the scale, in July 1952 No.7806 (and No.7801 of Laira) looked after the Royal train which operated in connection with the Royal Show at Newton Abbot. With its two engines, the train spent the night of 2/3 July stabled at Thorverton on the Exe Valley branch.

It was comparatively rare for any of Newton Abbot's Manors to stray very far afield, among the few recorded examples being No.7809, which was noted at Old Oak on 10 February 1958, and No.7808, observed with the 6.50am Reading-Southampton Terminus train on 26 July 1960. Conversely, the sight of 'foreign' Manors at Newton Abbot was less unusual, especially on peak summer Saturdays when almost any locomotive could turn up anywhere. Moreover, locomotives from other districts were sometimes sent to Newton Abbot Factory for repairs - for example, Banbury's No.7800 was dealt with there in 1952 and Gloucester's No.7810 in 1957.

On 11 June 1958 dynamometer tests had been undertaken between Newton Abbot and Plymouth with No.7813 (of Laira) and Warship diesel-hydraulic D601 - these were part of a series of tests to examine steam and diesel locomotives working together although, of course, the ultimate aim was to dispense with steam altogether. That year, the first of the two series of 'Warship' diesel-hydraulics - the D600 and D800 series - entered service and they soon took over the best West of England expresses. Although the D600

series were to prove embarrassingly unreliable, the D800s fulfilled most expectations and, before long, they displaced steam traction on many West Country express duties. Significantly, the Warships could haul all but the very heaviest trains unaided over the South Devon banks - previously, pilot duties had been among the Manors' customary duties. In instances where banking assistance was still required, the new 'Type 2' (D63XX series) diesel hydraulics had, by mid-1959, largely taken over; furthermore, the 'Type 2s' also proved eminently suitable for many of the secondary duties which, previously, had sometimes been Manor-hauled.

Despite the diesel insurgence in the West Country during 1959, five Manors were transferred *to* Newton Abbot in June and July of that year. Nevertheless, due to the successful diesel invasion all but one was considered surplus to requirements when the summer services ceased in September, and were transferred away. The remaining example was No.7808, which stayed at Newton Abbot until September 1960. A word of explanation about No.7808's departure from Newton Abbot is in order. The registers indicate that it was subsequently allocated to Exeter (q.v.), but it remained there for only three days before being noted as a Worcester engine. We suspect that No.7808 was stopped at Exeter, or possibly in temporary storage while *en route* to its new home.

While on the subject of 'grey areas', let's go back to 1956. In June and July of that year the turntable at Penzance was out of action and various tank engines were drafted in to work the trains between Truro and Penzance. (This is discussed in slightly greater depth in the section dealing with Truro). So - what has this got to do with Newton Abbot? To make good the loss at the depots which had loaned the tank engines, a number of tender engines from various Newton Abbot Division ('83' group) sheds were sent in exchange. Most of the temporary transfers were documented at the time and are included in this book, but there is a mystery surrounding two Newton Abbot Manors, Nos.7812 and 7813. Official records contain no mention of these two being involved in the exchanges but some secondary sources hint that both engines were loaned to Tyseley for a few weeks in June/July 1956. We certainly cannot rule that out, as a couple of sheds in the Wolverhampton Division (to which Tyseley belonged) were among those which sent tank engines to Truro and Penzance, and so there was clearly a minor shortage of locomotives in the Wolverhampton Division as a whole.

Excluding the alleged transfers of Nos.7812 and 7813 in 1956 (to Tyseley 6/56, back from Tyseley 7/56), the post-Nationalisation movement of Manors to and from Newton Abbot can be summarised as follows:

As related in the text, for a while Manors participated in the exchange workings between Exeter and Plymouth. On 20 June 1949, No.7804 BAYDON MANOR - still in GWR plain green - was in charge of the 6.51pm Exeter Central-Plymouth Friary (the last stage of the 2.50pm ex-Waterloo). PHOTOGRAPH: S.C. NASH

A regular task allotted to the Manors at Newton Abbot and Laira was piloting on the South Devon banks. This classic combination is No.7808 and No.6028 KING GEORGE VI. The date is July 1958, and the location Aller Junction. PHOTOGRAPH: DEREK CROSS

5/48: 7812 ex-Bath Road; 7813 ex-Oxley (2)
7/49: 7812 to St.Blazey; 7813 to Penzance (-)
10/49: 7812 ex-St.Blazey (1)
11/49: 7813 ex-Penzance (2)
9/50: 7805 ex-St.Blazey (3)
11/51: 7806 ex-St.Blazey (via Swindon Works) (4)
10/53: 7805 to Hereford (3)
6/54: 7824 ex-Laira (4)
7/54: 7815 ex-Laira (5)
12/54: 7824 to Laira (4)
1/55: 7815 to Laira (3)
7/55: 7806 to Truro (2)
6/56: 7814 ex-Reading (3)
12/56: 7812 to Laira (2)
10/57: 7809 ex-Laira (3)
12/57: 7813 to Laira (2)
9/58: 7809, 7814 to Canton (-)
6/59: 7806 ex-Aberystwyth; 7808 ex-Gloucester; 7818, 7821 ex-Tyseley; 7824 ex-Carmarthen (5)
9/59: 7824 to Tyseley, 7806 to St.Blazey; 7818 to store (transferred to Machynlleth 1/60); 7821 to Tyseley (1)
9/60: 7808 to Exeter/Worcester (-)
* see text, Exeter and Worcester.

Taunton (coded TN, then 83B)
No.7809 is shown in the registers as being allocated to Taunton between June and October 1954. Its regular weekday diagram seems to have been the 6.35am Taunton-Cardiff followed by the 11.25am Cardiff-Bristol, but we do not have details of how the engine usu-

ally returned from Bristol to Taunton on weekdays. On Saturdays, the 11.25 from Cardiff continued to Plymouth and Penzance, which probably meant that No.7809 worked through to Exeter or Newton Abbot

The summary is:
7/54: 7809 ex-Laira (1)
10/54: 7809 to Laira (-)

Exeter (coded EXE, then 83D)
According to the official registers, No.7808 was allocated to Exeter for just three days - from 13 September to 16 September 1960. It is, however, possible that the engine was under repair (or maybe even in temporary store) there before completing its transfer from Newton Abbot shed to Worcester, and so the entry in the registers could well be somewhat misleading. Manors were, of course, not infrequent visitors to Exeter but, that said, even the requirements of summer Saturday traffic didn't necessarily guarantee an appearance by the class in the city. Indeed, a report on traffic movements in Exeter on Saturday 14 July 1951 noted that 163 passenger trains (WR and SR) passed between 9.45am and 7.30pm, but not one was headed by a Manor.

Laira (coded LA, then 83D; recoded 84A in 9/63)
The story of Laira's Manors is similar to that of Newton Abbot's in that they were initially intended principally for

pilot duties over the South Devon banks. It will be noticed in the registers that Laira's five Manors were transferred elsewhere in June 1954 - this seemingly drastic move was due to the arrival of Standard 4MTs, principally for pilot duties during the summer season. Earlier, there had been rumours that 90XX class 4-4-0s would be drafted to South Devon for such duties, but the rumours had proved to be false and all concerned - especially Newton Abbot and Laira crews - had undoubtedly breathed a sigh of relief.

Although considerable emphasis has been placed (both here and elsewhere) on the pilot work undertaken by the Manors in Devon, a word of qualification is in order. Outside of the peak summer season many of the Plymouth expresses were within the loading limits of their charges, and so piloting was required far less frequently. There were, of course, alternative duties available for Laira's Manors - both passenger and goods - and there were also times when a Manor had to step into the breach under unusual circumstances. One example of this came on 8 November 1951 when, due to the failure of Castle No.7001 on the 3.30pm Paddington-Penzance, No.7804 took over at Newton Abbot and hauled the train as far as Plymouth unaided.

Among the other regular duties undertaken by Laira Manors were the well-known (but, sadly, seldom photographed) 'exchange' workings between Plymouth and Exeter, which involved GWR/WR locomotives working on the SR route via Okehampton while SR locomotives worked on the GWR/WR route via Newton Abbot. Those duties had been instigated during World War II so that crews could familiarise themselves with each other's routes in case of emergency, but they continued after the war and were retained until the end of steam.

In the late 1940s and early 1950s the SR trains involved in the exchange diagram were the 2.35pm Plymouth Friary-Okehampton-Exeter Central stopper and the 6.51pm Exeter Central-Okehampton-Friary semi-fast (a portion of the 2.50pm ex-Waterloo). An exception to this occurred during August and early September 1949 when only the up train was worked, the engine proceeding light from Exeter Central to St.David's and returning to Newton Abbot on the 5.45pm stopping train and then working the 7.30pm Newton Abbot-Plymouth stopper. During the mid-1950s a typical exchange diagram involved a Laira engine and crew taking the 2.25pm Plymouth Friary-Exeter Central stopping train and returning with the 6.35pm Exeter Central-Friary semi-fast, while an Exeter engine (not a Manor) and crew would work the 11.47am Exeter Central-Friary stopper and the 4.40pm Friary-Exeter stopper.

During the war, the usual GWR locomotives engaged on the exchange workings were 43XX class 2-6-0s, but

from 1948 until 1954 Laira Manors were regularly used. There were, however, other exceptions. Between 1949 and 1951 the Exeter-based exchange workings were frequently entrusted to an Exeter Hall, while on very rare occasions a Laira Hall was used. For a while in 1951, Star No.4054 PRINCESS CHARLOTTE might be seen on Laira's working. In 1951 the Halls were summarily barred from the Okehampton route upon accusations that they had 'reprofiled' some of the platform faces at the intermediate stations. Standard 4MT 4-6-0s took over most of the Laira-based exchange workings in 1954, but Moguls were later reinstated. Interestingly, by the early 1960s the official list of engines authorised for the Okehampton route included Castles, Counties and Halls (albeit in emergencies only, and subject to strict speed restrictions) but it did not include the Manors.

As for the role of the Manors on exchange duties in the early BR period, between 23 May 1949 and 9 June 1950 Mr Eric Youldon of Exeter observed the working on no less than 133 occasions, noting the following:

No.7801 - 51 appearances
No.7804 - 50 appearances
No.7809 - 5 appearances
No.7814 - 1 appearance
 Other classes - 26 appearances

Mr Youldon adds that Laira invariably turned out the engine in immaculate condition. Indeed, at that time, No.7804 was finished in a smart green

livery, principally for its regular duty as pilot to the 'Cornish Riviera' although, as is evident in the foregoing list, No.7804 wasn't kept exclusively for 'Riviera' duties. There were other points of interest on the exchange workings - on 10 September 1949 No.7801 was piloted on the up train by T9 4-4-0 No.30716 (that must have been a magnificent sight!), while on 15 March 1950 the down Waterloo (which provided the 6.35pm Exeter-Friary) was running late and so, instead of splitting the train at Exeter Central into the portions for Ilfracombe and Plymouth, the train left Central as a whole, double-headed by No.7804 and SR Pacific No.34009, to be divided at either Crediton or Yeoford. Somewhat ironically, the exchange workings provided the only *regular* sightings of Manors at Exeter. Members of the class were to be seen on Exeter-Kingswear stopping trains and long-distance workings on summer Saturdays, but those were casual rather than regular workings. There was also the one-off appearance of Nos.7801 (of Laira) and 7806 (of Newton Abbot) on Royal train duties on 2 and 3 July 1952; as mentioned earlier, the engines took the train from Newton Abbot (where it had arrived in connection with the Royal Show) and took it to Thorverton, on the Exe Valley branch, for overnight stabling.

The Laira-based Manors also worked west into Cornwall. Although they were officially restricted to ten-coach loadings between Plymouth

A heavy boat train - which includes at least two of the special 'Ocean Liner' saloons built in 1928 - leaves Millbay Quay at Plymouth on 2 July 1953. No.7815 FRITWELL MANOR pilots No.4088 DARTMOUTH CASTLE. PHOTOGRAPH: ALAN LATHEY

No.7812 ERLESTOKE MANOR pilots No.6957 NORCLIFFE HALL on the ascent of Hemerdon Bank, some time in 1954.
PHOTOGRAPH: MAURICE EARLEY

and Penzance, there are tentative reports of working solo with loads of up to 14 carriages on that section. The engines also worked to Newquay, and at other times, especially on peak summer Saturdays, were often used to assist Castles, Halls, Granges, Counties or BR Standards (including Britannias) to and from Penzance. One random example of a Manor piloting a Britannia occurred on 13 September 1952 when Laira's No.7809 and Britannia No.70024 double-headed the up 'Cornish Riviera' - loaded to fourteen coaches - out of Penzance. During summer Saturdays in 1959, a pair of Manors usually took charge of the 6am Penzance-Crewe between Plymouth and Newton Abbot.

The Laira Manors were not confined exclusively to the West Country. Various forays were reported, including those of No.7814, seen at Greenford with an up freight on 15 March 1955, No.7820 on the 2.35pm Paddington-Reading on 9 July 1955, No.7820 (again) at Portsmouth on 9 July 1958, and the same engine on a southbound parcels working at Bishops Cleeve (on the Stratford-Cheltenham line) in June 1959.

The arrival of the 'Warship' and 'Type 2' diesels in the West Country in 1958/59 prompted the transfer away of Laira's last Manors, in September 1959. Nevertheless, the Manors which were

allocated elsewhere in the area continued to appear in Plymouth for another year or so. One of the last reported sightings of a Manor at Plymouth - on this occasion at Laira shed - seems to be that of Canton's No.7805 on 27 May 1962. The fairly sudden disappearance of Manors, not only from Laira but also from other sheds in Devon and Cornwall, was the end of an era - for a decade or so, the class had been synonymous with the Southwest.

In the following summary, it will be noted that No.7809 was transferred to Landore briefly in 1956. This is not a misprint. It was a knock-on effect of the turntable at Penzance being out of action - this topic will be discussed in a little more detail under the section dealing with Truro.

As for Laira's Manors, they were:
5/48: 7801, 7804 ex-St.Philip's Marsh; 7814 ex-Bath Road (3)
6/48: 7809 ex-Bath Road (4)
8/52: 7815, 7824 ex-Cheltenham (6)
10/53: 7801 to Chester (5)
6/54: 7804 to Carmarthen; 7814 to Truro; 7824 to Newton Abbot (2)
7/54: 7809 to Taunton; 7815 to Newton Abbot (-)
10/54: 7809 ex-Taunton; 7814 ex-Truro (2)
12/54: 7820 ex-Chester; 7824 ex-Newton Abbot (4)
1/55: 7815 ex-Newton Abbot (5)

8/55: 7814 to Reading (4)
10/55: 7815 to Worcester; 7824 to Shrewsbury (2)
6/56: 7809 to Landore (1)
7/56: 7809 ex-Landore (2)
12/56: 7812 ex-Newton Abbot (3)
10/57: 7809 to Newton Abbot (2)
12/57: 7813 ex-Newton Abbot (3)
6/58: 7805 ex-Hereford; 7815 ex-Worcester (5)
9/58: 7805, 7815 to Canton (3)
9/59: 7812, 7813, 7820 to Truro (-)

St.Blazey (coded SBZ, then 83E; recoded 84B 9/63)
The distinctive part-roundhouse depot at St.Blazey accommodated the locomotives engaged on the china clay traffic in and from the St.Austell area; some of that traffic was exported via the ports of Par and Fowey and some taken by rail to other parts of Britain. St.Blazey also provided the locomotives for the passenger workings on the Lostwithiel-Fowey and Par-Newquay lines, although during the summer the Newquay line accommodated a number of through trains to and from Paddington, Wolverhampton, Manchester, York and Newcastle. The St.Blazey-based Manors were used on the Newquay line passenger trains, apparently working turn and turn about with Granges, and they also piloted heavy trains (most usually on summer Saturdays), sometimes right through between Plymouth

and Penzance or Plymouth and Newquay. Another regular working during the 1950s involved the 5.10am workmen's train from St.Austell to Plymouth and the 4.27pm return - these were used principally by workers at Devonport Dockyard, many of whom had lost their homes during the war and had had to be rehoused well away from Devonport.

As the Manors were mixed traffic engines, they also took their share of St.Blazey's four or five regular goods workings to Tavistock Junction and back. It might be thought that the Manors were also put to use on the china clay trains from the Par and St.Blazey area, but we have found no evidence of that.

It appears that St.Blazey Manors rarely ventured beyond Cornwall and Devon in normal service - the well known report of No.7806 bringing a Weymouth train into Paddington on 19 April 1960, departing with a Paddington-Oxford local and, two days later, working a Reading-Didcot goods would seem to be belated running-in turns. The engine underwent a 'heavy' at Swindon earlier that month, and so it might be assumed that, despite its 'book' return to St.Blazey on 8 April, it actually required further attention at Swindon and did not physically return to Cornwall until a little later.

In 1960 the North British 'Type 2' (D63XX) diesels took over many of the secondary duties in Cornwall, often running in almost permanently coupled pairs. However, the loadings of some trains were such that a Manor was routinely rostered to pilot a pair of diesels, thus forming a spectacular triple header with the Manor at the front. One such turn was the 8.55am SO Wolverhampton-Newquay/Penzance, which routinely had a Manor - usually No.7816 - piloting a pair of 'Type 2s' from Plymouth to Par.

The first Manor to be allocated to St.Blazey was No.7812, which was transferred from Newton Abbot in 1949. The engine was, however, certainly *NOT* the first of the class to visit St.Blazey - as discussed earlier, in 1947 No.7800 of Banbury had actually been repaired at St.Blazey. During the 1950s, the long-term resident at St.Blazey was No.7816. The summary is as follows:

7/49: 7812 ex-Newton Abbot (1)
10/49: 7812 to Newton Abbot (-)
9/50: 7805 ex-Banbury; 7805 to Newton Abbot (-)
12/50: 7806 ex-Penzance (1)
11/51: 7806 to Newton Abbot (-)
11/52: 7816 ex-Neyland (1)
12/55: 7823 ex-Croes Newydd (2)
1/56: 7823 to Truro (1)
9/59: 7806 ex-Newton Abbot (2)
6/60: 7820 ex-Truro (3)
9/60: 7806, 7816 to Tyseley; 7820 to Canton (-)

Truro (coded TR, then 83F; recoded 84C 9/63)
During much of the 1950s, Truro had an occasional allocation of just one Manor. However, three were transferred to Truro in the autumn of 1959 following their displacement at Laira by diesels. The Truro Manors were used mainly on goods workings and sometimes on secondary (stopping) passenger duties. They were also used as pilots on the main line when the need arose. In common with St.Blazey's Manors, those at Truro were occasionally to be seen triple heading in conjunction with a pair of 'Type 2' diesels, but in this instance it was usually due to the failure of one of the diesels.

As far as can be determined, Truro's Manors were also used on the Falmouth line - there is invariably an element of dispute whether that line should be described as a branch or a secondary main line, but we shall avoid that particular debate! The use of tender engines on the Falmouth branch is fairly well documented, although since the removal of the turntable at Falmouth in 1927 *all* tender engines had to run light to/from Truro for turning.

It will be noted that in June/July 1956, No.7823 had a very brief period away from Truro at, of all places, Neath. This was a comparatively long-distance transfer for a Manor, especially for such a short time, and despite initial suspicions that this was merely a 'book' transfer for some obscure purpose the engine, it turns out, *did* make the move. The transfer was, in fact, an indirect consequence of re-

No.7812 ERLESTOKE MANOR, this time with No.5057 EARL WALDEGRAVE passing through Brent with an up train in 1956.
PHOTOGRAPH: T.E. WILLIAMS

The new order cometh. No.7820 DINMORE MANOR pilots D601 ARK ROYAL on an up train through Totnes on 11 October 1958. PHOTOGRAPH: LES ELSEY

pairs to the turntable at Penzance. Rather than have tender-first running between Truro and Penzance, eighteen tank engines were temporarily transferred to Truro and Penzance to work the services between those points. Most of the incoming engines were 51XX 2-6-2Ts, some from sheds in the Wolverhampton and Worcester Divisions and others from sheds in South Wales. Among the latter were Nos.4106 and 4107 of Landore and No.5102 of Neath, and so it appears that Manor No.7823 was sent to Neath as a temporary replacement for 2-6-2T No.5102. When discussing the Manors at Laira (q.v.), mention was made of No.7809 going to Landore on loan - this was to help offset the loan of Landore's Nos.4106 and 4107 to Truro. Still on the subject of Truro Manors in South Wales, No.7823 made history of a minor sort in 1958, becoming the first of its class to be repaired at Caerphilly Works.

Truro's Manors were:
6/54: 7814 ex-Laira (1)
10/54: 7814 to Laira (-)
7/55: 7806 ex-Newton Abbot (1)
10/55: 7806 to Machynlleth (-)
1/56: 7823 ex-St.Blazey (1)
6/56: 7823 to Neath (-)
7/56: 7823 ex-Neath (1)
4/59: 7823 to Aberystwyth (-)
9/59: 7812, 7813, 7820 ex-Laira (3)
6/60: 7820 to St.Blazey (2)
9/60: 7812 to Oswestry; 7813 to Gloucester (-)

Penzance (coded PZ, then 83G; recoded 84D 9/63)
If the Truro complement was small and somewhat irregular, the same applied, but even more so, in the case of Penzance. Various suggestions have been put forward as to the purpose of basing Manors at Penzance. One is that they were intended to help out with heavy peak season passenger trains, but as will be seen from the summary (below), only one of the three allocations - that of No.7813 - coincided even approximately with the holiday period. Another suggestion is that the locomotives were required for the often intense broccoli traffic from Penzance, but the peak broccoli season was in the early spring and No.7824 was the only Manor to be at Penzance at the requisite time.

Assuming that we have hit on the probable reasons for the residency of Nos.7813 and 7824 at Penzance, this leaves No.7806, which was allocated there between September and December 1950. The transfer of No.7806 to Penzance from Banbury coincides with the transfer of 2-6-0 No.6354 *from* Penzance *to* Banbury, and so we can assume that this was an exchange. The departure of No.7806 (to St.Blazey) in December 1950 coincides with the transfer of four County 4-6-0s - Nos.1018, 1019, 1022 and 1023 - from Laira to Penzance, and it therefore seems that the newcomers rendered No.7806 superfluous to requirements. redundant.

The allocation of Manors to Penzance can be summarised thus:
7/49: 7813 ex-Newton Abbot (1)
11/49: 7813 to Newton Abbot (-)
9/50: 7806 ex-Banbury (1)
12/50: 7806 to St.Blazey (-)
11/56: 7824 ex-Shrewsbury (1)
7/57: 7824 to Carmarthen (-)

Stafford Road (SRD, then 84A)
The registers show that No.7810 was allocated to Stafford Road from June to September 1948. Although the engine had previously undergone a light repair at Stafford Road Works, this does not seem to be a case of it being retained as 'Stafford Road Stock' - the Swindon registers indicate that it was a 'proper' allocation.

To summarise:
6/48: 7810 ex-Leamington (1)
9/48: 7810 to Leamington (-)

Oxley (OXY, then 84B; recoded 2B 9-63)
Following the departure of No.7813 for Newton Abbot in May 1948, a little over four years elapsed before Oxley had its next permanent allocation of Manors. The renewed allocation was, however, short-lived, and was not revived until 1962. In 1952, the shed's two Manors seemed to be used principally on goods workings, although No.7811 was observed on a somewhat unusual passenger working on 1 August 1952 - this was the 5.13pm Paddington-Paignton, but although the Manor was seen taking the train out of Paddington, it is

unknown how far west it actually went. Oxley was transferred to the London Midland Region of BR at the end of 1962 and on 9 September 1963 was recoded 2B. Its engines, which included Nos.7806 and 7824, became LM Region stock, but as at other depots which were similarly transferred, it had no effect on the everyday lives of the engines. By then, Oxley's Manors had one goods diagram between them - 9.25am to Shrewsbury, on to Welshpool, and return with the 11.25am Welshpool-Victoria Basin (Wolverhampton) goods. By the beginning of 1965 - when withdrawal had already made significant inroads into the class - two of the survivors, Nos.7820 and 7821, were allocated to Oxley, although on 11 July it was reported that No.7820 was in store. Both engines were, however, transferred to Shrewsbury during the three-week period ending 2 October 1965.

Oxley's Manors were:
5/48: 7813 to Newton Abbot (-)
7/52: 7811 ex-Banbury; 7818 ex-Gloucester (2)
1/53: 7811 to Shrewsbury (1)
3/53: 7818 to Tyseley (-)
8/62: 7824 ex-Stourbridge (1)
9/62: 7806 ex-Stourbridge (2)
10/64: 7820 ex-Shrewsbury (3)
11/64: 7821 ex-Aberystwyth; 7806,

7824 withdrawn (2)
9/65: 7820, 7821 to Shrewsbury (-)

Banbury (BAN, then 84C; recoded 2D 9/63)
The Manors had a strong association with Banbury during their early lives, and at the time of Nationalisation four were still allocated there. However, by then one of their erstwhile star turns had been lost - the 'Ports-to-Ports Express' (Newcastle-Swansea) which, when reintroduced after the war, was re-routed via Swindon and Didcot. In the late 1940s and early 1950s Banbury's Manors seem to have been used more on goods workings than on passenger duties, but details of all the diagrams are not known. Nevertheless, it can be confirmed that one of the Banbury diagrams worked by Manors during that period comprised: 8.38am Banbury-Paddington, assist the 1.45pm Paddington-Stourbridge as far as Oxford; work home with the 5.12pm workmen's train from Morris Cowley to Banbury.

The association with Banbury came to an end in 1952 when the last was transferred away. Replacements for the Manors which departed in 1950/51 were 43XX 2-6-0s (Nos.7800, 7805 and 7806 replaced by Nos.5369, 5391 and 6354 respectively) while in 1952

Nos.7800 and 7811 were replaced respectively by Austerity No.90572 and 2-8-0 No.2835.

Bearing in mind that Nos.7800, 7805, 7806 and 7811 were allocated to Banbury on 1 January 1948, subsequent changes were:
6/49: 7800 to Tyseley (3)
9/50: 7805 to St.Blazey; 7806 to Penzance (1)
12/50: 7800 ex-Tyseley (2)
5/51: 7800 to Tyseley (1)
10/51: 7800 ex-Tyseley (2)
6/52: 7800 to Tyseley (1)
7/52: 7811 to Oxley (-)

Leamington (LMTN, then 84D; recoded 2L 9/63)
The only Manor to be allocated to Leamington was No.7810, which arrived there in February 1947 and was transferred away in October 1950. As discussed earlier, it also appears to have been transferred briefly to Stafford Road between June and September 1948.

To summarise:
6/48: 7810 to Stafford Road (-)
9/48: 7810 ex-Stafford Road (1)
10/50: 7810 to Shrewsbury (-)

Tyseley (TYS, then 84E; recoded 2A 9/63)
The Manors were not particularly renowned for their wanderlust, most of

The D800 series of Warship diesels were far more successful than their predecessors, the D600 series. Nevertheless, the emergence of the D800s did not bring about an immediate cessation of piloting in South Devon, as evidenced by No.7812 **ERLESTOKE MANOR** with D802 FORMIDABLE on the up 'Cornish Riviera' at Hemerdon on 16 May 1959. PHOTOGRAPH: ALAN LATHEY

St.Blazey No.7816 FRILSHAM MANOR - displaying its original chimney - heads an up express near Bodmin Road on 18 July 1953. The identity of the 2-6-2T is unknown, but the use of such an engine on this type of working suggests a holiday train, probably from Newquay. PHOTOGRAPH: E.R. MORTEN

the class spending much of their lives working within a modest distance of their home sheds. That, however, was no reflection on the engines' capability or reliability - it was simply an inescapable fact of life for almost every type of medium powered mixed traffic locomotive.

Among the Tyseley wanderings were those of No.7800, which in 1951 worked Birkenhead-Dover trains through to Redhill with reasonable regularity (normally the engine was changed at Oxford). The through engine workings to Redhill ceased in 1951, and as far as can be determined the next sighting of a Manor at Redhill was not until 3 July 1954, when Tyseley's No.7818 worked through. There were other unorthodox jaunts. For example, No.7800 was seen at Paddington on 11 October 1952, having brought in the 9.12am from Oxford, No.7821 was noted with a parcels train at Reading on 31 December 1953, and in February 1954 No.7818 was observed at Laira shed. Tyseley's Nos.7818 and 7821 (the latter having been transferred from Shrewsbury in December 1953) were both active in the Home Counties early in 1955, No.7818 being noted on the 6.15pm Paddington-Henley on 22 January, while No.7821 was seen on the 5.35pm Paddington-Didcot on 28 January and on the 12.05pm Paddington-

Reading on 5 February. The regularity of No.7821's activities in the London area at that time are, perhaps, evidenced by it having two stoppages for repair at Southall - one in October 1954 and the other in February 1955. During much of 1955, No.7818 worked into London fairly frequently, usually with a Birmingham line goods, and was reckoned to be the only Manor to be making regular appearances in the capital at that time. Some three years later - on 10 February 1958 - No.7821 was observed at Old Oak shed; apparently it was the third Manor at that shed in three days.

Between 1959 and 1963 Tyseley's Manors continued to make occasional appearances at Redhill. On 22 August 1959, for example, No.7824, recently transferred to Tyseley, worked a Birmingham - Hastings service through to Redhill, returning to Reading with the 4.04pm stopper from Redhill. On 23 and 30 June 1962 No.7808 worked the 10.35am Birmingham-Hastings train as far as Redhill while in late November 1963 No.7818 worked through to Redhill (with the daily Banbury-Reading-Redhill goods) on several occasions, and sometimes ventured as far as Merstham to pick up its return working. The Banbury-Redhill through goods ceased for the Christmas period of 1963, and did not

resume. Elsewhere in SR territory, No.7808 was observed at Eastleigh on 22 April 1962.

As for regular workings, for some time the core of duties undertaken by Tyseley Manors involved the Aberystwyth line. During the summer of 1957, for example, Tyseley's No.7818 was regularly engaged on the 7.55am Birmingham-Aberystwyth, returning the same day with the 2.15pm from Aberystwyth; also in that summer, Tyseley shared a cross-working with Aberystwyth (q.v.). During the summer of 1964 No.7823 was regularly observed at Aberystwyth, that same engine having been noted with a passenger working at Towyn on 6 July of the previous year.

During the early 1960s Tyseley Manors were also used on local passenger workings. For example, in January 1961 No.7806 was on a Wolverhampton-Dudley-Stourbridge Junction local while on 8 February 1963 No.7823, having worked to Gloucester, returned part of the way with the 4.08pm Gloucester-Hereford (apparently double heading with 2-6-0 No.6390). In June 1963 No.7818 was observed on the 5.45pm Birmingham (Snow Hill)-Stratford-on-Avon-Evesham (a regular duty for Tyseley Manors at that time) and on 18 April 1964 No.7818 worked the 8.00pm Evesham-Worcester. In the early part of 1963 - by which time

Tyseley had been transferred to the LM Region - its three Manors shared two regular goods diagrams. One turn involved a morning trip from Bordeseley Junction to Swindon, returning the following morning with the 2.15am Swindon-Bordesley. Other duties undertaken by Tyseley Manors in the 1960s - albeit less regularly - included summer Saturday trips to Weymouth with 7.30am Birmingham-Weymouth in 1960. One-off forays during that decade included No.7802's jaunt to Neath in February 1963 (it was noted on Neath shed on 3 February, but the manner of its arrival and departure seems to have gone unrecorded), and No.7818 on Banbury-Westbury goods workings in late 1964.

Before summarising the Manors at Tyseley, it should be pointed out that the list makes no mention of Nos.7812 and 7813 which were allegedly transferred from Newton Abbot to Tyseley for a few weeks in June/July 1956. This unconfirmed transfer - possibly only a loan - was discussed in the section dealing with Newton Abbot (q.v.).

Tyseley's Manors were:
6/49: 7800 ex-Banbury (1)
12/50: 7800 to Banbury (-)
5/51: 7800 ex-Banbury (1)
10/51: 7800 to Banbury (-)
6/52: 7800 ex-Banbury (1)

10/52: 7800 to Chester (-)
3/53: 7818 ex-Oxley (1)
12/53: 7821 ex-Shrewsbury (2)
6/59: 7818, 7821 to Newton Abbot (-)
9/59: 7824 ex-Newton Abbot (1)
9/60: 7806, 7816 ex-St.Blazey (3)
10/60: 7813 ex-Gloucester (4)
12/60: 7808 ex-Worcester (via Swindon) (5)
1/61: 7806 to Stourbridge (4)
2/61: 7824 to Stourbridge (3)
9/61: 7816 to Stourbridge (2)
9/62: 7808 to Reading (1)
10/62: 7813 to Reading (-)
11/62: 7802, 7823 ex-Aberystwyth; 7818 ex-Machynlleth (3)
6/63: 7805 ex-Cardiff East Dock (4)
9/63: 7802 to Machynlleth (3)
7/64: 7823 withdrawn (2)
12/64: 7805 withdrawn (1)
1/65: 7818 withdrawn (-)

Stourbridge (coded STB, then 84F, recoded 2C 9/63)
Only four Manors were ever allocated to Stourbridge - Nos.7806, 7816, 7817 and 7824. As will be seen from the summary (below), their stay at Stourbridge was brief. The usual passenger workings were on the Wolverhampton (LL)-Dudley-Worcester and Dudley-Birmingham (Snow Hill) routes, but they were also observed on the 6.05pm Snow Hill-Leamington (No.7824, 6 July 1961), the midday Wolverhampton-Stourbridge

service (No.7816, 2 December 1961), and the 4.10pm Kidderminster-Dudley-Snow Hill (No.7817, 28 April 1962). That said, the Stourbridge Manors were, if anything, more accustomed to goods workings.

Stourbridge Manors usually kept relatively low profiles, but on 28 April 1962 No.7824 (in conjunction with 2-6-0 No.6339) took over the 'Festiniog Railway Special' at Ruabon (from King No.6000 - a rather distinguished visitor to Ruabon) and worked the train to Minfford, returning later that day from Portmadoc to Shrewsbury. A few weeks later - on 24 May 1962 - Nos.7817 and 7824 were observed on Royal Train duties at Banbury.

To summarise:
1/61: 7806 ex-Tyseley; 7817 ex-Croes Newydd (2)
2/61: 7824 ex-Tyseley (3)
9/61: 7816 ex-Tyseley (4)
6/62: 7806 to Oxley (3)
8/62: 7824 to Oxley (2)
9/62: 7816, 7817 to Reading (via Stafford Rd) (-)

Shrewsbury (coded SALOP, then 84G; recoded 89A 1/61, then 6D 9/63)
Apart from the brief allocation of two Manors to Shrewsbury in 1939/40, it was October 1950 before the class reappeared on the shed's allocation lists. By the beginning of 1953 Shrewsbury

No.7820 DINMORE MANOR rests at St.Blazey shed in July 1960. PHOTOGRAPH: M. POPE

Somewhat late in the day - 18 September 1965 - Oxley's much neglected No.7821 (DITCHEAT MANOR) hauls an up fitted freight near Fenny Compton. In the distance, the overbridges carry the old SoA&MJ line. PHOTOGRAPH: MICHAEL MENSING

had four Manors but just two regular turns for them. Later that year they occasionally found another sphere of activity when WR engines displaced their LMR counterparts on the Saturdays Only 11.25am Shrewsbury-Wellington-Crewe train. Among the locomotives noted on that duty was Shrewsbury's No.7828, but it would seem that that working was not automatically given to a Manor or, indeed, to a Shrewsbury engine, as on one occasion a Bath Road-based County was noted! This was rather different to the late 1930s when the Manors themselves had been prohibited from the Wellington-Crewe section.

Until 1954, Shrewsbury Manors rarely ventured west of Welshpool, but the reintroduction of the 'Cambrian Coast Express' in that year's summer timetable resulted in Shrewsbury engines working the train through to Aberystwyth. The title of the 'Cambrian Coast Express' had been adopted in 1927 for a Fridays and Saturdays Only Paddington-Aberystwyth restaurant car train, although through carriages had operated *daily* on that route since before the grouping, albeit with no title for the service. Named trains disappeared from the timetables during the war, and in many cases were not reinstated until well into the 1950s; in the case of the 'Cambrian Coast', it was revived for summer Saturdays in 1952 and was reinstated as a daily train

(Sundays excepted) for the summer of 1954, the down service that summer usually being worked westwards from Wolverhampton by a Shrewsbury or Tyseley Manor. On Saturdays - with a Tyseley Manor in charge of the down working - the train avoided stopping at Shrewsbury by using the Abbey Foregate loop. The peak period loading for the train was usually twelve or thirteen carriages - a far from insignificant load for a Manor on the Welshpool route - but west of Welshpool, the train was routinely double headed if it comprised more than eight vehicles. During the winter of 1954/55, Shrewsbury's No.7828 was a very regular performer on the 'Cambrian Coast', alternating with Aberystwyth's No.7802. *(The use of Kings on the Paddington-Wolverhampton-Shrewsbury leg of the 'Cambrian Coast Express' is covered in* Peto's Register, Volume One).

During much of the 1950s and at the beginning of the 1960s Shrewsbury had either two or three Manors simultaneously, and apart from 'Cambrian Coast' duties from 1954 onwards, the engines undertook a variety of other duties. Somewhat ironically, perhaps, a sighting of No.7828 on empties from Ironbridge to Shrewsbury on 2 July 1958 was considered noteworthy. How things were to change twenty or so years later, when preserved Manors were commonplace on the southern end of the Severn Valley

line. Other forays reported in the contemporary railway press during that period included that of No.7811 which, on 27 July 1957, hauled the 10.37am Cardiff-Paignton relief and brought the empty stock (11 bogies) back to Gloucester. There was also No.7821 which, on several occasions in early October 1959 (shortly after its transfer to Shrewsbury), was noted working in the Oxford and Reading areas, and No.7821, observed on a Shrewsbury-Chester passenger working on 11 June 1960.

Between late 1961 and late 1962, Shrewsbury was completely devoid of an allocation of Manors, the shed's erstwhile 'Cambrian Coast' duty then being worked by Aberystwyth engines and crews. Manors returned to Shrewsbury in December 1962 due, as much as anything, to their partial (or total) displacement from duties elsewhere. Early in 1963 there were four Manor diagrams (one passenger and three goods) at Shrewsbury, but that, of course, did not imply a secure future for steam traction. The tenuous situation was reflected by Shrewsbury's recently acquired No.7809 which, in April 1963, claimed the dubious distinction of being the first Manor to be withdrawn.

Nevertheless, by the summer of 1963 four Manors were allocated to Shrewsbury. They were, by then, LM Region stock, Shrewsbury having been one of the sheds transferred to that region at the end of 1962. Among the duties performed by Shrewsbury's Manors at that time were the up *and* the down 'Cambrian Coast' on Saturdays. A further six Manors arrived at Shrewsbury (from Machynlleth and Aberystwyth) in January 1965 due to the dieselisation of most of the Cambrian Section passenger services, although the 'Cambrian Coast' remained steam hauled, as did the long established Aberystwyth-Crewe mail, which operated seven days a week. As a result of the changes to operations on the Cambrian Section, from January 1965 the mail train was routed via Shrewsbury. At that time, Nos.7802 and 7803, both immaculately kept, were the usual 'Cambrian Coast' engines, while Nos.7822 and 7828 were normally assigned to the mail.

Apart from the aforementioned duties, the Shrewsbury Manors made reasonably regular forays to Worcester and Hereford. The manner of their journeys to Worcester and Hereford is a little unclear, but it is thought that they worked either the Severn Valley goods or possibly the Croes Newydd-Worcester goods (assuming that the latter changed engines at Shrewsbury - the WTTs certainly allowed enough time for this to be done). Somewhat perversely,

once the engines had reached Worcester or Hereford, their activities seemed to be better reported - for example, on 18 April 1964 No.7801 was observed on a Worcester-Hereford local, on 22 June 1964 No.7800 worked a Gloucester-Hereford local, while on 31 October 1964 No.7801 headed another Gloucester-Hereford local.

A visitor to Shrewsbury shed on 24 March 1965 noted that Nos.7803 and 7827 were '....apparently out of use....' - indeed, the former was soon to be withdrawn. At that time Shrewsbury was the official home of eight of the remaining eighteen Manors but, as with virtually all other surviving types of steam locomotives at that time, their duties became increasingly sporadic. It is, however, evident that they continued to work southwards, as a visitor to Worcester on 11 July 1965 noted Shrewsbury's No.7822 under repair. (This repair is not shown on the Engine History Sheet but, as explained elsewhere in this book, repairs lasting under 14 days did not have to be recorded). The same engine was also observed at Worcester on 3 October 1965 - this time in action.

As for the other Shrewsbury Manors, No.7801 was withdrawn in July 1965 (but was still on shed until at least October), and Nos.7827 and

7828 were withdrawn in October 1965, although the previous month Nos.7820 and 7821 had *arrived* at Shrewsbury, having been transferred from Oxley. By the beginning of November 1965 there were six Manors left at Shrewsbury, but all had been withdrawn by the end of the month. This left just two Manors in BR stock - Nos.7808 and 7829 at Gloucester (q.v.). As a final word on the subject of Manors at Shrewsbury, a visitor to the shed on 15 April 1966 - i.e. over three months after the elimination of the class from BR stock - noted that eight representatives were still there, all with chimneys capped. They were: 7802, 7812, 7819, 7820, 7821, 7822, 7823 and 7828.

Shrewsbury's Manors were:

10/50: 7810 ex-Leamington (1)
11/52: 7828, 7829 ex-Neath (3)
1/53: 7811 ex-Oxley (4)
3/53: 7829 to Carmarthen (3)
10/53: 7821 ex-Oswestry (4)
12/53: 7810 to Cheltenham; 7821 to Tyseley (2)
10/55: 7824 ex-Laira (3)
11/56: 7824 to Penzance (2)
9/58: 7817 ex-Croes Newydd (3)
11/58: 7817 to Croes Newydd (2)
9/59: 7821 ex-Newton Abbot (3)
5/61: 7828 to Croes Newydd (2)
10/61: 7811, 7821 to Croes Newydd (-)

No.7827 LYDHAM MANOR departs from Shrewsbury with an Aberystwyth train on 27 August 1964. PHOTOGRAPH: DEREK CROSS

The down 'Cambrian Coast' approaches Wellington on 30 August 1952, with No.7818 GRANVILLE MANOR in charge. At this time, the train was operating only on Saturdays - all-week operation didn't commence until the summer of 1954. Note the style of the train headboard. **PHOTOGRAPH: BRIAN MORRISON**

12/62: 7800, 7801, 7809 ex-Oswestry; 7812 ex-Croes Newydd; 7819 ex-Machynlleth (5)
3/63: 7819 to Aberystwyth (4)
4/63: 7809 withdrawn; 7820 ex-Cardiff East Dock (4)
8/64: 7800 withdrawn (3)
10/64: 7820 to Oxley (2)
1/65: 7802, 7822, 7827 ex-Machynlleth; 7803, 7819, 7828 ex-Aberystwyth (8)
4/65: 7803 withdrawn (7)
7/65: 7801 withdrawn (6)
9/65: 7820, 7821 ex-Oxley (8)
10/65: 7827, 7828 withdrawn (6)
11/65: 7802, 7812, 7819, 7820, 7821, 7822 withdrawn (-)

Croes Newydd (coded CNYD, then 84J; recoded 89B 1/61 then 6C 9/63)
Croes Newydd's Manors worked mainly to and from Ruabon and Barmouth, sometimes staying overnight at Penmaenpool shed. They also visited Chester regularly. On 2 June 1952 Croes Newydd's No.7823 made history by being the first Manor to work between Barmouth and Machynlleth - it was commandeered from a goods working (the 3.05am Chester-Barmouth) to take over at Barmouth from the failed engine on the 5.35am Pwllheli-Machynlleth. In the easterly direction, more extravagant forays by Croes Newydd Manors weren't completely unknown - witness, for example, No.7817's appearance at Paddington, with a Forces leave train from Bicester, on 20 March 1954.

By the 1960s it was very unusual to see a Manor on a 'Class A' duty (other than the 'Cambrian Coast', of course), but on 8 June 1962 No.7821 worked the 3.33pm Wrexham-Paddington as far as Wolverhampton, returning north with the 6.08pm ex-Paddington. By the start of 1963 - when Croes Newydd was part of the LM Region - it had four Manors available for two diagrams (one passenger, one goods).

As will be seen in the summary (below), the shed's allocation of Manors was erratic - often just one, but occasionally as many as four. As a point of interest, at the time of Nationalisation the only Manor at Croes Newydd was No.7817 - it had arrived there in February 1939, and apart from a very brief sojourn at Shrewsbury in 1958, was to remain until February 1961 - a period of twenty-two years. The summary is:
12/50: 7825, 7826 new (3)
8/51: 7823 ex-Chester (4)
2/53: 7825, 7826 to Carmarthen (2)

12/55: 7823 to St.Blazey (1)
9/58: 7817 to Shrewsbury (-)
11/58: 7817 ex-Shrewsbury (1)
1/61: 7817 to Stourbridge (-)
5/61: 7828 ex-Shrewsbury (1)
10/61: 7811, 7821 ex-Shrewsbury (3)
12/61: 7812 ex-Oswestry (4)
9/62: 7803 ex-Aberystwyth (5)
12/62: 7812 to Shrewsbury (4)
2/63: 7811 to Llanelly (3)
3/63: 7803, 7821, 7828 to Aberystwyth (-)

Chester (coded CHR, then 84K; recoded 6E 2/58)
Chester was one of the sheds where, in the early and mid-1950s at least, Manors were used as all round mixed traffic engines. They were variously employed on passenger workings to and from Shrewsbury and Barmouth, on Saltney-Shrewsbury goods workings, and on the 'Class C' Manchester-Bristol night goods.

Chester Manors had occasional outings on express duties, including the Birkenhead-Paddington services as far as Shrewsbury, but the engines had a significant flurry of express activities during the so-called 'King Crisis' in 1956 (_see Peto's Register; Volume One_) when they took over a number of workings usually entrusted to Castles - this was a continuation of the 'knock-on' effect, the Castles being the immediate deputies for the Kings. One example was the 2.40pm Birkenhead-Paddington which, on 2 February 1956, was hauled from Chester by No.7827. Later that same year - on 27 December - No.7800 was observed well away from traditional territory at Totnes; it was hauling the 12.25pm Manchester (London Road)-Penzance which, inciden-

No.7827, now nameless, pulls away from Shrewsbury with the down 'Cambrian Coast Express' in April 1965. **PHOTOGRAPH: DEREK CROSS**

7815 FRITWELL MANOR, leaves Newton Abbot on 29 August 1954. PHOTOGRAPH: R.C.RILEY

tally, was reported to be running over two hours late - an engine failure somewhere *en route*, perhaps?

When Chester passed to the LM Region in February 1958 many GWR types were displaced from the shed, but the Manors were retained for several months, principally for workings to and from Barmouth. That incursion into LM territory lasted only until August, when Chester's five Manors were transferred to Oswestry. They were:

12/50: 7823, 7827 new (2)
8/51: 7823 to Croes Newydd (1)
10/52: 7800 ex-Tyseley (2)
10/53: 7801 ex-Laira (3)
12/53: 7807, 7820 ex-Oswestry (5)
4/54: 7822 ex-Oswestry (6)
12/54: 7820 to Laira (5)
8/58: 7800, 7801, 7807, 7822, 7827 to Oswestry (-)

Worcester (WOS, then 85A)
There is evidence to suggest that No.7824 might have been allocated to Worcester for a very brief period when new in December 1950, prior to moving to Cheltenham. However, this is not corroborated by the official Swindon registers - the transfer, it seems, was planned, but was subsequently abandoned. There seems to be only one report of the engine's early activities - this concerns the working of the 3.02pm Didcot-Oxford train on Sunday 17 December 1950 but, unfortunately, that duty does little to determine whether

the engine was based at Worcester or Cheltenham at the time.

Excluding the debatable allocation of No.7824, during the BR period only two Manors were ever based at Worcester. Little seems to have been recorded about the activities of either, although it is known that No.7815 made a rare appearances in London in 1958, being observed at Old Oak on 9 February of that year.

Ignoring No.7824, Worcester's Manors were:

10/55: 7815 ex-Laira (1)
6/58: 7815 to Laira (-)
9/60: 7808 ex-Exeter/Newton Abbot (1)
12/60: 7808 to Tyseley (-)

Gloucester (GLO, then 85B)
The shed we refer to is, of course, the ex-GWR premises, latterly suffixed 'Horton Road' in order to differentiate from the ex-LMS shed (itself suffixed 'Barnwood') which passed to Western Region control in February 1958.

At the start of the BR era, two Manors, Nos.7815 and 7818 were at Gloucester, although the latter was, in fact, outstationed at Cheltenham. They were used almost exclusively on the MSWJ line to Southampton, although No.7818 was on a somewhat different duty on 21 December 1951 when, due to the failure of gas-turbine No.18100 on the 12noon Bristol-Paddington, it took over for the rest of the journey. To all-round disappointment, that did

not end in a tale of dramatic recovery, No.7818 bringing the train into Paddington 110 minutes late.

As from 24 March 1952 the SR took over two of the daily return trips on the MSWJ line, leaving only one round trip - the 10.10am ex-Cheltenham and the 4.43pm ex-Southampton - to the Western Region. On 19 April 1952, following tests at Swindon, No.7818 returned to the MSWJ line, but its return was painfully brief as, in June, 43XX Moguls took over the remaining WR duties on the line. Gloucester's two Manors were transferred away, but the absence of the class from the MSWJ was not permanent as, in January 1954, Nos.7808 and 7810 were transferred to Gloucester for use on the route. No.7810 was regularly on the 4.10am Cheltenham-Southampton Docks fast goods, returning with the 11.30am Bevois Park-Cheltenham goods, while No.7808 frequently undertook the main passenger diagram on the MSWJ line - the 10.10am Cheltenham-Southampton, returning with the 4.43pm from Southampton; the typical weekday load was four carriages, but there could be up to eight on summer Saturdays. As mentioned earlier, the Manors couldn't be turned on the 'table at Southampton Terminus and so, in common with larger SR engines, they were turned on the Terminus-Tunnel Junction-Northam Junction triangle.

Even in its days as a Croes Newydd engine, No.7827 LYDHAM MANOR seemed to pop up for photographers at Shrewsbury with distinct regularity. Coaled and watered in readiness for working an Aberystwyth train, it passes Crewe Junction 'box on 28 August 1952. Note the original chimney, complete with capuchon. PHOTOGRAPH: BRIAN MORRISON

A South Coast trip with a difference was undertaken by No.7808 on 11 July 1954, the working in question being an excursion to Weymouth. As related earlier, Bristol-based Manors had been used on the Weymouth route in the 1940s, and so No.7808's appearance at the resort in 1954 certainly wasn't a 'first'.

In November 1954 the Manors lost their regular out and back passenger workings on the MSWJ to Standard 4-6-0s, but as can be seen from the lists, not only did Nos.7808 and 7810 remain at Gloucester/Cheltenham for alternative duties, but a further two (Nos.7809 and 7815) were transferred to Gloucester in December 1958. The

Manors' association with the MSWJ line diminished (probably in proportion with the decrease in services and traffic), but on the last day of through passenger services on the line - 10 September 1961 - No.7808 traversed the route with an SLS special.

Despite the emphasis on workings on the MSWJ, the Manors at Gloucester and Cheltenham were certainly not confined to that line. Among their other regular activities were passenger and goods workings to Cardiff and Hereford, while a 'one-off' involved No.7810 which was noted with a ballast train on the Tenbury Wells line on 2 July 1955. Following the departure of No.7808 from Gloucester to Tyseley late in 1960, Gloucester was without a complement of Manors until June 1964, when Nos.7814 and 7815, late of Llanelly, arrived. Other Manors were subsequently transferred from Swindon and Didcot, but did little more than see out their days at Gloucester.

Among the 'eleventh hour' workings undertaken by Gloucester Manors was a diagram which included the 5.20pm Weymouth-Bristol; No.7813, for example, was noted on that working on 19 December 1964. A few years earlier, Gloucester and Swindon Manors had sometimes substituted for diesel railcars on the Weymouth line. By 1964, Gloucester examples were also used

Gloucester's No.7809 CHILDREY MANOR returns to its former haunt of Canton, presumably in late 1958 or early 1959. The reason for narrowing down the date is that the engine was transferred from Canton to Gloucester in November/December 1959, and was placed in store at Gloucester in March 1959 before moving on to Oswestry. In fact, judging by the Canton-style cleanliness, this picture could well have been taken very soon after its move to Gloucester. PHOTOGRAPH: JOHN HODGE

on passenger workings on the Hereford line, Saturdays Only Gloucester-Swindon passenger trains, and humble pick-up goods turns. Almost all of Gloucester's remaining steam workings were dieselised as from 1 November 1964 but, ironically, a new steam working was created. This was the Saturdays Only 12.45pm Gloucester-Swindon, which was often hauled by a Manor, No.7814 being noted on 21 November 1964 and No.7808 on 15 May 1965, for example. Of those two engines, No.7814 had ventured farther afield on at least one occasion late in 1964, and was observed on shed at Reading on 28 December.

During 1965, in particular, various 'non-local' Manors were to be observed passing through Gloucester, but they were usually withdrawn engines in processions *en route* to South Wales scrapyards - dead engines were prohibited from the Severn Tunnel. Of the Manors withdrawn from Gloucester, No.7815 was noted in store at Barnwood (the ex-LMS shed) early in 1965; a visitor to the GWR shed in mid-July 1965 reported that Nos.7808 and 7829 were in steam, while No.7814 was stored. Of the aforementioned engines, No.7808 had been observed at Banbury on 26 March 1965, having brought in a Bournemouth-York train, and on 17 June had been noted on a Gloucester-Sharpness pick-up goods; the storing of No.7814 was apparently only temporary, as it was seen at Oxford on 16 July.

The report of the shed visit in July 1965 did not mention Gloucester's other Manor, No.7816, which, presumably, was at work somewhere. Confirmation of its still-active status was provided by a sighting at Oxford on 6 July. Two Gloucester Manors, Nos.7808 and 7829, were the last to be withdrawn from BR service, both retiring in December 1965.

As discussed in the section dealing with Worcester shed (q.v.) it has been suggested that No.7824 had a brief period there when new, before moving to Cheltenham, but as that is not recorded officially, it is not included it in the following summary. (For the sake of simplicity and standardisation, the summary deals only with 'parent shed' allocations - i.e. it does *not* note which engines were outstationed at Cheltenham). With Nos.7815 and 7818 allocated to Gloucester (albeit outstationed at Cheltenham) at the time of Nationalisation, subsequent transfers were:

1/51: 7824 (new) * see text (3)
7/52: 7818 to Oxley (2)
8/52: 7815, 7824 to Laira (-)
12/53: 7810 ex-Shrewsbury (1)
1/54: 7808 ex-St.Philip's Marsh (2)
12/58: 7809, 7815 ex-Canton (4)

4/59: 7809 to Oswestry (3)
5/59: 7810 to Oswestry (via Swindon) (2)
6/59: 7808 to Newton Abbot (1)
12/59: 7815 to Aberystwyth (-)
9/60: 7813 ex-Truro (1)
10/60: 7813 to Tyseley (-)
6/64: 7814, 7815 ex-Llanelly (2)
10/64: 7815 withdrawn (1)
11/64: 7808, 7813 ex-Swindon (3)
3/65: 7813 to Didcot (2)
5/65: 7814 to Didcot (1)
7/65: 7814, 7816, 7829 ex-Didcot (4)
9/65: 7814 withdrawn (3)
11/65: 7816 withdrawn (2)
12/65: 7808, 7829 withdrawn (-)

Hereford (HFD, then 85C)
During its 4½-year stint as Hereford's one and only Manor No.7805 was used mainly on goods workings, although it was far from unknown for it to undertake passenger workings to Cardiff and return. It was also used sometimes on excursion work from the Kidderminster area via the Tenbury Wells line to Barry Island or Porthcawl - on these duties, it occasionally picked up a portion from Shrewsbury at Woofferton. The engine also made the occasional noteworthy foray - for example it appeared at Paddington on 6 February 1954 (with a train from Gloucester) and again on 8 September 1956 (leaving with the 1.10pm Paddington-Wolverhampton, although the manner of its arrival in London seems not to have been recorded). As already remarked upon, during much of the 1950s Manors were rare visitors to London, and the appearance of the Hereford representative in the metropolis was, perhaps, all the more noteworthy.

On 14 June 1958 No.7805 was observed working the 9.15pm Cardiff-Tavistock Junction (Plymouth) goods - presumably a case of the engine working its passage to its new home at Laira. It is known that No.7815 (of Worcester) worked a Cardiff-Tavistock Junction goods at the time of its transfer, in June 1958, to Laira, and so one might conclude that that working was a fairly standard method by which an engine was transferred west.

To summarise:
10/53: 7805 ex-Newton Abbot (1)
6/58: 7805 to Laira (-)

Cardiff (Canton - CDF, then 86C, recoded 88A in 1/61; Cardiff East Dock - CED, then 88B, recoded 88L in 3/62 and 88A in 9/63)
Very occasionally, there is a discrepancy between what is recorded in the allocation registers and what actually happened. One such instance concerns the transfer of four Manors to Canton in September 1958 - the registers clearly show that Nos.7805, 7809, 7814 and 7815 were transferred, but in prac-

tice only Nos.7805 and 7814 actually made it. The other two engines went instead to Gloucester, although the relevant entries in the registers show them transferred from Canton to Gloucester in December 1958. Unfortunately, there might be a further inconsistency. According to the official registers, between February 1959 (when No.7814 was transferred from Canton to Aberystwyth) and September 1960 (when No.7820 was transferred to Canton from St.Blazey) Canton had just one Manor on its books. However, during the summer of 1959 the depot had *two* regular Manor diagrams. Unofficial sources state that No.7820 actually went to Canton in mid-1959 (where it joined No.7805), and in view of the depot's two Manor diagrams that summer, the unofficial story might possibly have greater credence than the official one.

Whatever the case, prior to the transfer of Manors to Canton the class had been relative strangers to Cardiff, their only regular duty (back in GWR days) having been on our old friend the 'Ports-to-Ports' between Swansea and Banbury. More often than not, their rare appearances had been on goods or excursions/specials - a Carmarthen representative might come up with a rugby or soccer special, or one might work through Cardiff with an excursion for Barry Island. Examples of excursion workings, quoted by Mr.John Hodge, involved No.7823 of Neath, which skirted the fringes of Cardiff with a ten-coach Barry Island excursion on 2 June 1956, and No.7818 of Tyseley, which headed an excursion from Worcester on 6 September 1958. There was also No.7817 of Croes Newydd - it was noted on Canton shed on 14 April 1957 and again on 4 June 1958, but we cannot confirm that it had worked in with excursions.

Somewhat curious was the appearance of No.7815 on the 11.15pm Pengam-Bordesley goods on 30 June 1958 and the 10.35pm Cardiff-Bristol on 12 July, as the engine had 'officially' been transferred to Laira on 12 June. Another slight discrepancy in transfer dates, maybe? A similar situation appears to have arisen with No.7801 of Oswestry which turned up in Cardiff with an excursion from Swindon on 9 July 1959. At the time, the engine had recently undergone a heavy intermediate repair at Swindon and so the Cardiff trip was probably a running-in turn, but the 'official' date of the engine's return to Oswestry is listed as 2 July.

As for routine matters, the Manors transferred to Canton in 1958 were primarily intended to replace 43XX 2-6-0s on stopping trains to Hereford, Gloucester, Bristol and Swansea. Those duties were, however, subse-

One of the more celebrated duties for Cheltenham-based Manors was the MSWJ route to Southampton. On 10 September 1955 it was the turn of No.7810 DRAYCOTT MANOR, seen emerging from the distinctive tunnel on the immediate approach to Southampton Central station with a northbound working. Note on the right the catenary supports for the generating station's electric locomotive. PHOTOGRAPH: E.R. MORTEN

quently given to Standard 'Class 4s', and Cardiff's humble stud of Manors were found alternative work, principally on goods duties. Nevertheless, during the summer of 1959 Canton had two Manor diagrams (but apparently only one Manor!), and both diagrams still incorporated passenger turns. These were: **Canton 80** - 10.30am Cardiff-Portsmouth (as far as Salisbury), 4.17pm Salisbury-Bristol, 10.50pm Bristol-Cardiff goods (1.05am on Sundays); **Canton 85** - 3.40pm Cardiff-Cheltenham, 7.45pm Cheltenham-Cardiff. On summer Saturdays, the duties included the 9.00am Cardiff-Portsmouth, coming off at Salisbury and returning with the 11.37am ex-Portsmouth-Cardiff, and also on the 5.43pm Cardiff-Gloucester. By the summer of 1960 the only Manor diagram was 'Canton 80', but this later became a BR7 turn. Summer Saturday activities during that year also took in - with reasonable frequency - the 8.30am Cardiff-Newcastle (as far as Gloucester) and the 9.35pm Cardiff-Chepstow.

In the best tradition of the railway press unusual workings by Canton's Manors were dutifully reported. For example, on 8 December 1958 No.7805 was seen heading the 12.45pm Oxford-Paddington, while on 8 April 1960 it was observed on an Oxford-Didcot local. It was noted with a goods working at Tondu on 17 October 1960, and on 29 July 1961 it worked through to Devon with the 8.50am Swansea-Paignton. On 15 March 1962 No.7820 was observed at Ledbury on the 12.05pm Hereford-Paddington. An interesting insight into the opposite angle - that of 'foreign' Manors working

into Cardiff - has been kindly provided by Mr.John Hodge, whose personal observations over a five-year period included the following:
7825 (Carmarthen) - up ECS 26.7.58; **7821** (Tyseley) - 3.40pm Birmingham-Cardiff relief 26.7.58: **7808** (Cheltenham) - 8.17am Carmarthen-Penzance from Swansea to Cardiff 30.8.58; **7811** (Shrewsbury) - 9.05am Birkenhead-Cardiff 4.7.59; **7819** (Oswestry) - 11.40am Birmingham-Cardiff 22.8.59; **7817** (Croes Newydd) - brought in an excursion via Newport 1.7.60; 7803 (Aberystwyth) - 10.35am Kensington-Whitland milk empties as far as Canton, then the 12.05am Cardiff-Shrewsbury 14.2.61 (this *might* have been the engine's journey home after repair at Swindon); **7816** (Tyseley) - 10.35am Pengam-Bordesley; **7808** (Tyseley) - 12.30pm Manchester-Cardiff 19.8.61; **7814** (Aberystwyth) - 11.37am ex-Portsmouth-Cardiff 1.9.62; **7816** (Reading) - 9.00am Bournemouth-Cardiff 17.8.63.

The closure of Canton shed to steam in September 1962 resulted in transfers to other sheds in the immediate area, most of the remaining tender engines going to the newly reopened Cardiff East Dock shed. At that time, the two Manors which made the move to East Dock, Nos.7805 and 7820, retained one passenger diagram between them, but both engines were transferred away in 1963. In 1965 Nos.7804, 7811 and 7826 had brief stints as East Dock engines, and when the shed closed in August 1965 the only Manor still allocated there was No.7804, which was subsequently transferred to Severn Tunnel Junction. Returning to 1962, in that year No.7805 underwent a Light

Casual repair at Caerphilly Works. As mentioned earlier, the first Manor to be repaired at Caerphilly was Truro's No.7823 (in 1958), and apart from an unconfirmed report that Canton's No.7820 was repaired at Caerphilly (presumably between 1962 and 1963), No.7805 is the only other member of the class known to have been repaired there. Our caution about the subject of No.7820 being repaired at Caerphilly stems from the lack of any such entry in the engine repair sheets. Repairs taking less than fourteen days did not *have* to be recorded (although they often were), but would an engine have been dispatched to an establishment such as Caerphilly Works for only a very minor repair? We have doubts. The other side of the argument is provided by the late Mr.Eric Mountford - an extremely well respected railway historian - who, in his book about Caerphilly Works, states that No.7820 was indeed repaired there. We would welcome substantiated details, if only to set the record straight once and for all.

Bearing in mind earlier remarks about possible discrepancies between the 'official' and the actual allocations of Manors to Cardiff, the following moves to and from Canton and East Dock are noted in the registers:
CANTON:
9/58: 7805, 7815 ex-Laira; 7809, 7814 ex-Newton Abbot (4)
12/58: 7809, 7815 to Gloucester (2)
2/59: 7814 to Aberystwyth (1)
9/60: 7820 ex-St.Blazey (2)
9/62: 7805, 7820 to CED (-)
CARDIFF EAST DOCK:
9/62: 7805, 7820 ex-Canton (2)
4/63: 7820 to Shrewsbury (1)
6/63: 7805 to Tyseley (-)
2/65: 7804, 7811, 7826 ex-Llanelly (3)
4/65: 7826 withdrawn (2)
7/65: 7811 withdrawn (1)
8/65: 7804 to Severn Tunnel Jct (-)

Severn Tunnel Junction (coded STJ, then 86E)
Following the closure of Cardiff East Dock shed at the beginning of August 1965, No.7804 was transferred to Severn Tunnel Junction, where it remained until being withdrawn the following month. Initially, we were prepared to suggest that the transfer might have been for book keeping purposes only, but the WR sales list for October/ November 1965 clearly shows that No.7804 was being offered for sale from Severn Tunnel Junction.

We have not found any reference to No.7804 undertaking any revenue earning activities during its brief stay at Severn Tunnel Junction, but comings and goings there - particularly goods activities - usually escaped the attention of most observers. This also meant that many visiting engines went unnoticed. The situation has been summarised by Mr.John Hodge: "On freight services from England which terminated at Severn Tunnel Downside Yard, many of the engines went straight to the shed and then returned from the Upside Yard to the likes of Acton, Bristol, Exeter, Tavistock Junction (Plymouth), Bordesley etc. These services would on occasions produce Manors from Reading, Swindon (ex-works), the West of England and Birmingham. As these did not penetrate beyond STJ, they were recorded by few people. A visit to STJ could sometimes reveal such workings as a Reading Manor on a Channel Islands produce freight via Reading, an ex-works engine working back to a West Wales shed, an out and back running-in trip from Swindon, or simply a Manor away from home appropriated for a trip through the Tunnel or via Gloucester to the Western's principal marshalling yard".

Severn Tunnel Junction's sole Manor was:

8/65: 7804 ex-CED (1)
9/65: 7804 withdrawn (-)

Neath (coded NEA, then 87A)
Neath was one of several sheds which had only a small - and somewhat short-lived - allocation of Manors. Nos.7828 and 7829, in Swindon stock since completion in December 1950, were dispatched to Neath during the four-week period ending 24 March 1951. Apart from the sighting of No.7828 on an up goods at Cardiff on 15 May 1952, little seems to have been recorded about regular duties from Neath. Predictably, though, unusual workings did not escape contemporary observers. Among the noteworthy forays by the two Neath Manors were those of No.7828, on the 7.45am Worcester-Paddington express on 5 April 1951, No.7829 on the 1.45pm Paddington-Worcester express (composed of '.....very old stock, mostly labelled "Wolverhampton".....', so the report goes) on 20 April 1951, No.7828 on a Carmarthen-Birmingham (Snow Hill) excursion in June 1952, and No.7829 taking out the 7.15pm Fishguard boat train from Paddington on 1 August 1952. Of those reports, those concerning Paddington workings were particularly noteworthy as the appearance of a Neath engine in London was wholly exceptional.

Nos.7828 and 7829 remained at Neath only until October 1952, and it was 1956 before the depot had another representative of the class. This was No.7823 which was transferred from Truro for less than a month in June/July 1956 as a temporary replacement for 51XX 2-6-2T No.5102 - the 2-6-2T had gone *from* Neath *to* Truro to assist with Truro-Penzance duties while the turntable at the latter point was out of

use. (This matter is dealt with at slightly greater length in the section about Truro shed). The activities of No.7823 at Neath seem to have gone largely unrecorded, save for the working of a school excursion from Neath to Barry Island on 2 June 1956.

To summarise:
2/51: 7828, 7829 new (2)
11/52: 7828, 7829 to Shrewsbury (-)
6/56: 7823 ex-Truro (1)
7/56: 7823 to Truro (-)

Landore (coded LDR, then 87E)
Another consequence of the repairs to Penzance turntable in 1956 was the temporary transfer of Landore's 51XX 2-6-2Ts Nos.4106 and 4107 to Truro, with the void at Landore partly filled by Manor No.7809 from Laira. This was the only time Landore ever had a Manor on its books, but no details of the duties undertaken by the engine during its stay at Swansea seem to have been reported. We would positively welcome substantiated information.

To summarise:
6/56: 7809 ex-Laira (1)
7/56: 7809 to Laira (-)

Llanelly (coded LLY, then 87F)
Llanelly shed didn't receive its first Manor until the summer of 1962, but less than two years later the shed's stud peaked -albeit very briefly - at six. Prior to spring 1964 the engines worked mainly west to and from Fishguard, but when Carmarthen shed (q.v.) closed in April 1964 Llanelly inherited the responsibility for the Carmarthen-Aberystwyth line, and with it came two ex-Carmarthen Manors. Previously, it had not been unknown for a Llanelly Manor to cover a Carmarthen turn, on 30 De-

cember 1963, for instance, when No.7814 had been noted at Aberystwyth.

During the summer of 1964 the Llanelly Manors were kept fairly busy on the Aberystwyth line, and they also undertook coal workings from Pantyffynnon to Swansea Docks (via the old Rhondda & Swansea Bay line at Swansea). However, by autumn 1964 steam working west of Llanelly had been almost completely eliminated, leaving the Aberystwyth services as virtually the only remaining steam working in the area. During that autumn, Nos.7804 and 7826 were in regular use on two of the three daily passenger trains on the Aberystwyth line, but those services were withdrawn on 22 February 1965 and Llanelly's three remaining Manors were transferred to Cardiff East Dock shed.

The Llanelly Manors were:
6/62: 7804 ex-Carmarthen (1)
2/63: 7811 ex-Croes Newydd (via Swindon) (2)
3/63: 7811 to Neyland (1)
9/63: 7814 ex-Neyland (2)
12/63: 7811 ex-Whitland (3)
1/64: 7826 ex-Carmarthen (via Swindon) (4)
4/64: 7815, 7829 ex-Carmarthen (6)
5/64: 7829 to Reading (5)
6/64: 7814, 7815 to Gloucester (3)
2/65: 7804, 7811, 7826 to Cardiff East Dock (-)

Carmarthen (coded CARM, then 87G)
In GWR days, Carmarthen had had No.7819 from new. As related earlier, it was used on the Carmarthen-Aberystwyth line at a fairly early date, until being transferred away in 1943. It was the 1950s before Carmarthen acquired

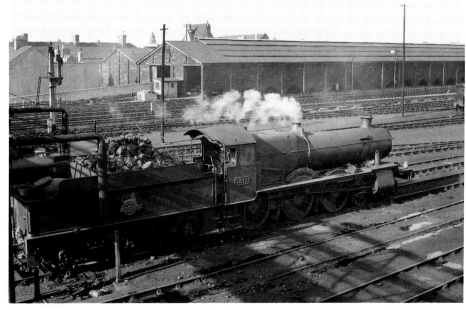

No.7817 GARSINGTON MANOR of Croes Newydd shed visited Cardiff on at least two occasions in 1957/58. This picture, at Canton shed, was taken in the course of its visit on 14 April 1957. PHOTOGRAPH: JOHN HODGE

Canton usually had a good reputation for keeping its main line engines in clean condition, as evidenced here by No.7805 BROOME MANOR, on shed some time during 1961 or 1962. PHOTOGRAPH: JOHN HODGE

any more Manors of its own. In December 1952 No.7826 of Croes Newydd was sent on loan to Carmarthen specifically for trials on the Aberystwyth line - on 7 January 1953 the engine was noted on the 10.45am from Carmarthen and returning with the 5.20pm from Aberystwyth, while on 9 January its duties included the 9.00am goods from Carmarthen. The trials were evidently satisfactory, as in February and March 1953 three Manors were transferred permanently to Carmarthen, where they - and their successors - forged a close association with the Aberystwyth route. Although the Manors' activities on Carmarthen-Aberystwyth passenger workings are well known, it should not be forgotten that the engines also undertook goods workings on that route. During the mid- and late-1950s, for example, Carmarthen Manors had two regular goods workings on the line - the 7.10am and 9.00am Carmarthen-Aberystwyth pick-up workings on Mondays, Wednesdays and Fridays, returning south with the 8.05am and 10.30am goods ex-Aberystwyth on Tuesdays, Thursdays and Saturdays. On alternating days, those diagrams were worked by Aberystwyth engines - usually 2-6-0s.

Carmarthen Manors were not confined to the Aberyswyth line, their other regular duties including local stopping trains and goods, the Neyland and Pembroke Dock portions of expresses, and the 'Pembroke Coast Express' (introduced in 1953). To the east, the engines sometimes ventured as far as Cardiff with goods, excursion and special workings. They also managed their share of straying, including No.7826, which was noted as far afield

as Old Oak Common on 4 February 1956, No.7825 at Exeter (with the 8.45am Liverpool-Penzance) on 28 July 1956, and No.7804 at Wolverhampton (piloting 2-6-0 No.6354 on a special to the Welsh Coast) on 27 July 1957. There were also the instances of No.7826 at Portsmouth on 8 July 1953 and No.7829 on the 7.54am Castle Cary-Weymouth on 5 June 1962, but both those occasions were ex-works running-in turns. (In the case of the latter No.7829 is shown as being ex-works on 31 May, but such a date was rarely that on which an engine physically returned to its home shed - as evidenced here).

As for the Carmarthen-Aberystwyth route, two of the three daily trains each way remained steam hauled (almost always with Manors in charge) until the cessation of passenger services on 22 February 1965. That said, it should be explained that as from 14 December 1964, the trains had run only as far as Strata Florida - flood damage at Llanilar had necessitated the substitution of a bus service between there and Aberystwyth. By then, Carmarthen shed had been closed for several months. Closure had in fact been effected in April 1964, with Llanelly (q.v.)subsequently looking after Carmarthen-Aberystwyth workings.

A summary of Carmarthen's Manors is:
2/53: 7825, 7826 ex-Croes Newydd (2)
3/53: 7829 ex-Shrewsbury (3)
6/54: 7804 ex-Laira (4)
7/57: 7824 ex-Penzance (5)
6/59: 7824 to Newton Abbot (4)
1/61: 7804 to Whitland (3)
10/61: 7825 to Neyland (Whitland); 7804 ex-Whitland (3)

6/62: 7804 to Llanelly (2)
12/62: 7814, 7815 ex-Aberystwyth (4)
3/63: 7814 to Neyland (3)
1/64: 7826 to Llanelly (2)
4/64: 7815, 7829 to Llanelly (-)

Neyland (coded NEY, then 87H)
The Manor allocated to Neyland at the time of Nationalisation, No.7816, was transferred away in 1952, and it was 1961 before the shed acquired another resident example of the class. However, the first new arrivals, No.7804 - replaced by No.7825 - were both, in fact, permanently outstationed at Whitland, the first 'proper' allocation to Neyland itself being that of Nos.7811 and 7814 in 1963.

By the summer of 1963 Neyland had an allocation of three Manors, four Halls and a County - believed to be the shed's biggest ever stud of 4-6-0s. The Manors were used principally on local duties, and the practice of outstationing at least one or two at Whitland was perpetuated. The somewhat parochial nature of their activities was best illustrated, perhaps, by what qualified as their 'star turn'. This roster - a comparatively modest one by the standards of many other sheds - took in the 10.45am Whitland-Pembroke Dock, then the 'Pembroke Coast Express' each way between Pembroke Dock and Carmarthen, and finished with the 6.15pm Pembroke Dock-Whitland. As far as can be determined, prior to 1961 that diagram had been worked by a Carmarthen Manor which was stationed at Whitland for a week at a time, while on at least one occasion in 1963 a Llanelly-based Manor was observed on that diagram. Neyland shed closed in September 1963, its former sub-shed, Whitland, assuming full shed status (as 87H) for the rest of its comparatively brief life.

To summarise:
11/52: 7816 to St.Blazey (-)
1/61: 7804 ex-Carmarthen (1) *
10/61: 7804 to Carmarthen; 7825 ex-Carmarthen (1) *
3/63: 7811 ex-Llanelly; 7814 ex-Carmarthen (3)
9/63: 7811 to Whitland; 7814 to Llanelly; 7825 to store (then to Reading) (-)
* Locos initially outstationed at Whitland (see text).

Whitland (coded 87H in 9/63; formerly sub to Neyland) For details, see Neyland.
The Manors at Whitland from 9/63 onwards were:
9/63: 7811 ex-Neyland (1)
12/63: 7811 to Llanelly (-)

Oswestry (coded OSW, then 89A, recoded 89D 1/61 and 6E 9/63)
Manors had been employed on the

Cambrian Section from 1942, and it eventually became a major stronghold of the class. The main shed on that section - at least, until 1961 - was the one-time Cambrian Railways shed at Oswestry, and although there was only one Manor on its books during the mid-1950s, the stud subsequently increased to nine, and remained at or near that number until late 1962. Furthermore, Oswestry works performed light and general repairs on most of the local Manors.

At the time of Nationalisation, Nos.7807, 7808 and 7819 were allocated to Oswestry, although No.7819 was, on the day in question, outstationed at the LMS shed at Whitchurch. The GWR practice of outstationing one or two Oswestry engines at Whitchurch was perpetuated by the Western Region of British Railways, but under the new regime the Manors were only rarely affected. For the record, the last Manor to be outstationed at Whitchurch was No.7808, which returned to base in July 1951.

As related earlier, in 1953 the WR requested permission to build ten new Manors for duties on the Cambrian Section, but the British Railways Board refused and, instead, allotted a small batch of Standard 4MT 4-6-0s. The 4MTs arrived at Oswestry during the latter part of 1953, and this resulted in the displacement of four Manors - Nos.7807 and 7820 (which moved to Chester), No.7808 (to Bristol) and No.7821 (to Shrewsbury). This left Nos.7819 and 7822. They were used indiscriminately with the 4MTs on passenger work and the morning Oswestry-Aberystwyth goods. The en-gine on the latter duty worked a fill-in pick-up goods to Machynlleth and back before returning to Oswestry with the last goods train of the day.

With the departure of No.7822 to Chester in April 1954, No.7819 was left as the sole representative of the class at Oswestry. It was usually employed on the stone trains from Oswestry to Ardley or High Wycombe, returning home with the empties (the stone, incidentally, originated at Llynclys) but in the summer of 1957 it was regularly rostered to the 2.40am Oswestry-Aberystwyth goods, returning with the 6.20pm goods from Aberystwyth.

During 1958 and 1959 Oswestry exchanged its Standard 4MTs for Manors, and by June of the latter year the shed had no less than nine on its books. Five of the new arrivals came from Chester, displaced by ex-LMS types after the shed's transfer to the LM Region. The majority of the duties undertaken by the Oswestry Manors were to the west (i.e. on the Cambrian Section), although a regular duty in the early 1960s was a trip to Crewe with the 12.35pm ex-Aberystwyth, returning with the 7.45pm Crewe-Whitchurch. At that time, the nine Oswestry Manors shared seven diagrams - two passenger, four goods and one 'special'.

Moving on to our customary summary of unusual workings, on 18 August 1951 No.7820 was observed at Crewe (presumably having worked in via Wellington), and on 13 February 1953 No.7821 was noted bringing in empty stock to Paddington and departing with the 7.10pm to Wolverhampton. On 25 February 1957 No.7819 was seen work-ing a Birmingham-Oxford parcels train via Stratford-on-Avon and Honeybourne - an unorthodox route, taken because of a blockage of the main line due to a collision at Leamington Spa. On 7 November 1960 No.7800 appeared at Paddington, heading the 8.02am from Oxford, while in October of that year the same engine was observed at Pontypool Road. That latter sighting might, however, have been nothing more than the engine's journey home after repair at Swindon. No.7809 was seen heading the 7.45am Crewe-Whitchurch on 19 September 1961, whereas a somewhat higher profile working was undertaken on 9 and 10 August 1963 when Nos.7819 and 7822 double-headed the Royal Train to Pwllheli. Nos.7827 and 7828 (the latter of Aberystwyth) were on standby. Coincidentally, all four engines on Royal duties at that time - Nos.7819, 7822, 7827 and 7828 - are now preserved.

The '89' Division sheds passed to LM Region control at the start of 1963, and on 9 September the sheds were recoded accordingly. By then, four of the Oswestry Manors had already departed for Shrewsbury and one for Croes Newydd, and the remaining four were all transferred away in December 1963. Oswestry remained active as a steam shed until 1965, closing on 17 January, after the cessation of steam workings on the Cambrian Section (the 'Cambrian Coast Express' and the evening Aberystwyth mail excepted).

The three Manors allocated to Oswestry at the time of Nationalisation were Nos.7807, 7808 and 7819. Subsequent changes were:

11/50: 7820, 7821 new (5)
12/50: 7822 new (6)
8/52: 7820 to Aberystwyth (5)
10/52: 7820 ex-Aberystwyth (6)
10/53: 7821 to Shrewsbury (5)
12/53: 7807, 7820 to Chester; 7808 to St.Philip's Marsh (2)
4/54: 7822 to Chester (1)
8/58: 7800, 7801, 7807, 7822, 7827 ex-Chester (6)
4/59: 7809 ex-Gloucester (7)
5/59: 7810 ex-Gloucester (via Swindon) (8)
6/59: 7814 ex-Aberystwyth (9)
7/59: 7814 to Aberystwyth; 7803 ex-Aberystwyth (9)
9/59: 7803 to Aberystwyth (8)
9/60: 7812 ex-Truro (9)
12/61: 7812 to Croes Newydd (8)
12/62: 7800, 7801, 7809, 7819 to Shrewsbury (4)
12/63: 7807, 7810, 7822, 7827 to Machynlleth (-)

Machynlleth (coded MCH, then 89C, recoded 6F 9/63)
and **Aberystwyth** (coded ABH but in 1932 became a sub-shed to Machynlleth)

A minor mystery..... No.7823 HOOK NORTON MANOR is known to have been transferred from Truro to Neath for a few weeks in June/July 1956, and the sight of the engine at St.Mellons West at Cardiff (believed to be with an excursion train returning to Neath) is therefore nothing untoward. The mystery is that the engine displays the 84J shed plate of Croes Newydd. PHOTOGRAPH: R.O. TUCK

No.7824 IFORD MANOR of Carmarthen shed stands at Neyland on 7 July 1958. PHOTOGRAPH: H.C. CASSERLEY

Elsewhere in this part of the book, we have discussed sub-sheds in conjunction with their parent sheds. Although Aberystwyth had been sub to Machynlleth since 1932, there seems to be a case for dealing with it separately - it certainly had a distinct identity of its own and, for most of the time, the Swindon registers identified which engines were officially outstationed there. In the last years of steam, however, the recording of sub-shed allocations was more or less abandoned. We have had to rely extensively on secondary sources for post-1963 events and will therefore discuss the workings of Machynlleth and Aberystwyth engines as a whole.

Bearing in mind the foregoing it might be considered a little ironic that, at the time of Nationalisation, the two Manors nominally allocated to Machynlleth, Nos.7802 and 7803, were actually resident at Aberystwyth. Indeed, No.7802 was recorded as an Aberystwyth engine from April 1946 right through to November 1962, and this prompts the question, whether any other main line tender engine remained at the same sub-shed for anything like 16$\frac{1}{2}$ years? Was No.7802's residency at Aberystwyth some sort of record? As will be seen in the summaries and the registers, until the end of 1963 there were more Manors based at the sub-shed of Aberystwyth than at the parent shed of Machynlleth. However, to fulfil its function as parent shed, Machynlleth had had a new 55ft turn-

table specially installed so that Manors could be turned there. The role of Machynlleth was discussed briefly in the previous chapter, but further comment about the working patterns and motive power requirements and restrictions affecting Machynlleth and Aberystwyth are now appropriate.

The Manors were to become synonymous with the Cambrian Section, and they also became well respected by the local crews. Although some crews elsewhere were critical of the Manors, the engines were a huge improvement on the antiquated 4-4-0s which Cambrian Section men had previously had to cope with. But despite the close association of the Manors with the area, prior to the summer of 1954 they had been seen on the Cambrian main line (Oswestry-Machynlleth-Aberystwyth) only infrequently. Indeed, a report made at the end of May 1954 noted that, during that entire month, the only Manor seen at Machynlleth was No.7819 (of Oswestry), which had been employed almost exclusively on goods duties. On the Machynlleth-Barmouth-Pwllheli section - the 'coast line' - the Manors had been used only since 1952. That, however, had been due to weight and clearance restrictions, as prior to the clearance tests undertaken by No.7802 (of Aberystwyth) in November 1951 the class had been prohibited from the coast line. The first recorded use of a Manor on that line was on 2 June 1952 when, due to an engine failure,

No.7823 (of Croes Newydd) took over the 5.35am Pwllheli-Machynlleth at Barmouth. No.7823, which had been commandeered from the 3.05am Chester-Barmouth goods, took the passenger train on to Dovey Junction, returned light to Barmouth, and then worked home with the 10.30am Barmouth-Ruabon.

By 1953 the Manors were seen on the coast line with slightly greater regularity. They undertook passenger and goods workings, and during the summer they gained a dominion of the Saturdays Only holiday camp train from Pwllheli (Abererch) to Swansea via Aberystwyth. On many summer Saturdays they could also be seen working the up 'Cambrian Coast Express' from Pwllheli. (To recap, the 'Cambrian Coast' was reintroduced as a Saturdays Only train for the summer of 1952 - it did not commence weekday operations until the summer of 1954). In the autumn of 1955 it looked as if Manors were set to make regular appearances on the coast line, as No.7806 was transferred to Machynlleth with the intention of using it between Pwllheli and Shrewsbury. However, the Locomotive Inspector at Oswestry opined that the use of a Manor on the coast line would be a waste of power, and after a year or so No.7806 was transferred to Aberystwyth principally for working the Cambrian main line. The foregoing provides ample evidence that Manors were permitted - and used - on the Dovey Junction-Pwllheli section from 1952 onwards, but in terms of axle weights that section nevertheless officially remained in the 'Yellow' route category, until the summer of 1957.

We have made various references to the 'Cambrian Coast Express' working to Pwllheli. To set the record absolutely straight, the train actually comprised two portions - one for Aberystwyth and one for Pwllheli - which, in the early 1950s at least, were divided/joined at Machynlleth (down train) or Dovey Junction (up train). Following the 'Cambrian Coast's' rebirth as a Mondays-Saturdays train for the summer of 1954, the usual practice was for a Manor to work the down train through to Aberystwyth, returning east with a stopper from Aberystwyth. In the up direction, at first the practice was for one of Aberystwyth's Standard 2MT 2-6-0s to work the train to Shrewsbury, but the timekeeping was often poor - especially after the Barmouth portion had been added at Dovey Junction, thereby making a seven coach loading for the haul over Talerddig. So, for the winter of 1954/55, a 43XX 2-6-0 or a Manor was substituted. That said, the old Duke class 4-4-0s were actually allowed seven coaches over Talerddig, but many drivers wouldn't take more than five with those engines. The Manors were officially allowed nine.

The pattern for working the 'Cambrian Coast' was for an Aberyst-wyth engine to work the up train to Shrewsbury, then work a local to Welshpool and back, and stay overnight at Shrewsbury. The following day, the engine would work a local to Baschurch and back, followed by one to Welshpool and back, before taking over on the down 'Cambrian Coast'. This two-day diagram was worked on alternate days by a Shrewsbury Manor.

Another regular duty undertaken by an Aberystwyth Manor in the mid-1950s (certainly by 1957, if not earlier) involved a 'cross working' with Tyseley. The outward working for the Aberystwyth engine was the 12.35pm Aberystwyth-Birmingham, the engine being accommodated overnight at Tyseley, returning to Aberystwyth the following day with the 8.05am ex-Birmingham.

During the summer of 1957 No.7817 of Croes Newydd was loaned for weeks at a time to Machynlleth. This was in connection with the 'Land Cruise' specials to and from Pwllheli, which involved a complex diagram. During the summer of 1959, No.7817 was regularly given the Saturday diagram which took in the down 'Cambrian Coast Express' - this started with the 7.20am ex-Pwllheli-Paddington (but only from Ruabon to Wolverhampton), returning with the down 'Cambrian Coast', usually assisted by a 2-6-0. As mentioned earlier, although Manors

had worked through to Pwllheli via the coast line since 1952, that route was not officially upgraded from 'Yellow' to 'Blue' until 1957.

Whereas some sheds used their Manors as all-round mixed traffic engines, or in some cases principally on goods workings, the Machynlleth and Aberystwyth Manors were used primarily as passenger engines, the majority of goods workings on the Cambrian Section being handled by 43XX 2-6-0s or 2251 0-6-0s. The Manors' highest profile duty was, of course, on the 'Cambrian Coast Express' west of Shrewsbury. The train was retimed for the 1959/60 winter timetable, and this meant that an Old Oak engine was no longer able to do Paddington-Shrewsbury Paddington in a day; instead, it permitted a Manor to do Aberystwyth-Shrewsbury-Aberystwyth in a day, allowing 51 minutes for the turnround at Shrewsbury. That working was usually entrusted to Machynlleth's best Manor - in early 1960 that was usually considered to be No.7818, fresh from its heavy general at Swindon.

By 1960, it was unusual to see Machynlleth or Aberystwyth Manors east of Shrewsbury, but during the Easter period of that year two of the class were observed in Birmingham - No.7815 (of Aberystwyth) heading the 8.5am Birmingham-Aberystwyth extra on 16 April and No.7823 (also of Aber-

No.7829 RAMSBURY MANOR was a Carmarthen engine from 1953 until the closure of the shed in 1964. While in West Wales, its star turn was the 'Pembroke Coast Express' - it was photographed with the down working at Tenby.

A splendid portrait of Oswestry's No.7809 CHILDREY MANOR at Crewe on 19 September 1961. Believed to be the 7.45pm to Whitchurch. PHOTOGRAPH: MICHAEL MENSING

ystwyth) heading the first part of the up 'Cambrian Coast' into Birmingham on 19 April. Even more noteworthy was the sight of Aberystwyth's No.7823 bringing a goods train into High Wycombe on 22 April (could this report have referred to the working of a stone train from Oswestry?).

At the other end of the GWR/WR empire, the official upgrading of the coast line (Dovey Junction-Pwllheli) in 1957 did not bring about the regular use of Manors right through to Pwllheli. The class was seen on the coast line only infrequently, as evidenced by a report which stated that, in 1960, the only

Manors seen on a weekday at Pwllheli were those hauling the 'Cambrian Coast'. Consequently, sightings such as those of No.7824 with the Ffestiniog Railway Special at Minnfford on 22 April 1961, No.7808 double heading with BR Standard No.78006 on the 8.20am ex-Dovey Junction as far as Morfa

No.7812 ERLESTOKE MANOR pauses at Welshpool with the 12.35pm Aberystwyth-Crewe/Shrewsbury train on 31 March 1962. Mogul No.7336 stands on the right. PHOTOGRAPH: HUGH BALLANTYNE

Mawddach on 24 July 1961 and No.7823 at Towyn heading for Pwllheli on 6 July 1963, were considered noteworthy. Other celebrated 'events' were No.7802 on the 6.40am Machynlleth-Pwllheli in September 1963, No.7823 (then of Tyseley) with a goods at Towyn in July 1964, and the same engine at the same location later that same month, but this time with an eight-coach excursion. Nevertheless, Manors continued to make very occasional appearances right through to Pwllheli as late as 1965, by which time any sort of steam traction on the coast line was regarded as something of a rarity. One such rarity that year was the sighting No.7819 (of Shrewsbury) at Pwllheli on 28 August.

Going back to late 1962, much of the GWR element had by then disappeared from motive power in mid-Wales. Indeed, a contemporary report noted that Machynlleth had only two ex-GWR locomotives left - Nos.7814 and 7815, which were, in fact, at Aberystwyth - the main function of which was to work the 'Cambrian Coast Express' between Aberystwyth and Shrewsbury, although there were rumours that, before long, that duty would be given to a Standard 4MT. The rumours were not without foundation, as at that time Standard types had largely taken over at Aberystwyth as well. A visitor to the area early in 1963 reported that Aberystwyth's Manors and GWR 2-6-0s were all stored, displaced by Standard 2-6-0s and 2-6-4Ts, the latter type even handling the coast portion of the 'Cambrian Coast Express'. Further evidence of change was seen in the servicing arrangements for steam locomotives - by early 1963 (if not before) boiler washouts were no longer being undertaken at Aberystwyth, and engines apparently had to travel to Machynlleth or Oswestry.

The general dilution of GWR/WR influence in the area had been evident even before the transfer of Machynlleth and Aberystwyth sheds to the LM Region in December 1962. A minor side-effect of the regional transfer was that, with Aberystwyth's Manors now officially LM engines, their workings to the south meant that LM Region engines reached Carmarthen.

Despite the changes on the old Cambrian Section, the total demise of steam traction - or even GWR types - in the area was certainly not imminent. At least, not quite yet. In March 1963 Nos.7803, 7819, 7821 and 7828 were transferred to Aberystwyth, and by the summer of that year one of the class was in regular charge of the 10.10am Pwllheli-Paddington as far as Wolverhampton (although the report failed to confirm whether the Manor actually started from Pwllheli). Late in 1963, No.7803, fresh from a 'heavy' at Swin-

Lined green No.7823 HOOK NORTON MANOR makes a lovely sight at Welshpool in the crisp spring sunshine, 31 March 1962, taking water before proceeding with the down 'Cambrian Coast' (11.10am ex-Paddington to Aberystwyth). The stock is in the chocolate and cream livery and in the leading carriage one compartment has been converted for vending machines, as evidenced by the blanked off window five from the front. Note the yard and BRS depot on the right - wholly different from to the present day scene. PHOTOGRAPH: HUGH BALLANTYNE

don and resplendent in a new coat of green paint and with what was described as '....shining silver painted buffers and smokebox door hinges....', was regularly engaged on the 9.50am portion of the 'Cambrian Coast', while a report of a visit to Aberystwyth on 30 December noted Nos.7801, 7827 and 7828 on shed. During the spring of 1964, Aberystwyth's No.7819 was reported as the regular 'Cambrian Coast' engine, while on 10 April a visitor reported seeing Nos.7803, 7810, 7819, 7822 and 7829 working in and out of

Aberystwyth. As from 18 January 1965, most of the passenger services on the Shrewsbury-Aberystwyth section were dieselised, only the 'Cambrian Coast' and the re-routed evening mail from Aberystwyth remaining steam hauled. In late 1964, incidentally, No.7803 had been the regular 'mail' engine. Following the dieselisation of passenger services, there was an exodus of steam locomotives from Machynlleth to Shrewsbury but the former shed remained open to steam until the end of 1966. Aberystwyth, on the other hand, closed on

A twin treat at Aberystwyth on 17 July 1963 - No.7800 TORQUAY MANOR and No.7819 HINTON MANOR. PHOTOGRAPH: P.J. LYNCH

10 April 1965, but remained available as a signing-on point. During those final months of Manor haulage, the 'Cambrian Coast' engine, usually one of Shrewsbury's, was normally stabled overnight at Machynlleth and ran light to Aberystwyth in the morning. Aberystwyth's No.7828 was active on the Cambrian on the last day of scheduled full steam workings - 16 January 1965 - but No.7822 claimed the distinction of hauling the very last train over the Welshpool-Whitchurch line - the 6.25pm ex-Aberystwyth mail - on that same day.

The Manors allocated to Machynlleth and Aberystwyth can be summarised thus:

MACHYNLLETH:
10/55: 7806 ex-Truro (1)
12/56: 7806 to Aberystwyth (-)
1/60: 7818 ex-Newton Abbot (via Swindon) (1)
9/62: 7818 to Aberystwyth (-)
9/63: 7802 ex-Tyseley (1)
12/63: 7807, 7810, 7822, 7827 ex-Oswestry (5)
9/64: 7810 withdrawn (4)
11/64: 7807 withdrawn (3)
1/65: 7802, 7822, 7827 to Shrewsbury (-)

As already mentioned, at the time of Nationalisation Nos.7802 and 7803 were allocated to Aberystwyth.

ABERYSTWYTH:
8/52: 7820 ex-Oswestry (3)
10/52: 7820 to Oswestry (2)
12/56: 7806 ex-Machynlleth (3)
2/59: 7814 ex-Canton (4)
4/59: 7823 ex-Truro (5)
6/59: 7806 to Newton Abbot; 7814 to Oswestry (3)
7/59: 7803 to Oswestry; 7814 ex-Oswestry (3)
9/59: 7803 ex-Oswestry (4)
12/59: 7815 ex-Gloucester (5)
9/62: 7803 to Croes Newydd; 7818 ex-Machynlleth (5)
11/62: 7802, 7818, 7823 to Tyseley (2)
12/62: 7814, 7815 to Carmarthen (-)
3/63: 7803, 7821, 7828 ex-Croes Newydd; 7819 ex-Shrewsbury (4)
11/64: 7821 to Oxley (3)
1/65: 7803, 7819, 7828 to Shrewsbury (-)

Shrewsbury station was not an ideal location for faint-hearted photographers. When it came to 'interior' shots the overall roof presented technically difficult lighting conditions, while the angles for 'exterior' shots were a little restricted. But for those photographers whose skill matched their enthusiasm, the results could be extremely rewarding. This superb view of No.7802 BRADLEY MANOR departing with the 3.10pm Shrewsbury-Pwllheli was taken on 28 August 1952. PHOTOGRAPH: BRIAN MORRISON

Aberystwyth shed, July 1961. No.7809 CHILDREY MANOR and one of the 'new breed' - Standard 2-6-0 No.78003. PHOTOGRAPH: ERIC SAWFORD

Aberystwyth's No.7823 HOOK NORTON MANOR pulls away from Whitchurch with a southbound train, presumably ex-Crewe, on 27 August 1959. A southbound diesel-hauled LM line train waits at the adjacent platform. In the distance to the right of No.7823 can be seen the ex-LMS engine shed at which GWR/WR locos from Oswestry were regularly outstationed until the 1950s. PHOTOGRAPH: R.C. RILEY COLLECTION

Chapter Five

Working with the Manors

Mr Ron Hacker, a former GWR engineman, speaks to Bryan Wilson.

Ron Hacker remembers the Manors well. He started on the GWR in 1936 at Andover Junction shed (alongside the SR premises) and in May 1938 was promoted to fireman and sent to Swindon. In those days, the railway 'grapevine' was every bit as good as it is now, and Ron had word that, following successful route clearance trials, a Manor would be put on the 10.29am Cheltenham-Southampton Terminus and 4.36pm return. Ron arranged the necessary call from bed (having been on night duty) and went to Andover Junction to see the brand new engine on both journeys. In his words, "It looked a treat".

The Manor was the first 4-6-0 intended to run on the old M&SWJ line, although it should be pointed out that a Saint had previously worked a special into Andover and had run to Ludgershall to turn before returning to Swindon. At Southampton Terminus, it was necessary for the Manor to use the Terminus-Tunnel Junction-Northam Junction triangle for turning as the turntable at the Terminus was too small. Similarly, the 'table at Andover couldn't accommodate a Manor.

After a period at Swindon, Ron Hacker returned to Andover Junction as a fireman. This was at the end of the 1938 summer service, and in the following May he moved to Bristol where, at the time, the Bath Road and St.Philip's Marsh main line work was combined into the various links with men working between the two depots, depending on the duty. The top goods link held 72 turns, divided into six links of twelve turns - the links were the Plymouth, Banbury, Birkenhead, Carmarthen, Worcester and London. Ron fired in the London link, ten of the twelve turns of which were lodging or 'double homes'.

When Ron arrived at Bristol, three Manors were allocated there - Nos.7809, 7812 and 7814. Their regular duties included trips to Salisbury, Weymouth and Cardiff, but they were also frequently used on the 9.35am Bristol-Paddington (as far as Swindon, where a Castle took over), returning from Swindon with the 1.00pm all stations to Weston-Super-Mare, and finishing with a local back to Bristol. That duty covered a fairly modest 130-odd miles, and was regarded by crews as a comfortable job in 'office hours' - the Manors, with their smaller wheels, had no difficulties on 'all stations' jobs provided, of course, that the load wasn't excessive.

Like most engine types, the Manors had their idiosyncrasies. One potential problem was that the inclined tube plate made for a firebox with a curved front end, instead of the normal straight end - an unwary fireman might put too much coal up at the front end, and this could build up too close to the brick arch, causing poor combustion with loss of steam. Another trap for the unwary was the single cone ejector, which could cause problems when

HINTON MANOR at Oswestry, 28 August 1952. PHOTOGRAPH: BRIAN MORRISON

7806 COCKINGTON MANOR with the 4.35pm Stourbridge Junction - Birmingham Snow Hill, leaving Brettell Lane station, through the local steel works haze. 26 August 1961. PHOTOGRAPH: MICHAEL MENSING

releasing the vacuum brake on a lengthy train. With a single cone ejector, if leaks on the train could not be overcome by the vacuum pump, frequent use of the ejector was necessary. However, if this method was used almost constantly it was a further drain on the boiler - particularly noticeable on types such as 63XXs and Manors.

Another potential pitfall was that if the pressure fell to 170lb or thereabouts, the ejectors would not release the brakes efficiently.

One regular Manor turn which required full awareness of any possible problems was the 8.05pm Paddington Goods-Kingsland Road (Bristol), which was always loaded to the maxi-

mum of 59 goods wagons and a brake van. On this job, Bristol men travelled to Reading and walked to Oxford Road Junction, where they relieved London men and brought the train to Bristol. Before the war, this duty was the 'home leg' of a lodging turn to London, but it was abandoned during the war when it was considered too risky to stay in London. Having taken charge of the train at Reading, the Bristol crew worked non-stop to Kingsland Road except for a compulsory examination stop at Newbury (remember the days of hot axle boxes?) and for water at Devizes. It was a hard slog with a full load up to Savernake and over the single line from Patney to Devizes. Ron Hacker describes working the 8.05pm goods as a 'balancing act all the way' - a full head of steam was essential to ensure efficient operation of the brakes under all circumstances, but if there were too much fire up front, it was deadened and pressure dropped.

For Bristol crews, another difficult trip was the Sundays Only 12.10am mail train from Temple Meads (the Penzance-Manchester train) as far as Hereford via the Severn Tunnel. This became a regular Manor duty, the class taking over from the 43XX Moguls, which had previously dominated. Ron Hacker worked this train many times between 1943 and 1947, and recalls that it was always very heavy, particularly with a string of vans from the West Country. A banking engine was

7819 HINTON MANOR at Oswestry on 28 August 1952, with the 10.50 Oswestry - Pwllheli. PHOTOGRAPH: BRIAN MORRISON

sometimes available for the climb from Bristol towards Filton, but if not, it was a case of 'flat out and hope', nearly draining the boiler in he process. From Filton, the downhill run to the tunnel gave the opportunity to recover, then it was another bout of hard work on the climb at the Welsh end of the tunnel, with a further slog required from Maindee up to Pontypool Road. After all this came the severe climb from Abergavenny to Llanvihangel - sometimes an LNW 0-8-0 was available to give assistance at the rear, but it was far from unknown for the banker to give up before the train had reached the summit.

That mail train was the last working of the week through the Severn Tunnel. After the train had cleared the tunnel, it was closed for maintenance (and remained closed to traffic all day Sunday), and so the return working from Hereford was routed via Ross-on-Wye to Gloucester (which was weight restricted - hence the need for a Manor), thence via Yate and Stoke Gifford. The return working was also with a heavy train, but was rather more comfortable than the outward trip through 'The Hole'. The Manors, with their larger boilers, were unanimously considered preferable to Moguls on that duty. The part of the return run between Gloucester and Yate was, of course, on LMS metals, and GWR crews were quick

More Manors in the Midlands - 7816 FRILSHAM MANOR on the 4.35pm Stourbridge Junction - Snow Hill, setting off on the Dudley line out of Stourbridge Junction. Whit Monday, 11 June 1962. PHOTOGRAPH: MICHAEL MENSING

to find out if they had delayed an LMS train over that section - on arrival at Temple Meads, almost side by side with the LMS men, the latter were not slow to express their disapproval!

In the other direction, a Bristol Manor was often used on the 5.45am all stations to Salisbury, which usually comprised four carriages. An easy trip? Not at all - during the night, parcels vans from all over the system had congregated at Bristol for Salisbury and beyond, and sometimes as many as 16 vans were tacked on behind the passenger vehicles. With fifteen stops and the climb up Upton Scudamore Bank, it was a very hard duty - in fact, a Grange (68XX) was usually preferred for this

7824 IFORD MANOR at Newton Abbot, around 1958.

Talerddig, perhaps the most celebrated of the Manors' haunts, one which in the last years they made very much their own. PHOTOGRAPH: E.R. MORTEN

task, although a 43XX could be rostered, in which case it was a very hard turn, especially if the engine was in anything other than excellent condition. The return trip was a little easier - all stations (except Avoncliff Halt and St.Anne's Park) with a four-coach loading.

Crews worked all the time on locomotives from other sheds, and Ron Hacker tells of the 11.22am Bristol-Reading passenger (via Devizes), which made no less than twenty stops (plus Manningford Halt on Thursdays). This was usually a job for a Reading Hall but the crew worked home with a

Manor, which had left Paddington at 2.45pm for Newbury, where the train divided - the front four carriages continued semi-fast to Bristol (a fairly easy duty, Ron recalls), while the other carriages worked all stations to Devizes and Temple Meads. Apart from working on 'foreign' locomotives, crews often

7802 BRADLEY MANOR at Shrewsbury shed. 7802 was one of the Manors which passed to the London Midland Region. This had little effect at first, though an inevitable outcome was the survival of (often utterly woebegone) ex-GW engines after all their brethren had gone on the Western Region. Another odd circumstance was that the ex-WR territory became an LM 'frontier', and while dieselisation went on apace on the rest of the 'new' region, the former WR lines first went through a phase where native steam was supplanted by Black 5s, 8Fs and Standards. PHOTOGRAPH: R.K. BLENCOWE

Front ends at Shrewsbury - GRANVILLE MANOR alongside CALCOT GRANGE, and an earnest conversation. PHOTOGRAPH: R.K. BLENCOWE

worked diagrams which took them outside their 'home' area. At Bath Road shed in Bristol, men working the Super Spare link signed for 12 of the 15 Working Timetables which the GWR published! Consequently, the two Bristol sheds had, between them, a greater route mileage than any other GWR depot, although it seems that did not unduly affect the Manors.

Of all the duties undertaken by footplate crews, there were few which were regarded as 'comfortable' in terms of the hours and the degree of hard graft. One of Bristol's 'comfy' turns was the 8.5am Bristol-Weymouth and 12.25pm return, normally a job for a diesel railcar set with a coach sandwiched in the middle, but in the event of non-availability the usual substitute was a Manor and a five-coach train. As if to add to the icing on the crew`s cake, Weymouth men usually serviced the engine while the Bristol men had a break. Ron Hacker opines - with tongue partly in cheek! - that the most taxing part of this duty was remembering to stop at places such as Sparkford and Marston Magna on Wednesdays or Saturdays, depending on when market day was!

In 1950 Ron became a driver at Frome, but at the end of 1952 he took the opportunity of returning to Bristol. By this time Manors were no longer allocated to Bristol, but Ron occasionally took charge of one from another shed which had worked through, and did so virtually until the end of the

steam era. He remembers the Manors as capable engines, but emphasises that, to get the best out of them, it was essential to take into account the two significant departures from the norm - the design of the firebox and the single-cone ejector - and to remember that with Stephenson link motion, cut-off could not be reduced below 25% to avoid rough riding or jerking the train. Ron confirms that although the Manors had a 'bit in hand' over the 43XXs, they were certainly not up to

the Granges, despite sharing the same power classification - 'D' under GWR auspices, 5MT under BR.

Below. Newton Abbot, and 7814 rumbles along in company with a 2-6-2T.

Chapter Six
Preservation

No less than nine Manors - almost *one third* of the class - are now preserved. Furthermore, four of the preserved engines have spent almost as long in preservation as they did under GWR/BR ownership, while the other five have spent virtually *twice* as long in preservation as they did in BR service. For those of us who recall the demise of BR steam as being 'not very long ago', that is a sobering (or ageing!) thought.

Eight of the Manors which are now preserved were rescued from the Woodham Bros. yard at Barry. Between 1959 and 1968 Woodham's purchased a total of 288 locomotives (of which 163 were of GWR pedigree) from BR. The locomotives were purchased solely as scrap - BR had realised that it could not cut up or dispose of all of its 16,000-odd steam locomotives, and so it had invited outside contractors to bid for the scrap metal. Woodham Bros. was one of a couple of dozen or so contractors whose bids were accepted by BR.

Dai Woodham became regarded by many as the saviour of steam, but in fact he had negligible interest in railways. He purchased the locomotives solely for their scrap value, and the fact that many of them lingered intact at Barry for several years was due partly to the weight of numbers. As a rule of thumb it took two men one week to cut up a medium size steam locomotive, and as Woodham's had only a relatively small workforce it was inevitable that a backlog would develop. Another factor in the equation was that until 1973 the price of scrap metal was subject to controls - with the relaxation of controls in the offing, it is not surprising that there was no rush to convert locomotives into scrap at the old prices.

Woodham's did not actually dispense with their last steam locomotive until 1990, when 2-6-2T No.5553 left the yard - still substantially intact - for static display locally, although it has since moved to the Great Central Railway (at Loughborough) for full restoration to working order. The fact that No.5553 had escaped cutting up reflected Dai Woodham's unintentional role in the British railway preservation movement as, by that time, some 200 of the 288 BR locomotives which he had purchased for scrap had been rescued.

No.7802 BRADLEY MANOR
Although withdrawn from BR service in November 1965, No.7802 was noted 'in store' at Shrewsbury shed in June the following year. It was later sold as scrap to Woodhams, but was rescued in November 1979 and taken to the Severn Valley Railway for restoration. It was steamed again in April 1993. In September 1994, when on loan to the West Somerset Railway, it was involved in a tragic accident - a woman, trying to rescue her dog who had strayed on to the line, was run over by the locomotive and received fatal injuries.

No.7802 was earmarked for several main line outings in 1995 - among them Worcester-Didcot-Bristol on 27 May and Bristol to Paignton and return on 29 May and 30 July - but its activities were severely curtailed by the ban on main line steam, as a possible fire risk, during the prolonged spell of very dry weather. Furthermore, during that same summer the relationship between steam locomotive operators and the Special Trains Unit of BR deteriorated significantly and placed a longer-term question mark over the feasibility (and viability) of main line steam specials. Adopting a fatalistic stance, if main line steam outings were to be drastically reduced in the future, that wouldn't affect the Manors as much as some other types as only three have ever performed 'preserved' main line duties. At the time of writing (spring 1996) No.7802 is the only representative to have a

No.7808 COOKHAM MANOR participated in the Stockton & Darlington anniversary celebrations in 1975, and was photographed passing through York station *en route* to Darlington on 11 July. PHOTOGRAPH: LES NIXON

On more familiar territory, No.7808 COOKHAM MANOR works in conjunction with No.6998 BURTON AGNES HALL on an excursion near Ledbury on 14 June 1975. PHOTOGRAPH: LES NIXON

current 'main line' ticket; since returning to traffic it has been paired with Collett-pattern 4000-gallon tender No.2792.

No.7808 COOKHAM MANOR
In January 1966, BR sold No.7808 in working order to a private purchaser. It was, therefore, the only Manor to enter the preservation arena from a source other than Woodham's. Following its sale, No.7808 was stored at Gloucester shed while awaiting outings on rail tours during the summer of 1966, but the planned tours were thwarted by the locomotive requiring new piston rings. No.7808 nevertheless returned to action on 14 July, working from Gloucester to Honeybourne and return, and on 17 September worked to Taplow where it was exhibited during the Great Western Society's open day. The locomotive was also a guest at the open day at Bath Road diesel depot in Bristol on 22 October, and returned for the following year's open day on 19 October.

After a period at Messrs Dowty's at Ashchurch, during which it had at least one outing (Tyseley open day on 28 September 1969), No.7808 was transferred to the GWR Society headquarters at Didcot in August 1970. It took part in the Stockton & Darlington 150th anniversary celebrations in 1975, the main event being the grand cavalcade on 31 August, and subsequently returned to Didcot, where it still resides as a static exhibit. At the time of writing, there seem to be no proposals to return it to work.

No.7812 ERLESTOKE MANOR
No.7812 was withdrawn in November 1965 and sold as scrap to Woodhams. On 28 June 1973, it was purchased at a cost of £4,400 (including 10% VAT - how times change!), by a quartet of enthusiasts. The locomotive was subsequently found a temporary home at the premises of Messrs Dowty at Ashchurch in Gloucestershire before moving to the Severn Valley Railway. When purchased from Woodham's No.7812 was in comparatively good condition, but it was still necessary to raise additional funds to restore it to full working order. It was 11 May 1979 before No.7812 undertook a test steaming, and test runs on the SVR were made during the following month. It finally returned to full-time action on 1 September after being ceremonially 'named' at Bewdley station by Mr.H.Roberts, the Swindon Works Manager. The engine is currently being overhauled at Swindon.

No.7819 HINTON MANOR
Apart from No.7802 the only Manor to undertake main line outings in recent years has been No.7819, and it is the latter which has had the lion's share.

Rescued from Woodham's, No.7819 arrived at the Severn Valley Railway in January 1973 for restoration to full running order. It returned to steam in September 1977. During 1985 - the GWR 150th anniversary year (in which, in a case of abysmal timing, the closure of Swindon Works was announced) No.7819 was rostered to work a Bristol-Plymouth special on 7 April, double-heading with No.6000 KING GEORGE V. It was an ill fated trip, No.6000 succumbing to an overheated tender axlebox and having to be taken off at Taunton. No.7819 continued the journey, albeit with the ignominy of a pair of Class 37 diesels at the rear of the 13-coach train, but itself developed a hot tender axlebox at Tiverton Junction. It was taken off at Exeter. After receiving attention, it proceeded to Plymouth in order to work the return journey the following day, Hall class 4-6-0 No.4930 HAGLEY HALL substituting at short notice for No.6000, which was unable to be repaired in time. Later in 1985 - in August - No.7819 had a series of less eventful outings on Swindon-Gloucester specials, also as part of the GWR anniversary celebrations.

On 22 May 1987 No.7819 returned to once familiar territory, working the 'Cardigan Bay Express' over part of Cambrian system. The trip was from Machynlleth (where No.7819 had arrived the previous day) to Pwllheli, and further trips from Machynlleth to Barmouth were made between 21 and 24 of that same month. The following year - on 20 May - No.7819 arrived at Great Malvern at the head of a special train. This was part of the festivities to mark the ceremonial reopening of the station buildings, which had been impressively restored after being badly damaged by fire. As for the special train, appearances were not all they seemed - No.7819 had been attached to the train only at Ledbury (a mere seven miles away), and the train actually left Great Malvern behind diesel traction. In June and September 1991 No.7819 returned to the Cambrian section, and later went on loan from the SVR to the Nene Valley Railway near Peterborough. No.7819's boiler certificate expired in 1992, and it is currently undergoing its ten-year overhaul.

No.7820 DINMORE MANOR
In September 1979 No.7820 was purchased from Woodham's by the Gwili Railway, which was based at Bronwydd Arms station on the old Carmarthen-Aberystwyth line. However, no restoration work was done by the Gwili, and in March 1985 No.7820 moved to the West Somerset Railway so that the job could be undertaken. The bulk of the

work, however, was done in the workshops of the Birmingham Railway Museum at Tyseley, and No.7820 finally returned to traffic on the West Somerset in September 1995.

No.7821 DITCHEAT MANOR
Another of the class to be rescued from Woodham's, No.7821 was purchased by the Gloucestershire & Warwickshire Railway and taken to the Toddington headquarters for restoration in June 1981. No.7828 also made the trip from Barry to Toddington about the same time. No.7821 moved to the Llangollen Railway in June 1989, where it still remains.

No.7822 FOXCOTE MANOR
The locomotive was purchased from Woodham's by the specially created Foxcote Manor Society, and in January 1975 was taken to Oswestry for restoration. A considerable amount of work was done there, but in November 1985 No.7822 moved to the Llangollen Railway for the completion of the works. It returned to action in April 1988.

No.7827 LYDHAM MANOR
It was June 1970 when No.7827 left Woodham's for Newton Abbot, and it was 30 March 1973 when it left for its

new home under its own steam - a remarkably swift restoration job. That new home was the Torbay Steam Railway - later retitled the Paignton & Dartmouth Steam Railway, despite the fact that it didn't go to Dartmouth and it wasn't exclusively steam worked - which had been formed late in 1972 following BR's announcement that services on the Paignton-Kingswear section were to be withdrawn. No.7827 soon gained, and maintained, a position as the metaphorical flagship of the P&D fleet, but at the time of writing it awaits its compulsory boiler overhaul.

No.7828 ODNEY MANOR
This was the second of the Manors to be purchased from Woodham's by the Gloucestershire & Warwickshire Railway and taken to Toddington in June 1981. Although No.7828 was restored at Toddington, the work being completed in May 1988, its first real outings were actually on the Gwili Railway. The locomotive continued its peripatetic existence, moving to the Llangollen Railway in March 1989 and on to the East Lancashire Railway at Bury in March 1991. It currently resides on the West Somerset Railway.

A winter's evening photographic event at Bridgnorth, on the Severn Valley Railway - preserved No.7819 HINTON MANOR. PHOTOGRAPH: PETER HERRING

Chapter 7
Summary of MANOR class 4-6-0s

Above. Perhaps the highest profile working undertaken regularly by the Manors was the 'Cambrian Coast Express' west of Shrewsbury. On 10 August 1956, No.7803 BARCOTE MANOR departs from Welshpool with the up working. Note the style of the train headboard - as will be seen in other photographs, this and the new style were in use simultaneously. **PHOTOGRAPH: BRIAN MORRISON**

			BR liveries		
No.	Name	Built	ul.black	l.green	Withdrawn
7800	TORQUAY MANOR	1/38	5/51	3/58	8/64
7801	ANTHONY MANOR	1/38	8/49	2/57	7/65
7802	BRADLEY MANOR	1/38	2/51	9/58	11/65
7803	BARCOTE MANOR	1/38	7/49	4/58	4/65
7804	BAYDON MANOR	2/38	*	6/57	9/65
7805	BROOME MANOR	3/38	2/49	8/56	12/64
7806	COCKINGTON MANOR	3/38	6/49	12/56	11/64
7807	COMPTON MANOR	3/38	6/49	3/57	11/64
7808	COOKHAM MANOR	3/38	12/48	1/58	12/65
7809	CHILDREY MANOR	4/38	8/49	11/57	4/63
7810	DRAYCOTT MANOR	12/38	8/50	4/57	9/64
7811	DUNLEY MANOR	12/38	3/49	11/57	7/65
7812	ERLESTOKE MANOR	1/39	8/51	1/59	11/65
7813	FRESHFORD MANOR	1/39	3/51	2/59	5/65
7814	FRINGFORD MANOR	1/39	*12/48?*	*6/59?*	9/65
7815	FRITWELL MANOR	1/39	*9/50?*	*9/56?*	10/64
7816	FRILSHAM MANOR	1/39	9/49	*9/56?*	11/65
7817	GARSINGTON MANOR	1/39	11/50	12/58	6/64
7818	GRANVILLE MANOR	1/39	2/50	11/56	1/65
7819	HINTON MANOR	2/39	2/50	2/60	11/65
7820	DINMORE MANOR	11/50	+1/55	6/58	11/65
7821	DITCHEAT MANOR	11/50	+8/55	12/57	11/65
7822	FOXCOTE MANOR	12/50	+12/55	12/57	11/65
7823	HOOK NORTON MANOR	12/50	+4/56	*11/58?*	7/64
7824	IFORD MANOR	12/50	+8/53	5/58	11/64
7825	LECHLADE MANOR	12/50	+4/56	10/58	5/64
7826	LONGWORTH MANOR	12/50	+1/56	11/58	4/65
7827	LYDHAM MANOR	12/50	+8/55	5/57	10/65
7828	ODNEY MANOR	12/50	+12/53	7/56	10/65
7829	RAMSBURY MANOR	12/50	+11/53	*11/56?*	12/65

* No.7804 retained a livery of unlined green as it was, at the time, designated the regular pilot engine for the 'Cornish Riviera Express'.
+ When new, Nos.7820-7829 were painted in lined black

Nos.7800-7819 - Lot 316; Nos.7820-7829 - Lot 377
The dates of livery changes quoted left have been deduced by cross-referencing reports (usually of 'first locos to be repainted') in the contemporary railway press with officially documented dates of works visits. Consequently, we cannot guarantee that this is a wholly definitive list. It will be noted that some dates are appended with question marks - these dates are the ones of which we are least certain and are given in italics. If any reader has different (and substantiated) information, we would be very interested to hear from them.

Chapter Eight

THE REGISTERS

The following listings have been collated from the official Swindon registers. It is possible that the original documents included the occasional slip of the pen and where an entry is questionable, it is discussed it the appropriate section of the text. A few words about the presentation of the listings are in order.

Shed allocations: Until the mid-1950s it was the usual practice for all allocations to sub-sheds to be recorded in the Swindon registers, but from then on this seems to have been undertaken with less rigour. By 1963, it was rarely done at all. In the allocation lists for the Manors this is most evident in the case of Aberystwyth, which was a sub-shed to Machynlleth - for the purpose of this book, allocations to Aberystwyth from 1963 onwards have had to be deduced almost exclusively from secondary sources.

The year 1963 also marked the transfer of the Western Region's '84' and '89' division sheds to the London Midland Region, and of course the LMR did not inform the WR of all subsequent transfers. Furthermore, the Western Region itself was less and less concerned with recording transfers. Consequently, we have cross-referenced the allocations listed in the registers with those which appeared in contemporary issues of the *Railway Observer* magazine - arguably, the most reliable such source. In the following listings, allocations which have been gleaned from the *RO* are given in *italic* type. We have no reason to doubt their veracity - we use italics simply to show that they came from a different source.

In the summary of sheds (at the start of each listing), transfers direct to sub-sheds at Cheltenham, Whitchurch (LMS), and Whitland are noted under the respective parent sheds of Gloucester, Oswestry and Neyland. At the risk of being inconsistent, transfers direct to Aberystwyth are included in their own right because of that shed's 'semi autonomous' status.

Dates: Where allocations and transfers are discussed, we quote either precise dates (if known) or 'four weeks ending' dates. In the case of the latter, we have standardised by quoting the month at the end of the relevant four-week period - for example, four weeks ending 20.4.46 is quoted as April 1946. Similarly, four weeks ending 1.4.39 is quoted as April 1939, although the allocation/transfer in question almost certainly occurred during the previous month.

'Wait': Many routine overhauls to locomotives were scheduled in advance, and a locomotive was often held at its running shed before the date of the works visit. Such instances are identified in the registers by the word 'wait'. The term was also used when an engine failed and had to be taken to the nearest running shed to await entry to Swindon works. Occasionally, the registers do not make it wholly clear where a 'wait' occurred, and in such instances a question mark is appended.

The period a locomotive spent waiting to enter the works was used for administration purposes - once the word 'wait' had been entered against a locomotive, it came under the jurisdiction of Swindon Works, even if it was physically at Laira, Old Oak or wherever. It was considered acceptable for up to 5% of GWR stock to be under works jurisdiction simultaneously, but some serious explaining had to be done by the Swindon management if the figure crept above 5%.

Repairs: Minor repairs which took less than 14 days did not have to be entered on the Engine History Sheets and were not costed, but some shed officials nevertheless recorded such repairs on the EHS as a matter of routine. Conversely, some very minor repair stoppages (usually lasting only a day or two) are noted in the allocation registers but were not recorded on the Engine History Sheets. In such minor matters it was the chance hand of the

GWR Engine History sheet No. 7814, for a 4-6-0 locomotive built 1939 at Swindon, Lot 316.

Manor in the undergrowth. The 2.47pm Gloucester - Ross - Hereford train approaching Longhope, 15 August 1964, with 7814 FRINGFORD MANOR in charge. PHOTOGRAPH: W. POTTER

local clerk at work. Although the following listings note the dates and locations of all significant repairs and the vast majority of minor ones, a few very minor repairs might have been overlooked.

The repair codes used are those which were in effect at the relevant time. Between January 1929 and the end of 1948, these were: **G** - General; **H** - Heavy; **I** - Intermediate; **L** - Light; **R** - Running. After Nationalisation, BR adopted LMSR-style repair codes, and these came into use on the Western Region at the end of 1948. They were: **HC** - Heavy Casual; **HG** - Heavy General; **HI** - Heavy Intermediate; **LC** - Light Casual; **LI** - Light Intermediate; **U** - Unclassified.

Places of repair: As a general guide, 'Factory' denotes works (such as Swindon and Newton Abbot), whereas 'Shops' denotes workshops at a running shed. The Swindon registers were sometimes confusing when it came to the categories of 'Factory' and 'Shop'. For example, they occasionally referred to 'Bath Road Factory' but, of course, such entries referred to the running shed workshops as Bath Road had had no 'locomotive works' (in the accepted sense) since Bristol & Exeter days.

In the following listings, where neither 'Factory' nor 'Shop' were quoted in the original GWR documents, we have assumed that the repair in question was undertaken at the running shed itself.

Swindon/Swindon Stock: From the late 1920s onwards, locomotives arriving at Swindon for repairs were usually recorded as entering 'Swindon Factory Pool' (written in the registers as 'Swindon F.Pool'), but for the sake of simplicity we have omitted that designation. The 'Swindon Works' dates given here are for a locomotive's arrival at Swindon, be it the date of entry into 'Swindon F.Pool' or the date of reception at the works themselves. When a repair at Swindon Works had been completed, the engine usually spent a couple of days or so at Swindon Stock shed (a building almost alongside the running shed) before despatch to its designated home. The 'Swindon Stock' dates are shown here, albeit only until August/September 1944 when, apart from a few isolated instances, they ceased to be recorded in the official registers. It was not unknown for an engine under the jurisdiction of Swindon Works (i.e. in Swindon Factory Pool or Swindon Stock) to be returned temporarily to traffic in the event of a locomotive shortage at the running shed. There is, incidentally, no evidence that this happened in the case of the Manors.

Boilers: An asterisk (*) denotes that a boiler was brand new.

Mileages: As noted in the text, the Western Region ceased to record the mileages of steam locomotives after 28 December 1963.

Tenders: Some 90% of tender record cards were destroyed by BR, but from 1929 the tender numbers were recorded on the Engine History Sheets and so their absence does not present a problem with the Manors. It should be emphasised that although the tender details in the following registers were taken directly from the Engine History Cards, it was not the usual practice to list short-term tender transfers on the sheets. Consequently, transfers lasting only a few days may not be shown.

Below. GRANVILLE MANOR again, waiting to leave Shrewsbury with the 3.50pm to Aberyswyth, 5 August 1961. PHOTOGRAPH: MICHAEL MENSING

Above. A unexpected combination of engines came about for a while on the Cambrian Coast Express, that of Manor and 2251 class 0-6-0. Here is the up train with 7818 GRANVILLE MANOR and 2200, approaching Shrewsbury on 24 September 1960. The disused Shropshire and Montgomeryshire line runs a weed-strewn course on the left. PHOTOGRAPH: MICHAEL MENSING

No.7800 TORQUAY MANOR underwent its last heavy general at Swindon in August/September 1960, and it is seen fresh from the works. PHOTOGRAPH: R.C. RILEY

7800 TORQUAY MANOR
To stock: 19 January 1938
Summary of sheds:

First	Stafford Road
3.38	Banbury
6.49	Tyseley
12.50	Banbury
3.5.51	Tyseley
10.51	Banbury
6.52	Tyseley
10.52	Chester
26.8.58	Oswestry
12.62	Shrewsbury

Engine history:

6.2.38	Stafford Road
3.38	Banbury
9.7.40	Swindon Factory **I**
14.8.40	Swindon Stock
23.8.40	Banbury
5.4.43	Banbury (wait)
6.4.43	Swindon Factory **G**
4.6.43	Swindon Stock
5.6.43	Banbury
6.1.45	Severn Tunnel Junct. (wait)
16.1.45	Swindon Factory **L**
1.2.45	Banbury
2.5.45	Banbury (wait)
23.5.45	Swindon Factory **G**
27.6.45	Banbury
21.7.45	Tyseley Shops **R**
30.8.45	Banbury
5.9.45	Banbury Shops **R**
2.10.45	Banbury
16.11.45	Banbury (wait)
17.11.45	Swindon Factory **R**
14.12.45	Swindon Stock
20.12.45	Swindon (wait)
24.12.45	Swindon Factory **R**
7.1.46	Banbury
20.2.47	Canton Shops **R**
11.4.47	Banbury
9.5.47	Didcot Shops **L**
19.6.47	Banbury
28.8.47	St.Blazey Shops **R**
25.9.47	Banbury

3.10.47	Newton Abbot Fty **R**
7.10.47	Banbury
4.4.48	Oxford Shops **R**
27.4.48	Banbury
16.6.48	Taunton Shops **R**
1.7.48	Banbury
3.7.48	Laira (wait)
26.8.48	Swindon Factory **I**
5.10.48	Banbury
6.49	Tyseley
12.50	Banbury
9.4.51	Swindon Factory **HI**
3.5.51	Tyseley
10.51	Banbury
27.4.52	Taunton (wait)
7.5.52	Newton Abbot Fty **LC**
29.5.52	Banbury
6.52	Tyseley
10.52	Chester
9.3.53	Chester (wait)
18.3.53	Swindon Factory **HG**
4.5.53	Chester
23.9.55	Swindon Factory **HG**
25.10.55	Chester
23.10.57	Chester Shops **U**
7.11.57	Chester
23.2.58	Swindon Factory **HI**
13.3.58	Chester
26.8.58	Oswestry
23.10.58	Oswestry Shops **U**
18.11.58	Oswestry
8.8.60	Oxley (wait)
13.8.60	Swindon Factory **HG**
3.10.60	Oswestry
27.2.62	Oswestry (*wait*)
16.3.62	Swindon Factory **HI**
16.5.62	Oswestry
12.62	Shrewsbury
10.3.64	Hereford Shops **U**
3.4.64	Shrewsbury
8.64	**Withdrawn**
5.10.64	Sold as scrap to John Cashmore, Great Bridge

N.B: Loco was LM Region book stock from 23.2.58 to 7.9.58 and from 30.12.62 until withdrawal

Boilers and mileages:

First	6400	
14.8.40	..	(89,299)
4.6.43	6408	(177,885)
27.6.45	6407	(242,644)
5.10.48	6401	(325,132)
3.5.51	6409	(409,472)
4.5.53	6429	(464,183)
25.10.55	6423	(564,377)
13.3.58	6421	(649,832)
3.10.60	6418	(749,839)
16.5.62	..	(815,870)
28.12.63	..	(877,781)

Tenders:

First	1824
14.8.40	1878
4.6.43	1922
1.2.45	1716
27.6.45	1669
5.10.48	2213
3.5.51	2228
29.5.52	2125
4.5.53	2358
25.10.55	2346
9.3.57	2120
13.3.58	1879
29.11.58	2317
3.10.60	2019
16.5.62	1758

...............ooo...............

7801 ANTHONY MANOR
To stock: 21 January 1938
Summary of Sheds (parent sheds only)**:**

First	Bath Road
29.11.39	St.Philip's Marsh
5.48	Laira
10.53	Chester
26.8.58	Oswestry
12.62	Shrewsbury

Engine history:

2.2.38	Bath Road

6.38	Weston-s-Mare
7.38	Bath Road
10.38	Weston-s-Mare
11.38	Bath Road
12.38	Weston-s-Mare
1.39	Bath Road
4.39	Weston-s-Mare
5.39	Bath Road
6.39	Weston-s-Mare
7.39	Bath Road Shops **R**
14.8.38	Bath Road
24.10.39	Swindon Factory **I**
25.11.39	Swindon Stock
29.11.39	St.Philip's Marsh
11.1.41	Swindon Factory (no repair)
15.1.41	St.Philip's Marsh
10.4.42	St.Philip's Marsh (wait)
23.4.42	Swindon Factory **I**
5.6.42	Swindon Stock
7.6.42	St.Philip's Marsh
18.12.43	Old Oak Common (wait)
5.1.44	Swindon Factory **G**
2.2.44	Swindon Stock
11.2.44	St.Philip's Marsh
5.44	Weston-s-Mare
6.44	St.Philip's Marsh
23.9.46	St.Philip's Marsh (wait)
30.9.46	Swindon Factory **I**
1.11.46	St.Philip's Marsh
26.2.47	Tyseley Shops R
17.4.47	St.Philip's Marsh
25.9.47	St.Philip's Mh Shps **L**
2.10.47	St.Philip's Marsh
5.48	Laira
10.6.48	Newton Abbot Ftry **L**
17.6.48	Laira
16.10.48	Laira (wait)
29.10.48	Newton Abbot Ftry **L**
22.12.48	Laira
19.4.49	Laira Shops **U**
26.4.49	Laira
23.6.49	Swindon Factory **HG**
5.8.49	Laira

In June 1965 - the month before its withdrawal - No.7801 ANTHONY MANOR undertakes station pilot duties at Shrewsbury.
PHOTOGRAPH: DEREK CROSS

13.9.51	Newton Abt Ftry **LC**	28.12.63	..	(909,469)	7.2.57	2072	18.5.46	Aberystwyth
9.10.51	Laira				2.7.59	1773	12.11.62	Tyseley
21.1.52	Swindon Factory **HI**	**Tenders:**			29.6.62	1954	9.9.63	Machynlleth
19.2.52	Laira	First	1876		................ooo..............		*1.65*	*Shrewsbury*
30.3.53	Laira Shops **U**	28.5.38	2081					
13.4.53	Laira	3.11.38	2078		**7802 BRADLEY MANOR**		**Engine history:**	
10.53	Chester	25.11.39	1938		**To stock: 22 January 1938**		2.2.38	Old Oak Common
21.10.53	Chester Shops **U**	4.6.42	2327				5.38	St.Philip's Marsh
6.11.53	Chester	2.2.44	1891		**Summary of sheds:**		4.39	Bath Road
14.7.54	Chester (wait)	1.11.46	1929		First	Old Oak Common	6.7.39	Bath Road Shops **R**
21.7.54	Swindon Factory **HG**	5.8.49	1923		5.38	St.Philip's Marsh	21.7.39	Bath Road
24.8.54	Chester	19.2.52	2342		4.39	Bath Road	8.39	Weston-s-Mare
2.5.56	Chester Shops **U**	18.4.53	1856		12.39	St.Philip's Marsh	9.39	Bath Road
25.5.56	Chester	24.8.54	1881		27.4.46	Oswestry	12.39	St.Philip's Marsh
20.11.56	Croes Newydd Shops **U**							
5.12.56	Chester							
28.12.56	Swindon Factory **HG**							
7.2.57	Chester							
26.8.58	Oswestry							
18.9.58	Oswestry Shops **LC**							
10.58	Oswestry							
12.1.59	Aberystwyth Shops **U**							
30.1.59	Oswestry							
25.5.59	Swindon Factory **HI**							
2.7.59	Oswestry							
14.9.59	Oswestry (wait)							
18.9.59	Stafford Road Ftry **HC**							
13.10.59	Oswestry							
1.5.62	Swindon Factory **HG**							
29.6.62	Oswestry							
12.62	Shrewsbury							
7.65	**Withdrawn**							
c.10.65	Sold as scrap to Birds of Swansea							

Boilers and mileages:

First	6401	
25.11.39	..	(87,804)
5.6.42	..	(176,463)
2.2.44	6419	(232,908)
1.11.46	6412	(316,891)
5.8.49	6421	(398,259)
19.2.52	6419	(476,713)
24.8.54	6407	(554,650)
7.2.57	6430	(647,992)
2.7.59	..	(738,899)
29.6.62	6426	(855,858)

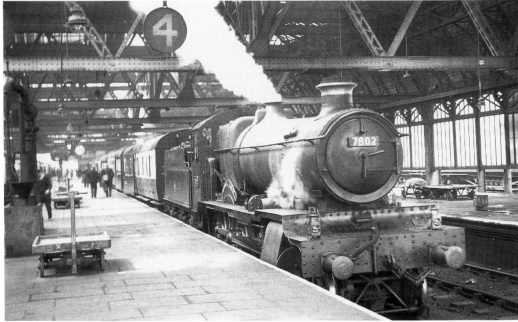

No.7802 BRADLEY MANOR - in its original condition, save for the smokebox number plate - waits at Shrewsbury with an Aberystwyth train. The date is 18 May 1949. **PHOTOGRAPH: P.J. LYNCH**

Ex-works picture No.7803 BARCOTE MANOR (minus its 6F shedplate - a tactical Swindon 'oversight', maybe?) fresh from its last heavy intermediate on 20 October 1963. Note the intermediate pattern tender. PHOTOGRAPH: M. JOHN STRETTON

14.5.40	Swindon Factory **G**
17.6.40	Swindon Stock
25.6.40	St.Philip's Marsh
2.12.42	Swindon Factory **G**
8.1.43	Swindon Stock
10.1.43	St.Philip's Marsh
10.3.44	Westbury Shops **R**
25.3.44	St.Philip's Marsh
16.6.44	St.Philip's Marsh (wait)
9.8.44	Stafford Rd Fcty **L**
28.9.44	St.Philip's Marsh
20.2.46	St.Philip's Marsh (wait)
21.3.46	Swindon Factory **I**
27.4.46	Oswestry
18.5.46	Aberystwyth
25.9.46	Aberystwyth (wait)
18.10.46	Swindon Factory **L**
13.11.46	Aberystwyth
20.12.46	Machynlleth Shops **R**
6.1.47	Aberystwyth
13.5.47	Aberystwyth (wait)
14.6.47	Oswestry Shops **L**
20.6.47	Aberystwyth
29.11.47	Aberystwyth Shops **R**
22.12.47	Aberystwyth
16.4.48	Aberystwyth Shops **R**
5.5.48	Aberystwyth
20.7.48	Aberystwyth Shops **R**
19.8.48	Aberystwyth
20.9.48	Aberystwyth (wait)
8.10.48	Swindon Factory **R**
1.11.48	Aberystwyth
27.12.50	Aberystwyth Shops **U**
12.1.51	Aberystwyth (wait)
14.1.51	Stafford Road (wait)
5.2.51	Stafford Road Fcty **HI**
14.3.51	Aberystwyth
25.9.52	Aberystwyth Shops **U**
11.10.52	Aberystwyth
26.11.52	Aberystwyth (wait)
8.12.52	Stafford Road Fcty **LC**
22.1.53	Aberystwyth
7.4.53	Machynlleth (wait)
17.4.53	Oswestry Shops **U**
23.4.53	Aberystwyth
26.5.53	Oswestry Shops **U**
9.6.53	Aberystwyth

22.9.53	Swindon Factory **HI**
23.10.53	Aberystwyth
12.8.55	Aberystwyth Shops **U**
23.9.55	Aberystwyth
21.2.56	Oswestry Shops **U**
5.3.56	Aberystwyth
25.4.56	Swindon Factory **HG**
28.5.56	Aberystwyth
27.2.58	Oswestry Shops **U**
18.3.58	Aberystwyth
3.4.58	Aberystwyth (wait)
29.7.58	Swindon Factory **HG**
24.9.58	Aberystwyth
18.7.61	Aberystwyth (wait)
1.8.61	Swindon Factory **HG**
15.9.61	Aberystwyth
23.5.62	Machynlleth Shops **U**
6.6.62	Aberystwyth
12.11.62	Tyseley
9.9.63	Machynlleth
17.6.64	Swindon Factory **HG**
28.8.64	Machynlleth
1.65	*Shrewsbury*
6.11.65	**Withdrawn**
	Sold as scrap to Woodham Bros.
11.79	Purchased for preservation by Severn Valley Railway

N.B: Loco was LM Region book stock from 30.12.62 until withdrawal

Boilers and mileages:
First	6402	
17.6.40	..	(94,122)
8.1.43	6420 *	(185,200)
27.4.46	6414	(280,207)
1.11.48	6406	(346,613)
14.3.51	..	(434,884)
23.10.53	6416	(519,480)
28.5.56	6402	(599,345)
24.9.58	6410	(681,456)
15.9.61	6413	(786,657)
28.12.63	..	(861,965)
28.8.64	6421	(?)

Tenders:
22.1.38	2372

17.6.40	2146
8.1.43	1936
27.4.46	2211
13.11.46	2137
19.8.48	1644
1.11.48	2368
17.6.50	1922
29.12.51	2327
23.10.53	2353
28.5.56	1931
28.12.57	2089
24.9.58	1975
15.9.61	2103
28.8.64	2128

...............ooo...............

7803 BARCOTE MANOR
To stock: 27 January 1938

Summary of sheds: (parent sheds only)
First	Neyland
4.46	Aberystwyth
24.7.59	Oswestry
22.9.59	Aberystwyth
10.62	Croes Newydd
3.63	*Aberystwyth*
1.65	*Shrewsbury*

Engine history:
3.2.38	Neyland
11.8.39	Carmarthen Shops **L**
15.8.39	Neyland
8.12.39	Swindon Factory **I**
12.1.40	Swindon Stock
26.1.40	Neyland
21.2.42	Swindon Factory **I**
27.2.42	Factory Stock
28.3.42	Neyland
27.5.42	Carmarthen Shops **L**
27.5.42	Neyland
18.11.43	Carmarthen Shops **L**
22.11.43	Neyland
30.10.44	Neyland (wait)
10.11.44	Swindon Factory **G**
16.12.44	Neyland
4.46	Aberystwyth
9.46	Whitchurch LMS
10.46	Aberystwyth
12.46	Machynlleth
3.1.47	Machynlleth (wait)
30.1.47	Swindon Factory **I**
7.2.47	Aberystwyth
1.7.48	Aberystwyth Shops **R**
21.7.48	Aberystwyth
30.5.49	Machynlleth (wait)
7.6.49	Swindon Factory **HG**
8.7.49	Aberystwyth
2.9.49	Swindon Factory **U**
15.9.49	Aberystwyth
5.5.50	Oswestry Shops **U**
12.5.50	Aberystwyth
3.10.50	Oswestry Shops **U**
11.10.50	Aberystwyth
29.6.51	Aberystwyth (wait)
9.7.51	Swindon Factory **HI**
7.9.51	Aberystwyth
2.3.53	Aberystwyth (wait)
9.3.53	Swindon Factory **HG**
10.4.53	Aberystwyth
7.2.55	Aberystwyth (wait)
14.2.55	Stafford Road Frty **LC**
11.3.55	Aberystwyth
3.9.55	Swindon Factory **HG**
6.10.55	Aberystwyth
5.3.58	Swindon Factory **HI**
11.4.58	Aberystwyth
9.10.58	Machynlleth Shops **U**
23.10.58	Aberystwyth
24.7.59	Oswestry
22.9.59	Aberystwyth
6.1.60	Swindon Factory **U**
22.1.60	Aberystwyth
7.12.60	Swindon Factory **HG**
27.1.61	Aberystwyth
7.9.62	Croes Newydd
3.63	*Aberystwyth*
19.8.63	Swindon Factory **HI**
8.11.63	Aberystwyth
31.7.64	Swindon Factory **LC**
21.10.64	Aberystwyth
1.65	*Shrewsbury*
17.4.65	**Withdrawn**
	Sold as scrap to R.S.Hayes of Bridgend

N.B: Loco was LM Region book stock from 30.12.62 until wthdrn.

Mileages and boilers:
First	6403	
12.1.40	..	(85,409)
27.3.42	..	(168,694)
16.12.44	6411	(260,807)
7.2.47	6421	(326,785)
8.7.49	6410	(409,812)
7.9.51	..	(483,105)
10.4.53	6408	(545,187)
6.10.55	6420	(630,057)
11.4.58	..	(725,447)
27.1.61	6400	(803,341)
8.11.63	6432	(901,696)
28.12.63	..	(904,013)

Tenders:
First	1725
12.1.40	1866
27.3.42	2316
16.12.44	1764
7.2.47	1644
4.9.48	2137
9.7.49	1740
15.7.49	2204
22.6.52	1780
10.4.53	2138
8.8.53	2140
14.8.54	1708
16.7.55	2223
6.10.55	2358
11.4.58	1699
13.8.60	1656
17.1.61	2380 *

* 2380 was a Churchward intermediate (see text)

...............ooo...............

7804 BAYDON MANOR
To stock: 1 February 1938

Summary of sheds (parent sheds only):

First	Bath Road
2.2.40	St.Philip's Marsh
5.48	Laira
6.54	Carmarthen
18.1.61	Neyland *
24.10.61	Carmarthen
15.6.62	Llanelly
2.65	*Cardiff East Dock*
2.8.65	*Severn Tunnel Jct*

Engine history:

14.2.38	Bath Road
6.38	Weston-s-Mare
7.38	Bath Road
12.38	Weston-s-Mare
22.1.39	Bath Road
4.39	Weston-s-Mare
4.39	Bath Road
1.5.39	Bath Road Shops R
19.5.39	Bath Road
20.12.39	Swindon Factory I
29.1.40	Swindon Factory
2.2.40	St.Philip's Marsh
4.8.41	St.Philip's Mh Shops R
31.8.41	St.Philip's Marsh
15.12.41	St.Philip's Mh Shops R
31.12.41	St.Philip's Marsh
4.4.42	Swindon Factory L
6.5.42	Swindon Stock
9.5.42	St.Philip's Marsh
27.7.42	St.Philip's Marsh (wait)
30.7.42	Swindon Factory I
5.9.42	Swindon Stock
8.9.42	St.Philip's Marsh
10.12.42	Swindon Factory L
12.12.42	St.Philip's Marsh
21.1.44	St.Philip's Marsh (wait)
23.2.44	Swindon Factory L
5.4.44	Swindon Stock
7.4.44	St.Philip's Marsh
17.4.45	Westbury Shops R
7.5.45	St.Philip's Marsh
8.1.46	St.Philip's Marsh (wait)
19.1.46	Swindon Factory I
21.2.46	St.Philip's Marsh
4.46	Weston-s-Mare
5.46	St.Philip's Marsh
11.46	Weston-s-Mare
12.46	St.Philip's Marsh
26.2.47	Leamington Shops R
12.3.47	St.Philip's Marsh
5.48	Laira
25.5.48	Laira Shops R
14.6.48	Swindon Factory G
16.6.48	Laira
28.7.48	Laira (wait)
30.5.50	Swindon Factory LC
6.6.50	Laira
29.6.50	Laira
28.10.50	Laira Shops U
12.11.50	Laira
22.8.51	Swindon Factory HG
20.9.51	Laira
13.4.53	Laira Shops U
26.4.53	Laira
8.2.54	Newton Abbot Fty LC
8.3.54	Laira
22.3.54	Laira Shops U
30.3.54	Laira
6.54	Carmarthen
17.1.55	Swindon Factory HG
18.2.55	Carmarthen
9.5.57	Swindon Factory HI
7.6.57	Carmarthen
11.8.59	Carmarthen Shops U
16.9.59	Carmarthen
9.1.60	Carmarthen (wait)
4.2.60	Swindon Factory HI
22.3.60	Carmarthen
18.1.61	Whitland
3.8.61	Danygraig Shops U
25.8.61	Whitland
24.10.61	Carmarthen
11.12.61	Carmarthen (wait)
22.2.62	Stafford Road Ftry HC
6.4.62	Carmarthen
15.6.62	Llanelly
30.4.63	Swindon Factory HI
3.7.63	Llanelly
2.65	*Cardiff East Dock*
2.8.65	*Severn Tunnel Jct*
10.9.65	**Withdrawn**

Sold as scrap to
J.Cashmore
of Newport.

Mileages and boilers:

First	6404	
29.1.40	..	(87,123)
5.9.42	..	(172,086)
5.4.44	6401	(225,461)
21.2.46	..	(284,399)
28.7.48	6417	(368,862)
20.9.51	6414	(461,062)
18.2.55	6400	(554,333)
7.6.57	6407	(630,698)
22.3.60	6416	(726,830)
6.4.62	6415	(787,512)
3.7.63	..	(811,590)
28.12.63	..	(826,812)

Tenders:

First	2069
29.1.40	1632
5.9.42	1792
5.4.44	1982
21.2.46	1867
12.3.47	2230
29.6.50	2010
20.9.51	2162
1.11.52	2016
18.2.55	2372
7.6.57	1797
22.3.60	1560 *
3.7.63	1983

* 1560 was 4,000gall (see text)

...............ooo...............

7805 BROOME MANOR
To stock: 14 March 1938

Summary of sheds:

First	Shrewsbury
11.39	Banbury
12.39	Shrewsbury
2.40	Banbury
9.50	St.Blazey
21.9.50	Newton Abbot
10.53	Hereford
12.6.58	Laira
26.9.58	Canton
21.9.62	Cardiff East Dock
17.6.63	Tyseley

Engine History:

27.3.38	Shrewsbury
11.39	Banbury
12.39	Shrewsbury
2.40	Banbury
30.12.40	Swindon Factory I
5.2.41	Swindon Stock
10.2.41	Banbury
23.12.42	Banbury R
17.1.43	Banbury
24.9.43	Banbury R
2.10.43	Banbury
8.11.43	Swindon Factory G
12.12.43	Swindon Stock
14.12.43	Banbury
4.6.46	Banbury (wait)
18.6.46	Swindon Factory I
2.8.46	Swindon Stock
2.8.46	Banbury
27.8.48	Banbury R
14.9.48	Banbury
26.1.49	Swindon Factory HG
18.2.49	Banbury
29.3.50	Reading Shops U
12.4.50	Banbury
9.50	St.Blazey

No.7804 BAYDON MANOR of Laira approaches Tigley signal box (just to the south-west of Totnes) with a down goods on 27 June 1951. PHOTOGRAPH: ALAN LATHEY

No.7805 BROOME MANOR, still almost immaculate from its recent heavy intermediate at Swindon, poses at its home depot of Canton in November 1959. PHOTOGRAPH: JOHN HODGE

6.9.50	St.Blazey Shops **U**
21.9.50	Newton Abbot
23.7.51	Swindon Factory **HI**
27.8.51	Newton Abbot
10.53	Hereford
27.11.53	Hereford (wait)
7.12.53	Swindon Factory **HG**
11.1.54	Hereford
3.12.54	Stafford Road Ftry **LC**
23.12.54	Hereford
2.4.55	Worcester Shops **U**
18.4.55	Hereford
26.10.55	Hereford (wait)
28.10.55	Stafford Road Ftry **LC**
18.11.55	Hereford
30.7.56	Swindon Factory **HI**
31.8.56	Swindon Stock
3.9.56	Hereford
12.6.58	Laira
26.9.58	Canton
7.9.59	Canton (wait)
17.9.59	Swindon Factory **HI**
28.10.59	Canton
4.5.61	Gloucester Shops **U**
31.5.61	Canton
26.9.61	Canton (wait)
11.10.61	Swindon Factory **HG**
23.11.61	Canton
21.7.62	Cardiff East Dock
7.9.62	Caerphilly Factory **LC**
21.9.62	Cardiff East Dock
17.6.63	Tyseley
12.64	**Withdrawn**
	Sold as scrap to
	J.Cashmore
	of Great Bridge, Staffs.

N.B: Loco was LM Region book stock from 17.6.63 until withdrawal

Boilers and mileages:

First	6405	
5.2.41	..	(91,443)
12.12.43	6412	(189,722)
2.8.46	6410	(278,997)
18.2.49	6400	(368,844)
27.8.51	6403	(437,131)
11.1.54	6432*	(508,868)
31.8.56	..	(597,896)
28.10.59	6415	(709,232)
23.11.61	6428	(782,109)
28.12.63	..	(828,098)

Tenders:

First	1964
12.12.43	1651
2.8.46	1922
18.2.49	2369
25.2.50	2343
27.8.51	1837
11.1.54	2148
18.4.55	1927
3.9.56	1820
18.4.59	1990
28.10.59	1879
23.11.61	2114

..............ooo..............

7806 COCKINGTON MANOR
To stock: 16 March 1938

Summary of sheds:

First	Shrewsbury
3.40	Banbury
9.50	Penzance
12.50	St.Blazey
2.11.51	Newton Abbot
7.55	Truro
10.55	Machynlleth
17.12.56	Aberystwyth
18.6.59	Newton Abbot
30.9.59	St.Blazey
16.9.60	Tyseley
18.1.61	Stourbridge
15.6.62	Oxley

Engine history:

25.3.38	Shrewsbury
25.4.39	Shrewsbury Shops **R**
2.5.39	Shrewsbury
3.40	Banbury
17.5.40	Banbury **R**
5.6.40	Banbury
23.1.41	Swindon Factory **I**
6.3.41	Swindon Stock
8.3.41	Banbury
18.11.42	Banbury **R**
12.12.42	Banbury
24.1.44	Banbury (wait)
7.2.44	Swindon Factory **G**
7.3.44	Swindon Stock
8.3.44	Banbury
24.11.45	Oxford Shops **R**
10.1.46	Banbury
29.1.46	Banbury **R**
12.2.46	Banbury
13.1.47	Banbury (wait)
4.2.47	Swindon Factory **I**
28.2.47	Banbury
12.7.48	Canton Shops **R**
20.8.48	Banbury
26.5.48	Swindon Factory **HG**
23.6.49	Banbury
9.50	Penzance
12.50	St.Blazey
15.1.51	St.Blazey Shops **U**
30.1.51	St.Blazey
6.9.51	(wait) for Swindon
5.10.51	Swindon Factory **HG**
2.11.51	Newton Abbot
13.5.54	Swindon Factory **HG**
14.6.54	Newton Abbot
7.55	Truro
10.55	Machynlleth
10.11.56	Swindon Factory **HI**
17.12.56	Aberystwyth
4.2.57	Oswestry Shops **LC**
9.2.57	Aberystwyth
9.11.57	Aberystwyth Shops **U**
28.11.57	Aberystwyth
4.8.58	Oswestry Shops **LC**
14.8.58	Aberystwyth
17.2.59	Stafford Road Ftry **LC**
20.3.59	Aberystwyth
18.6.59	Newton Abbot
30.9.59	St.Blazey
25.2.60	Swindon Factory **HG**

No details are known about this photograph of No.7806 COCKINGTON MANOR. However, an 83A shed plate is discernible, the first style of BR emblem is displayed on the tender, and the engine's cosmetic condition possibly indicates a recent visit to Swindon. As will be seen from the registers, while allocated to Newton Abbot in the first half of the 1950s, No.7806 underwent heavy generals at Swindon in October 1951 and May/June 1954. This gives a choice of two approximate dates, though given the leafy state of the tree, the October date can be ruled out. *Where* this scene might be is another matter........ PHOTOGRAPH: R.C. RILEY COLLECTION

No.7807 COMPTON MANOR, carrying a 6E shed plate. Chester shed was thus recoded in February 1958 and as No.7807 was transferred to Oswestry (89A) in August 1958, the date of the photograph can be narrowed down accordingly. Nevertheless, the location is unknown. One possible curiosity - No.7807 was repainted in lined green (at Wolverhampton) in March 1957, which was about the time the old 'ferret and dartboard' BR emblem was replaced by the new style emblem. Yet the tender still carried the old crest. All we can add to this little mystery is the fact that, while at Stafford Road Works in February/March 1957, No.7807's intermediate pattern tender (No.2222) was not changed. PHOTOGRAPH: BRYAN WILSON COLLECTION

8.4.60	St.Blazey
16.9.60	Tyseley
18.1.61	Stourbridge
21.5.61	Stourbridge Shops **U**
6.6.61	Stourbridge
18.4.62	Stourbridge Shops **U**
14.5.62	Stourbridge
15.6.62	Oxley
16.7.62	Oxley (wait)
9.8.62	Swindon Factory **HC**
6.11.62	Oxley
11.2.63	Ebbw Junction Shops **U**
8.3.63	Oxley
11.64	**Withdrawn**
	Sold as scrap to
	J.Cashmore Ltd
	of Great Bridge, Staffs.

N.B: Loco was LM Region book stock from 30.12.62 until withdrawal

Boilers and mileages:

First	6406		
6.3.41	..	(92,099)	
7.3.44	6405	(188,651)	
28.2.47	6411	(290,508)	
23.6.49	6407	(366,297)	
2.11.51	6400	(433,111)	
14.6.54	6418	(508,980)	
17.12.56	..	(590,567)	
8.4.60	6405	(678,525)	
28.12.63	..	(750,993)	

Tenders:

First	1662
6.3.41	1929
7.3.44	1703
28.2.47	2000
23.6.49	2382 *
5.10.49	2010
17.6.50	2321
2.11.51	2370
14.6.54	2366
17.12.56	1864
6.11.62	1897
13.6.64	2049

* 2382 was 'intermediate pattern' (see text)

................ooo................

7807 COMPTON MANOR
To stock: 22 March 1938
Summary of sheds (parent sheds only):

First	Neyland
3.43	Oswestry
7.43	Aberystwyth
9.43	Oswestry
11.43	Aberystwyth
12.43	Oswestry
12.53	Chester
26.8.58	Oswestry
28.12.63	*Machynlleth*

Engine history:

5.4.38	Neyland
15.1.40	Swindon Factory **I**
23.2.40	Swindon Stock
25.2.40	Neyland
3.9.41	Neath Shops **L**
16.9.41	Neyland
10.6.42	Swindon Factory **I**
30.7.42	Swindon Stock
1.8.42	Neyland
3.43	Oswestry
7.43	Aberystwyth
9.43	Oswestry
10.43	Whitchurch LMS
11.43	Aberystwyth
12.43	Oswestry
1.44	Whitchurch LMS
12.2.44	Tyseley Shops **L**
16.3.44	Oswestry
17.8.44	Oswestry (wait)
23.8.44	Swindon Factory **G**
4.10.44	Oswestry
4.45	Whitchurch LMS
5.45	Oswestry
9.45	Whitchurch LMS
10.45	Oswestry
1.46	Whitchurch LMS
2.46	Oswestry
3.46	Whitchurch LMS
3.4.46	Oswestry (wait)
24.4.46	Stafford Road Factory **L**

10.7.46	Oswestry
11.46	Whitchurch LMS
11.46	Oswestry
2.47	Whitchurch LMS
3.47	Oswestry
9.4.47	Oswestry Shops **L**
15.4.47	Oswestry
16.9.47	Swindon Factory **L**
14.10.47	Whitchurch LMS
11.47	Oswestry
2.48	Whitchurch LMS
5.48	Oswestry
7.48	Whitchurch LMS
8.48	Oswestry
10.48	Whitchurch LMS
11.48	Oswestry
29.1.49	Oswestry **U**
18.2.49	Oswestry
12.5.49	Oswestry (wait)
23.5.49	Swindon Factory **LC**
16.6.49	Oswestry
25.5.50	Swindon Factory **HG**
23.6.50	Oswestry
29.5.52	Swindon Factory **HG**
1.7.52	Oswestry
12.53	Chester
22.3.54	Chester Shops **U**
5.4.54	Chester
5.1.55	Swindon Factory **HG**
2.2.55	Chester
26.10.56	Croes Newydd Shops **U**
10.11.56	Chester
19.2.57	Chester (wait)
26.2.57	Stafford Road Ftry **HI**
28.3.57	Chester
26.8.58	Oswestry
26.1.59	Oswestry (wait)
9.3.59	Swindon Factory **HG**
28.5.59	Swindon Stock
29.5.59	Oswestry
14.2.62	Oswestry (wait)
26.2.62	Swindon Factory **HI**
27.4.62	Oswestry
28.12.63	*Machynlleth*
11.64	**Withdrawn**
	Sold as scrap to John Cashmore

	Ltd. of Great Bridge, Staffs.

N.B: Loco was LM Region book stock from 23.2.58 to 7.9.58 and from 30.12.62 until withdrawal

Boilers and mileages:

First	6407		
23.2.40	..	(83,752)	
30.7.42	..	(174,675)	
4.10.44	6409	(258,002)	
14.10.47	6418	(369,159)	
23.6.50	6420	(470,426)	
1.7.52	6412	(552,879)	
2.2.55	6411	(643,855)	
28.3.57	..	(721,727)	
28.5.59	6424	(782,204)	
27.4.62	..	(895,838)	
28.12.63	..	(949,807)	

Tenders:

First	1901
30.7.42	2089
15.9.43	2055
4.10.44	1799
14.10.47	2108
16.6.49	1805
31.12.49	2054
23.6.50	2319
5.4.54	1794
2.2.55	2222
28.5.59	1636
4.62	1952

................ooo................

7808 COOKHAM MANOR
To stock: 29 March 1938
Summary of sheds (parent sheds only):

First	Old Oak Common
3.39	Gloucester
4.46	Oswestry*
12.53	St.Philip's Marsh
1.54	Gloucester*
18.6.59	Newton Abbot
13.9.60	Exeter

31.12.65 Withdrawn
1.66 Purchased privately for preservation

Boilers and mileages:

First	6408	
2.10.40	..	(40,653)
31.3.43	6421*	(175,095)
13.12.46	6400	(317,410)
10.12.48	6415	(395,225)
18.12.50	6416	(475,147)
31.7.53	6409	(582,783)
15.2.56	..	(679,103)
16.1.58	6417	(749,855)
21.12.60	6408	(841,535)
28.12.63	6407	(913,744)

Tenders:

First	1970
2.10.40	2347
31.3.43	1715
4.5.45	2154
13.12.46	2349
9.9.50	2177
18.12.50	1811
14.6.52	2080
31.7.53	1917
18.4.59	1856
21.12.60	2107
7.1.64	2316

Hauling empty mineral wagons, No.7808 COOKHAM MANOR approaches Eastleigh on 2 July 1954, heading for Andover and then, presumably, on to Cheltenham (where it was allocated at the time) via the MSWJ line. PHOTOGRAPH: BRIAN MORRISON

...............ooo...............

7809 CHILDREY MANOR
To stock: 13 April 1938
Summary of sheds (parent sheds only):

First	Westbury
20.3.40	Bath Road
6.48	Laira
7.54	Taunton
11.54	Laira
6.56	Landore
7.56	Laira
10.57	Newton Abbot
26.9.58	Canton
2.12.58	Gloucester
16.4.59	Oswestry

16.9.60	Worcester	14.11.54	Cheltenham	18.6.59	Newton Abbot
21.12.60	Tyseley	4.1.55	Worcester Factory **HG**	13.9.60	Exeter
7.9.62	Reading	1.2.55	Cheltenham	16.9.60	Worcester
8.64	Swindon	11.1.56	Stafford Road Ftry **HI**	14.10.60	Gloucester (wait)
11.64	Gloucester	15.2.56	Cheltenham	2.11.60	Swindon Factory **HG**

* Upon being transferred, went immediately to sub-shed (see engine history).

21.4.56	Gloucester Shops **U**	21.12.60	Tyseley
13.5.56	Cheltenham	29.12.60	Old Oak Com'n Shps **U**
25.3.57	Worcester Shops **LC**	26.1.61	Tyseley
10.4.57	Cheltenham	7.9.62	Reading
6.12.57	Gloucester (wait)	9.10.63	Reading (wait)
17.12.57	Swindon Factory **HG**	22.10.63	Swindon Factory **HI**
16.1.58	Cheltenham	7.1.64	Reading
20.1.58	Swindon Factory **LC**	8.64	Swindon
30.1.58	Cheltenham	11.64	Gloucester

Engine history:

3.4.38	Old Oak Common
3.39	Gloucester
19.8.40	Swindon Factory **I**
2.10.40	Swindon Stock
9.10.40	Gloucester
17.2.42	Gloucester Shops **R**
22.2.42	Gloucester
22.2.43	Swindon Factory **G**
31.3.43	Swindon Stock
3.4.43	Gloucester
19.11.44	Gloucester Shops **R**
29.11.44	Gloucester
12.3.45	Gloucester (wait)
29.3.45	Swindon Factory **I**
5.45	Gloucester
2.46	Cheltenham
4.46	Whitchurch LMS
6.46	Oswestry
28.9.46	Oswestry (wait)
5.11.46	Swindon Factory **I**
13.12.46	Whitchurch LMS
2.47	Oswestry
1.48	Whitchurch LMS
2.48	Oswestry
6.48	Whitchurch LMS
7.48	Aberystwyth
8.48	Oswestry
10.48	Whitchurch LMS
4.11.48	Oswestry (wait)
12.11.48	Swindon Factory **G**
10.12.48	Oswestry
1.49	Whitchurch LMR
13.11.50	Swindon Factory **HG**
18.12.50	Whitchurch LMR
7.51	Oswestry
17.6.53	Swindon Factory **HG**
31.7.53	Oswestry
12.53	St.Philip's Marsh
1.54	Cheltenham
28.10.54	Worcester Factory **U**

No.7809 CHILDREY MANOR at Aberystwyth, July 1961. The engine was allocated to Oswestry, which at the beginning of that year had been recoded 89D. PHOTOGRAPH: ERIC SAWFORD

12.62 Shrewsbury

Engine history:
13.4.38 Westbury
4.8.38 Westbury Shops **R**
18.8.38 Westbury
9.38 Salisbury
10.38 Westbury
7.11.39 (wait) for Swindon
21.11.39 Swindon Factory (tender work)
8.12.39 Westbury
22.1.40 Salisbury
22.1.40 Bath Road (wait)
6.2.40 Swindon Factory **I**
14.3.40 Swindon Stock
20.3.40 Bath Road
4.40 Weston-s-Mare
5.40 Bath Road
8.40 Weston-s-Mare
9.40 Bath Road
27.11.40 Swindon (No work)
3.12.40 Bath Road
14.2.41 Bath Road Shops **R**
11.3.41 Bath Road
28.3.42 Bath Road (wait)
30.3.42 Swindon Factory **I**
6.5.42 Swindon Stock
7.5.42 Bath Road
8.42 Weston-s-Mare
10.42 Bath Road
7.43 Weston-s-Mare
8.43 Bath Road
4.44 Weston-s-Mare
5.44 Bath Road
8.6.44 (wait) for Swindon
22.6.44 Swindon Factory **G**
5.8.44 Swindon Stock
7.8.44 Bath Road
2.45 Weston-s-Mare
3.45 Bath Road
12.45 Weston-s-Mare
12.45 Bath Road
10.46 Weston-s-Mare
23.10.46 (wait) for Swindon
6.12.46 Swindon Factory **I**
16.1.47 Bath Road
10.47 Weston-s-Mare
12.47 Bath Road
6.48 Laira
20.9.48 Newton Abbot Ftry **L**
7.10.48 Laira
14.3.49 Laira Shops **U**
29.3.49 Laira
16.5.49 Laira Shops **U**
1.6.49 Laira
25.7.49 Swindon Factory **HG**
25.8.49 Laira
1.5.51 Newton Abbot Ftry **LC**
10.5.51 Laira
5.3.52 Swindon Factory **HG**
3.4.52 Laira
21.7.52 Truro Shops **R**
23.8.52 Laira
26.11.52 Swindon Factory **U**
8.12.52 Laira
20.1.53 Laira Shops **U**
3.2.53 Laira
2.9.53 Laira Shops **U**
8.9.53 Laira
7.54 Taunton
31.10.54 Laira Shops **U**
30.11.54 Laira
29.12.54 Laira Shops **U**
3.1.55 Laira
31.3.55 Swindon Factory **HG**
6.5.55 Laira
6.56 Landore
7.56 Laira
23.1.57 Laira Shops **U**
29.1.57 Laira
10.57 Newton Abbot
14.10.57 Swindon Factory **HG**
19.11.57 Newton Abbot

26.9.58 Canton
2.12.58 Gloucester
9.3.59 Gloucester (in store)
16.4.59 Oswestry
30.11.59 Oswestry Shops **LC**
4.12.59 Oswestry
22.11.60 Stafford Road Ftry **HI**
6.1.61 Oswestry
12.62 Shrewsbury
8.4.63 **Withdrawn**
    Cut up at Swindon w/e
15.6.63
N.B: Loco was on LM Region book stock from 30.12.62 until withdrawal

Boilers and mileages:
First 6409
14.3.40 .. (84,257)
6.5.42 .. (166,779)
5.8.44 6416 (245,464)
16.1.47 6419 (328,820)
25.8.49 6412 (418,776)
3.4.52 6417 (485,032)
6.5.55 6412 (579,227)
19.11.57 6414 (657,655)
6.1.61 .. (761,611)
28.12.63 .. (846,823)

Tenders:
First 1866
8.12.39 2080
14.3.40 2162
6.5.42 1953
5.8.44 1818
16.1.47 2151
29.3.49 2232 ?
23.4.49 1910
29.12.51 1723
3.4.52 2206
28.1.56 2224
19.11.57 1990
18.4.59 2028
5.62 1973
9.48 Leamington
10.50 Shrewsbury
12.53 Gloucester *
29.5.59 Oswestry
28.12.63 *Machynlleth*
* On being transferred, went direct to

sub-shed (see engine history).

Engine history:
18.12.38 Banbury
1.1.40 Stafford Road Shops **R**
15.1.40 Banbury
6.12.40 Banbury
21.12.40 Banbury
18.8.41 Swindon Factory **I**
3.10.41 Swindon Stock
10.10.41 Banbury
6.2.43 Banbury
3.3.43 Banbury
9.10.43 Banbury *(wait)*
26.10.43 Stafford Road Factory **I**
5.2.44 Banbury
18.7.44 St.Blazey Shops **R**
25.8.44 Banbury
24.3.45 Banbury
4.5.45 Banbury
15.1.46 Shrewsbury Shops **R**
9.3.46 Banbury
18.3.46 Banbury *(wait)*
28.3.46 Swindon Factory **G**
4.5.46 Banbury
2.47 Leamington
6.4.48 Leamington (wait)
29.4.48 Stafford Road Factory **L**
11.6.48 Stafford Road ?
9.48 Leamington
25.1.49 Banbury Shops **U**
26.2.49 Leamington
16.2.50 Tyseley Shops **U**
17.3.50 Leamington
21.4.50 Leamington Shops (tender work)
28.4.50 Leamington
26.7.50 Swindon Factory **HG**
29.8.50 Leamington
10.50 Shrewsbury
16.3.53 Stafford Road Ftry **HI**
24.4.53 Shrewsbury
12.53 Cheltenham
9.7.54 Worcester Shops **U**
5.8.54 Cheltenham
14.3.55 Swindon Factory **HI**
12.4.55 Cheltenham
4.7.56 Gloucester Shops **U**
26.7.56 Cheltenham

24.11.56 Worcester Shops **U**
9.12.56 Cheltenham
25.2.57 Gloucester (wait)
26.2.57 Swindon Factory **HG**
10.4.57 Cheltenham
1.8.57 Cheltenham (wait)
13.8.57 Newton Abbot Shps **LC**
21.8.57 Cheltenham
22.2.59 Gloucester (wait)
4.3.59 Swindon Factory **HI**
1.5.59 In store
29.5.59 Oswestry
30.9.61 Oswestry (wait)
15.11.61 Swindon Factory **HG**
30.1.62 Oswestry
28.12.63 *Machynlleth*
9.64 **Withdrawn**
    Sold as scrap to Birds of Morriston
N.B: Loco was LM Region book stock from 30.12.62 until withdrawal

Boilers and mileages
First 6410
3.10.41 .. (95,617)
5.2.44 .. (168,860)
4.5.46 6402 (228,371)
29.8.50 6406 (326,449)
24.4.53 6405 (407,781)
12.4.55 6414 (484,296)
10.4.57 6431 (562,681)
1.5.59 .. (638,333)
30.1.62 6402 (734,489)
28.12.63 .. (818,074)

Tenders:
First 1865
3.10.41 1907
4.5.46 1782
29.8.50 1671
24.4.53 1935
16.5.53 2132
12.4.55 1817
10.4.57 2371
19.4.58 2122
1.5.59 2226
1.1.61 1921
30.1.62 2368
18.5.63 2347

The 'Cambrian Coast Express', headed by No.7810 DRAYCOTT MANOR, pulls into Abermule.
PHOTOGRAPH: A.J.B. DODD/PAUL CHANCELLOR COLLECTION

**No.7811 DUNLEY MANOR of Croes Newydd heads a Chester-Barmouth train across the Dee Bridge at Chester on 9 August 1962.
PHOTOGRAPH: DEREK CROSS**

7.63   1560 *
* 1560 was Churchward
   4,000gall (see text)

...............ooo...............

7811 DUNLEY MANOR
To stock: 10 December 1938
Summary of sheds:

First	Banbury
7.52	Oxley
1.53	Shrewsbury
10.61	Croes Newydd
5.2.63	Llanelly
4.3.63	Neyland
7.9.63	*Whitland*
12.63	*Llanelly*
2.65	*Cardiff East Dock*

Engine history:

18.12.38	Banbury
26.8.40	Banbury Shops **L**
18.9.40	Banbury
25.2.41	Swindon Factory **I**
7.4.41	Swindon Stock
12.4.41	Banbury
15.10.42	Swindon Factory **L**
13.11.42	Swindon Stock
16.11.42	Banbury
27.6.44	Southall (wait)
1.7.44	Swindon Factory **G**
10.8.44	Swindon Stock
9.44	Banbury
31.3.47	Banbury (wait)
25.4.47	Swindon Factory **I**
2.6.47	Swindon Stock
8.6.47	Banbury
19.7.48	Banbury Shops **U**
3.8.48	Banbury
25.1.49	Banbury (wait)
2.2.49	Swindon Factory **LC**
11.3.49	Banbury
16.1.50	Banbury Shops **U**
31.1.50	Banbury
24.4.50	Southall (wait)
2.5.50	Swindon Factory **HG**
30.5.50	Banbury
24.11.50	Leamington Shops **U**
6.12.50	Banbury
21.6.51	Banbury Shops **U**
7.7.51	Banbury
7.52	Oxley
6.9.52	Oxley Shops **U**
11.9.52	Oxley
30.9.52	Swindon Factory **HI**
27.10.52	Oxley
1.53	Shrewsbury
23.12.53	Shrewsbury Shops **U**
7.1.54	Shrewsbury
7.4.54	Shrewsbury Shops **U**
22.4.54	Shrewsbury
19.7.54	Shrewsbury Shops **U**
7.8.54	Shrewsbury
21.5.55	Swindon Factory **HG**
23.6.55	Shrewsbury
22.10.57	Swindon Factory **HI**
27.11.57	Shrewsbury
21.10.58	Shrewsbury (wait)
23.10.58	Stafford Road F'cty **LC**
3.11.58	Shrewsbury
13.1.60	Shrewsbury Shops **U**
27.1.60	Shrewsbury
28.3.60	Shrewsbury (wait)
13.4.60	Swindon Factory **HG**
2.6.60	Shrewsbury
12.10.61	Croes Newydd
27.11.62	Swindon Factory **HI**
5.2.63	Llanelly
4.3.63	Neyland
27.6.63	Carmarthen Shops **U**
17.7.63	Neyland
7.9.63	*Whitland*
9.9.63	In store (Whitland ?)
12.63	*Llanelly*
2.65	*Cardiff East Dock*
21.7.65	**Withdrawn**
c.10.65	Sold as scrap to Birds
	of Morriston

Boilers and mileages:

First	6411	
7.4.41	..	(82,574)
10.8.44	6418	(185,967)
2.6.47	6405	(278,719)
30.5.50	6408	(363,543)
27.10.52	6420	(438,460)

**The 8.20am Oswestry-Aberystwyth, headed by No.7812 ERLESTOKE MANOR, stands at
Welshpool in pouring rain on 21 April 1962. PHOTOGRAPH: MICHAEL MENSING**

23.6.55	6421	(516,660)
27.11.57	6408	(594,157)
2.6.60	6419	(670,745)
5.2.63	6411	(760,315)
28.12.63	..	(777,149)

Tenders:

First	1796
13.11.42	1889
10.8.44	1831
2.11.46	1949
2.6.47	2134
11.3.49	1922
30.5.50	1718
27.10.52	1992
7.53	2379 *
18.3.54	1865
23.6.55	2019
11.57	1941
2.6.60	2056
5.2.63	2112

* 2379 was 'intermediate
pattern' (see text)

...............ooo...............

7812 ERLESTOKE MANOR
To stock: 4 January 1939
Summary of sheds (parent sheds
only):

First	Bath Road
12.39	St.Philip's Marsh
2.40	Bath Road
5.48	Newton Abbot
7.49	St.Blazey
10.49	Newton Abbot
12.56	Laira
22.9.59	Truro
16.9.60	Oswestry
12.61	*Croes Newydd*
12.62	Shrewsbury

Engine history:

9.1.39	Bath Road
12.39	St.Philip's Marsh
2.40	Bath Road
16.9.40	Bath Road Shops **R**
3.10.40	Bath Road
11.40	Weston-s-Mare
12.40	Bath Road
25.2.41	Swindon Factory **I**
8.4.41	Swindon Stock
10.4.41	Bath Road
12.41	Weston-s-Mare
1.42	Bath Road
10.42	Weston-s-Mare
11.42	Bath Road
6.1.43	Swindon Factory (ten der change)
12.1.43	Bath Road
8.43	Weston-s-Mare
10.9.43	Swindon Factory **G**
6.10.43	Swindon Stock
11.43	Bath Road
3.45	Weston-s-Mare
4.45	Bath Road
9.45	Weston-s-Mare
12.45	Bath Road
12.3.46	Bath Road Shops **R**
27.3.46	Bath Road
24.5.46	Bath Road (wait)
4.6.46	Swindon Factory **I**
4.7.46	Bath Road
6.47	Weston-s-Mare
7.47	Bath Road
11.47	Weston-s-Mare
11.47	Bath Road
10.1.48	Bath Road Shops (tender)
24.1.48	Bath Road
5.48	Newton Abbot
3.7.48	Newton Abbot (wait)
16.7.48	Swindon Factory **I**
12.8.48	Newton Abbot

7.49	St.Blazey
10.49	Newton Abbot
6.11.50	Newton Abbot Ftry **LC**
9.11.50	Newton Abbot
20.6.51	Swindon Factory **HG**
7.8.51	Newton Abbot
30.12.53	Swindon Factory **HI**
29.1.54	Newton Abbot
7.12.55	Newton Abbot (wait)
10.12.55	Swindon Factory **HG**
13.1.56	Newton Abbot
12.56	Laira
19.9.58	Laira Shops **U**
4.6.58	Laira
3.12.58	Laira (wait)
6.12.58	Swindon Factory **HI**
14.1.59	Laira
22.9.59	Truro
5.6.60	Penzance Shops **U**
23.6.60	Truro
16.9.60	Oswestry
27.5.61	Swindon Factory **HG**
11.7.61	Oswestry
12.61	*Croes Newydd*
12.62	Shrewsbury
18.11.63	Swindon Factory **HI**
30.1.64	Shrewsbury
6.11.65	**Withdrawn**
	Sold as scrap to Woodham Bros of Barry.
28.6.73	Purchased for preserva-tion
4.76	Moved to Severn Valley Railway

N.B: Loco was LM Region book stock
from 30.12.62 until withdrawal

Boilers and mileages:

First	6412	
8.4.41	..	(86,750)
6.10.43	6415	(177,170)
4.7.46	6406	(260,724)
12.4.48	6403	(333,339)
7.8.51	6401	(398,849)
29.1.54	6426	(473,849)
13.1.56	6429	(532,061)
14.1.59	6428	(620,770)
11.7.61	6412	(694,571)
30.1.64	6400	(789,376)

Tenders:

First	2373
8.4.41	2353

12.1.43	1921
6.10.43	2110
4.7.46	2160
31.10.53	2351
29.1.54	1976
24.2.55	1837
13.1.56	1807
14.1.59	2345
25.6.60	2170
25.2.61	2068
30.1.64	1719

...............ooo...............

7813 FRESHFORD MANOR
To stock: 12 January 1939
Summary of sheds:

First	Oxley
13.5.48	Newton Abbot
7.49	Penzance
11.49	Newton Abbot
12.57	Laira
22.9.59	Truro
16.9.60	Worcester
31.10.60	Tyseley
5.10.62	Reading
8.64	Swindon
11.64	Gloucester
3.65	Didcot

Engine history:

20.1.39	Oxley
14.4.41	Oxley (wait)
14.4.41	Stafford Road Factory **L**
20.6.41	Oxley
3.10.42	Oxley Shops **R**
16.10.42	Oxley
22.3.43	Oxley (wait)
9.1.46	Swindon Factory **G**
4.2.46	Oxley
1.3.47	Southall Shops **R**
16.3.47	Oxley
7.7.47	Swindon Factory
7.47	Oxley
13.11.47	Oxley Shops **R**
27.11.47	Oxley
2.4.48	Landore (wait)
12.4.48	Swindon Factory **I**
6.48	Newton Abbot
13.9.48	Newton Abbot Shops **R**
1.10.48	Newton Abbot
7.49	Penzance
11.49	Newton Abbot
27.2.50	Newton Abbot Shops **U**

22.3.50	Newton Abbot
18.7.50	Newton Abbot **U**
9.8.50	Newton Abbot
20.1.51	Newton Abbot Shops **U**
13.2.51	Newton Abbot
22.2.51	Swindon Factory **HG**
22.3.51	Newton Abbot
8.7.52	Newton Abbot **U**
17.7.52	Newton Abbot
30.10.52	Newton Abbot Ftry **U**
4.11.52	Newton Abbot
7.1.53	Newton Abbot **U**
21.1.53	Newton Abbot
11.3.53	Newton Abbot Ftry **LC**
30.3.53	Newton Abbot
28.11.53	Swindon Factory **HG**
1.1.54	Newton Abbot
14.2.56	Newton Abbot Ftry **HI**
26.3.56	Newton Abbot
2.5.57	Newton Abbot Ftry **LC**
16.5.57	Newton Abbot
12.57	Laira
3.2.58	Laira Shops **U**
16.2.58	Laira
5.1.59	Laira (wait)
14.1.59	Swindon Factory **HG**
25.2.59	Laira
22.9.59	Truro
16.9.60	Worcester
31.10.60	Tyseley
27.1.61	Tyseley Shops **U**
15.2.61	Tyseley
25.5.62	Tyseley Shops **U**
8.6.62	Tyseley
16.6.62	Tyseley (wait)
23.7.62	Swindon Factory **HI**
5.10.62	Reading
8.2.63	Reading (wait)
18.2.63	Swindon Factory **U**
15.3.63	Reading
8.64	Swindon
11.64	Gloucester
3.65	Didcot
10.5.65	**Withdrawn**
	Sold as scrap to Birds of Morriston

Boilers and mileages:

First	6413	
7.5.43	6402	(138,494)
4.2.46	6417	(222,349)
13.5.48	6409	(300,819)
22.3.51	6404	(364,957)
1.1.54	6406	(443,072)

**No.7813 FRESHFORD MANOR (with original chimney) and No.5094 TRETOWER CASTLE work
hard on the ascent of Hemerdon Bank. The year is 1954. PHOTOGRAPH: MAURICE EARLEY**

Newton Abbot's No.7814 FRINGFORD MANOR (seemingly with its original capuchon chimney) runs light into Plymouth Millbay on 4 August 1957. The station had closed to passengers in April 1941, but remained in use to accommodate empty stock. PHOTOGRAPH: E.R. MORTEN

26.3.56	..	(507,043)
25.2.59	6422	(581,600)
5.10.62	..	(676,752)
28.12.63	..	(704,558)

Tenders:

First	1852
7.5.43	1878
4.2.46	1785
8.7.44	2357
13.5.48	2012
22.3.51	2148
1.1.54	2377 *
25.2.59	1897
14.7.62	2233
5.10.62	2367

* 2377 was 'intermediate pattern' (see text)

..............ooo...............

7814 FRINGFORD MANOR
To stock: 16 January 1939
Summary of sheds (parent sheds only):

First	Westbury
2.40	Bath Road
5.48	Laira
6.54	Truro
10.54	Laira
8.55	Reading
6.56	Newton Abbot
26.9.58	Canton
16.2.59	Aberystwyth
23.6.59	Oswestry
24.7.59	Aberystwyth
21.12.62	Carmarthen
4.3.63	Neyland
9.9.63	Llanelly
6.64	Gloucester
5.65	*Didcot*
7.65	*Gloucester*

Engine history:

19.1.39	Westbury
3.2.40	Bath Road
12.6.40	Bath Road Shops **R**
27.6.40	Bath Road
2.9.40	Bath Road (wait)
13.9.40	Swindon Factory **L**
10.10.40	Swindon Stock
27.11.40	Bath Road
14.2.41	Swindon Factory **L**
7.3.41	Swindon Stock
9.3.41	Weston-s-Mare
4.41	Bath Road
4.11.41	Swindon Factory **I**
9.12.41	Swindon Stock
11.12.41	Bath Road
1.42	Weston-s-Mare
2.42	Bath Road
7.42	Weston-s-Mare
8.42	Bath Road
9.42	Weston-s-Mare
10.42	Bath Road
20.7.43	Bath Road (wait)
7.8.43	Swindon Factory **L**
17.9.43	Swindon Stock
18.9.43	Bath Road
11.43	Weston-s-Mare
12.43	Bath Road
5.7.44	Bath Road (wait)
26.7.44	Swindon Factory **I**
30.8.44	Bath Road
3.45	Weston-s-Mare
4.45	Bath Road
6.45	Weston-s-Mare
7.45	Bath Road
10.45	Weston-s-Mare
4.46	Weston-s-Mare
5.46	Bath Road
2.8.46	Southall (wait) (failed ?)
26.8.46	Swindon Factory **G**
23.9.46	Bath Road
19.3.47	Hereford Shops **R** (failed?)
19.4.47	Bath Road
17.5.47	Bath Road Shops **R**
28.5.47	Bath Road
31.5.47	Taunton Shops **R**
24.6.47	Bath Road
1.48	Yatton
2.48	Bath Road
5.48	Laira
4.6.48	Newton Abbot Shops **L** (tender)
8.48	Laira
7.9.48	Newton Abbot Shops **L** (tender)
8.9.48	Laira
25.10.48	(wait) for Swindon
29.10.48	Swindon Factory **I**
29.11.48	Laira
3.12.48	Swindon Factory **L**
13.12.48	Laira
7.7.49	Newton Abbot Shops **U**
4.8.49	Laira
28.6.50	Newton Abbot Ftry **LC**
4.8.50	Laira
22.4.51	Swindon Factory **HC**
22.5.51	Laira
24.10.52	Laira Shops **U**
11.11.52	Laira
9.1.53	Laira Shops **U**
3.2.53	Laira
15.9.53	Laira Shops **U**
2.10.53	Laira
20.3.54	Swindon Factory **HG**
23.4.54	Laira
6.54	Truro
10.54	Laira
8.55	Reading
6.56	Newton Abbot
10.10.56	Stafford Road F'cty **HI**
13.11.56	Newton Abbot
26.9.58	Canton
16.10.58	Canton Shops **U**
30.10.58	Canton
16.2.59	Aberystwyth
1.4.59	Aberystwyth (wait)
9.5.59	Swindon Factory **HG**
23.6.59	Oswestry

No.7815 FRITWELL MANOR passes Sutton Bridge Junction at Shrewsbury with the 3.55pm to Aberystwyth on 24 September 1960. PHOTOGRAPH: MICHAEL MENSING

An unadvertised Marsh Mills (Plymouth) - St.Austell workmen's train climbs the bank to the west of St.Germans. The engine is No.7816 FRILSHAM MANOR and the date is 27 April 1954.
PHOTOGRAPH: ALAN LATHEY

24.7.59	Aberystwyth
31.5.62	Swindon Factory **HI**
15.8.62	Aberystwyth
21.12.62	Carmarthen
4.3.63	Neyland
9.9.63	Llanelly
27.4.64	Llanelly Shops (tender)
5.6.64	Llanelly
6.64	Gloucester
5.65	*Didcot*
7.65	*Gloucester*
10.9.65	**Withdrawn**
	Sold as scrap to Birds of Swansea; cut up at Long Marston yard.

Boilers and mileages:

First	6414	
9.12.41	..	(113,826)
17.9.43	6400	(172,331)
30.8.44	..	(204,973)
23.9.46	6415	(271,226)
29.11.48	6414	(336,667)
22.5.51	6415	(398,811)
23.4.54	6401	(483,936)
13.11.56	..	(570,736)
23.6.59	6406	(636,507)
15.8.62	6404	(739,174)

Tenders:

First	2133
10.10.40	2099
9.12.41	1748
17.9.43	1645
30.8.44	2373
23.9.46	1743
29.11.48	1919
22.5.51	2346
21.3.53	2152
23.4.54	2108
12.7.58	2330
15.8.62	2153

...............ooo...............

7815 FRITWELL MANOR
To stock: 21 January 1939
Summary of sheds (parent sheds only):

First	Gloucester
8.52	Laira
7.54	Newton Abbot

1.55	Laira
10.55	Worcester
12.6.58	Laira
26.9.58	Canton
2.12.58	Gloucester
9.12.59	Aberystwyth
18.1.63	Carmarthen
4.64	Llanelly
6.64	Gloucester

Engine history:

31.3.39	Gloucester
26.9.40	Stafford Road F'cty **I**
15.11.40	Gloucester
5.5.42	Stafford Road **R**
14.5.42	Gloucester
31.5.43	Swindon Factory **G**
16.7.43	Swindon Stock
21.7.43	Gloucester
14.2.44	Hereford (wait)
29.2.44	Stafford Road F'cty **L**
13.3.44	Gloucester
10.3.45	Gloucester (wait)
4.4.45	Worcester F'cty **L**
19.6.45	Cheltenham
5.11.45	Worcester F'cty **L**
31.1.46	Gloucester
7.8.46	Gloucester Shops **R**
18.8.46	Gloucester
10.2.47	Gloucester (wait)
5.3.47	Swindon Factory **I**
9.4.47	Gloucester
2.48	Cheltenham
1.7.48	Swindon (wait)
5.8.48	Swindon Factory **R**
24.8.48	Cheltenham
3.1.49	Worcester F'cty **U**
19.1.49	Cheltenham
8.2.49	Swindon Factory
18.2.49	Swindon Factory **HI**
23.3.49	Cheltenham
19.7.49	Cheltenham (wait)
30.8.49	Swindon Factory **LC**
23.9.49	Cheltenham
9.7.50	Gloucester (wait)
10.8.50	Swindon Factory **HC**
11.9.50	Cheltenham
11.6.51	Swindon Factory **HI**
27.7.51	Cheltenham
8.52	Laira
4.11.52	Laira Shops **U**

22.11.52	Laira
27.10.53	Laira Shops **U**
30.11.53	Laira
20.2.54	Swindon Factory **HG**
26.3.54	Laira
7.54	Newton Abbot
1.55	Laira
25.3.55	Laira Shops **U**
1.4.55	Laira
10.55	Worcester
14.4.56	Worcester Shops **U**
1.5.56	Worcester
14.8.56	Swindon Factory **HI**
25.9.56	Worcester
12.6.58	Laira
25.8.58	Laira (wait)
9.9.58	Newton Abbot Shps **LC**
18.9.58	Laira
26.9.58	Canton
2.12.58	Gloucester
29.5.59	(wait) for Swindon
19.6.59	Swindon Factory **HG**
26.8.59	Gloucester
9.12.59	Aberystwyth
1.2.60	Stafford Road F'cty **LC**
9.3.60	Aberystwyth
22.10.62	Aberystwyth (wait)
12.11.62	Swindon Factory **HI** (PART)
18.1.63	Carmarthen
16.3.63	Carmarthen (wait)
27.3.63	Swindon Factory **HI** (FINISH)
5.6.63	Carmarthen
25.4.64	Llanelly Shops **U**
4.64	Llanelly
6.64	Gloucester
23.10.64	**Withdrawn**
3.65	Sold as scrap to R.S.Hayes of Bridgend

Boilers and mileages:

First	6415	
15.11.40	..	(91,729)
16.7.43	6413	(170,907)
9.4.47	6416	(278,901)
23.3.49	..	(347,225)
11.9.50	6418	(403,808)
27.7.31	..	(438,945)
26.3.54	6403	(533,531)
25.9.56	..	(606,060)

26.8.59	6411	(695,800)
18.1.63	6403	(800,452)
28.12.63	..	(822,506)

Tenders:

First	2208
22.2.40	1870
3.3.43	1873
16.7.43	2027
24.5.45	1899
9.4.47	1741
24.8.48	1911
23.3.49	1646
19.8.49	1720 *
23.9.49	2020
11.9.50	2345
27.7.51	2230
26.3.54	2229
25.9.56	1856
18.4.59	1917
26.8.59	2112
18.1.63	2065
5.6.63	2345

* Attached for repair period only

...............ooo...............

7816 FRILSHAM MANOR
To stock: 23 January 1939
Summary of sheds:

First	Neyland
11.52	St.Blazey
16.9.60	Tyseley
11.9.61	Stourbridge
30.8.62	Reading
8.64	Swindon
11.64	Didcot
7.65	*Gloucester*

Engine history:

7.2.39	Neyland
6.6.40	Swindon Factory **L**
3.7.40	Swindon Stock
11.7.40	Neyland
28.12.40	Swindon Factory **I**
3.2.41	Swindon Stock
6.2.41	Neyland
10.3.42	Neyland (wait)
6.4.42	Stafford Road F'cty **L**
21.5.42	Neyland
11.7.42	Newton Abbot F'cty **L**
21.7.42	Neyland
28.3.43	Carmarthen Shops **L**
9.6.43	Neyland Shops **R**
24.6.43	Neyland
20.9.43	Neyland Shops **R**
6.10.43	Neyland
22.1.44	Neyland Shops **R**
15.2.44	Neyland
1.4.44	Neyland (wait)
14.4.44	Swindon Factory **G**
24.5.44	Swindon Stock
25.5.44	Neyland
13.3.46	Neyland (wait)
24.3.46	Ebbw Jctn. Shops **L**
9.4.46	Danygraig Shops **L**
29.4.46	Neyland
21.6.47	Neyland (wait)
23.6.47	Swindon Factory **I**
31.7.47	Neyland
15.8.49	Neyland (wait)
19.8.49	Swindon Factory **G**
23.9.49	Neyland
12.7.51	Llanelly Shops **U**
2.8.51	Neyland
16.11.51	Swindon Factory **HI**
12.12.51	Neyland
11.52	St.Blazey
3.3.54	Swindon Factory **HG**
5.4.54	St.Blazey
22.11.54	Newton Abbot Ftry **HC**
27.11.54	St.Blazey
27.3.56	St.Blazey Shops **U**
11.4.56	St.Blazey

10.9.55	2157
28.1.56	1657
25.2.56	1641
18.9.56	1778
9.6.59	1889
5.62	1936

...............ooo...............

7817 GARSINGTON MANOR
To stock: 30 January 1939

Summary of sheds:

First	Croes Newydd
26.9.58	Shrewsbury
9.12.58	Croes Newydd
25.1.61	Stourbridge
7.9.62	Reading

Engine history:

6.2.39	Croes Newydd
10.9.39	Stafford Road F'cty **L**
25.10.39	Croes Newydd
9.3.40	Stafford Road F'cty **L**
21.3.40	Stafford Road
5.40	Croes Newydd
10.10.40	Croes Newydd (wait)
17.10.40	Stafford Road F'cty **L**
30.11.40	Croes Newydd
28.12.40	Croes Newydd (wait)
29.12.40	Stafford Road F'cty **L**
11.1.41	Croes Newydd
31.1.41	Croes Newydd Shops **L**
10.4.41	Croes Newydd
27.11.41	Croes Newydd Shops **R**
12.12.41	Croes Newydd
28.4.42	Croes Newydd (wait)
6.5.42	Swindon Factory **I**
12.6.42	Swindon Stock
15.6.42	Croes Newydd
12.12.42	Stafford Road (wait)
18.12.42	Stafford Road F'cty **L**
26.2.43	Croes Newydd
17.2.44	Croes Newydd (wait)
2.3.44	Tyseley Shops **L**
24.5.44	Stafford Road F'cty **L**
1.7.44	Stafford Road

A returning holiday express formed of SR stock (possibly the 1.28pm Portsmouth Harbour-Birmingham), hauled by No.7817 GARSINGTON MANOR, passes through Harbury cutting, near Leamington, on 17 August 1963. PHOTOGRAPH: MICHAEL MENSING

7.8.56	Swindon Factory **HI**	**18.11.65**	**Withdrawn**	30.8.62	..	(777,585)
18.9.56	St.Blazey		Sold as scrap to	28.12.63	..	(806,006)
25.3.59	St.Blazey (wait)		Cashmores of Newport			
13.4.59	Swindon Factory **HG**			**Tenders:**		
9.6.59	St.Blazey	**Boilers and mileages:**		First	1933	
16.9.60	Tyseley	First	6416	3.7.40	2220	
11.9.61	Stourbridge	3.2.41	.. (88,297)	24.5.44	2098	
20.1.62	Stourbridge Shops **U**	24.5.44	6404 (190,581)	31.7.47	1998	
7.2.62	Stourbridge	31.7.47	6413 (280,505)	10.7.48	2334	
14.6.62	Stafford Road F'cty **HI**	23.9.49	6411 (360,665)	23.9.49	1720	
30.8.62	Reading	12.12.51	6407 (442,827)	20.5.50	2162	
8.64	Swindon	5.4.54	6464 (533,601)	8.9.51	1926	
11.64	Didcot	18.9.56	.. (619,213)	?	2209	
7.65	*Gloucester*	9.6.59	6429 (700,244)	5.4.54	1981	

Dovey Junction, 9 June 1960 - No.7818 GRANVILLE MANOR has just arrived with the up 'Cambrian Coast', and connects with the Pwllheli train, hauled by 43XX No.6392 (on the right). PHOTOGRAPH: HUGH BALLANTYNE

9.44	Croes Newydd
1.1.45	Croes Newydd (wait)
31.1.45	Swindon Factory **G**
6.3.45	Swindon Stock (?)
6.45	Croes Newydd
28.7.45	Tyseley Shops **L**
31.8.45	Croes Newydd
27.9.46	Croes Newydd (wait)
1.11.46	Swindon Factory **L**
14.12.46	Croes Newydd
10.10.47	Croes Newydd (wait)
21.10.47	Swindon Factory **I**
18.11.47	Croes Newydd
25.12.47	Chester (wait)
9.1.48	Birkenhead Shops **R**
18.2.48	Croes Newydd
20.6.48	Croes Newydd Shops **L**
1.7.48	Croes Newydd
4.8.48	Croes Newydd (wait)
23.9.48	Tyseley Shops **L**
10.11.48	Croes Newydd
9.12.49	Tyseley Shops
10.1.50	Croes Newydd
12.10.50	Swindon Factory **HG**
8.11.50	Croes Newydd
11.7.51	Tyseley Shops **LC**
26.7.51	Croes Newydd
22.8.52	Tyseley Shops **U**
18.9.52	Croes Newydd
29.1.53	Croes Newydd Shops **U**
12.2.53	Croes Newydd
1.4.53	Stafford Road F'cty **HI**
20.5.53	Croes Newydd
7.7.54	Tyseley Shops **U**
21.7.54	Croes Newydd
18.5.55	Croes Newydd Shops **U**
1.6.55	Croes Newydd
26.7.55	Tyseley Shops **U**
23.8.55	Croes Newydd
11.1.56	Swindon Factory **HG**
9.2.56	Croes Newydd
27.2.57	Stafford Road F'cty
28.2.57	Croes Newydd
4.1.58	Croes Newydd Shops **U**
18.1.58	Croes Newydd
26.9.58	Shrewsbury
28.10.58	Swindon Factory **HG**
9.12.58	Croes Newydd
25.1.61	Stourbridge
17.6.61	Stourbridge (wait)
13.7.61	Stafford Road F'cty **HI**
8.9.61	Stourbridge
13.8.62	In store
7.9.62	Reading
4.4.63	Reading Shops **LC**
30.4.63	Reading
15.6.64	**Withdrawn**
18.8.64	Sold as scrap to Birds, and cut up at Risca

Boilers and mileages:

First	6417	
12.6.42	..	(116,896)
6.3.45	6403	(208,228)
18.11.47	6404	(301,631)
8.11.50	6402	(380,551)
20.5.53	..	(464,088)
9.2.56	6424	(547,003)
9.12.58	6423	(636,384)
28.12.63	..	(773,502)

Tenders:

First	1987
12.6.42	2051
6.3.45	2137
14.12.46	1873
18.11.47	2150
8.11.50	1950
20.5.53	1935
23.8.55	2017
6.1.56	2314
9.2.56	1777
9.12.58	2148
3.12.61	1936

...............ooo...............

7818 GRANVILLE MANOR
To stock: January 1939
Summary of sheds (parent sheds only):

First	Worcester
24.5.44	Gloucester
7.52	Oxley
27.1.53	Tyseley
18.6.59	Newton Abbot
7.1.60	Machynlleth
21.11.62	Tyseley

Engine history:

9.2.39	Worcester
27.7.40	Worcester Shops **L**
26.8.40	Worcester
7.4.41	Worcester Shops **R**
17.5.41	Worcester
19.5.41	Worcester Shops **R**
25.6.41	Worcester
6.10.41	Worcester **R**
18.10.41	Worcester
17.3.42	Swindon Factory **I**
30.4.42	Swindon Stock
2.5.42	Worcester
21.3.44	Worcester (wait)
11.4.44	Swindon Factory **G**
20.5.44	Swindon Stock
24.5.44	Cheltenham
10.6.45	Gloucester Shops **R**
17.6.45	Gloucester
10.45	Cheltenham
7.12.45	Worcester Shops **L**
24.1.46	Gloucester
22.4.46	Gloucester (wait)
22.5.46	Swindon Factory **I**
21.6.46	Gloucester
22.8.47	Gloucester (wait)
9.9.47	Swindon Factory **I**
10.10.47	Cheltenham
11.6.48	Gloucester Shops **R**
29.6.48	Cheltenham
23.9.48	Swindon Factory **L**
14.10.48	Cheltenham
10.1.49	Worcester Shops **LC**
6.4.49	Cheltenham
7.1.50	Gloucester (wait)
20.1.50	Swindon Factory **HG**
14.2.50	Cheltenham
27.11.50	Swindon Factory
1.12.50	Cheltenham
3.51	Gloucester
2.1.52	Swindon Factory **HI**

EXPERIMENTS

5.2.52	Swindon Stock
31.3.52	Gloucester
7.52	Oxley
7.1.53	Worcester Shops **U**
27.1.53	Tyseley
15.5.53	Tyseley Shops **U**
22.5.53	Tyseley
7.4.54	Tyseley (wait)
19.4.54	Swindon Factory **HI**
17.5.54	Tyseley
28.5.56	Tyseley Shops **U**
11.6.56	Tyseley
31.10.56	Swindon Factory **HG**
30.11.56	Tyseley
20.1.58	Stafford Rd F'cty **LC**
11.2.58	Tyseley
18.6.59	Newton Abbot
30.9.59	In store
24.11.59	Swindon Factory **HG**
7.1.60	Machynlleth
25.9.62	Aberystwyth
5.10.62	Swindon Factory **HG**
21.11.62	Tyseley
23.1.65	**Withdrawn**
	Sold as scrap to Cashmore's of Great Bridge.

N.B: Loco was on LM Region book stock from 30.12.62 until withdrawal

Boilers and mileages:

First	6418	
30.4.42	..	(103,246)
20.5.44	6406	(168,960)
21.6.46	6420	(249,762)
10.10.47	..	(311,011)
14.2.50	6419	(406,346)
5.2.52	6411	(494,073)
17.5.54	6415	(576,176)
30.11.56	6416	(660,260)
7.1.60	6401	(738,135)
21.11.62	6406	(833,244)
28.12.63	..	(866,194)

Tenders:

First	2166
20.5.44	2097
21.6.46	2380 *
10.10.47	2368
14.10.48	2062
29.1.49	2161
26.3.49	1720
19.8.49	1646
14.2.50	2318
1.12.50	2002
5.2.52	2233
17.5.53	2150
17.5.54	1864
30.11.56	1921
7.1.60	1674
21.11.62	2082

* 2380 was 'intermediate pattern' (see text)

...............ooo...............

7819 HINTON MANOR
To stock: February 1939
Summary of shed (parent sheds only):

First	Carmarthen
7.43	Oswestry
9.46	Aberystwyth
10.46	Oswestry
12.62	*Shrewsbury*
14.3.63	*Aberystwyth*
1.65	*Shrewsbury*

Engine history:

13.2.39	Carmarthen
29.11.40	Swindon Factory **L**
6.1.41	Swindon Stock
11.1.41	Swindon
2.41	Carmarthen
8.7.41	Swindon Factory **I**
2.9.41	Swindon Stock
7.9.41	Carmarthen
12.4.43	Severn Tunnel Jct **R**
9.5.43	Carmarthen
7.43	Oswestry
8.43	Whitchurch LMS
31.8.43	Oswestry (wait)
17.10.43	Swindon Factory **G**

No.7819 HINTON MANOR takes on water at Welshpool before continuing with the down 'Cambrian Coast' on 26 August 1963. PHOTOGRAPH: ANDREW MUCKLEY

1.10.51	Oswestry Shops **U**	
10.10.51	Oswestry	
2.5.52	Swindon Factory **HG**	
3.6.52	Oswestry	
4.11.53	Oswestry (wait)	
9.11.53	Stafford Road F'cty **LC**	
11.12.53	Oswestry	
25.1.55	Swindon Factory **HG**	
21.2.55	Oswestry	
18.3.57	Stafford Road F'cty **HI**	
18.4.57	Oswestry	
26.11.57	Oswestry Shops **U**	
10.12.57	Oswestry	
1.10.58	Oswestry Shops **U**	
18.10.58	Oswestry	
29.12.58	Oswestry (wait)	
2.1.60	Swindon Factory **HG**	
9.2.60	Oswestry	
25.5.61	Worcester Shops **LC**	
16.6.61	Oswestry	
12.62	*Shrewsbury*	
18.1.63	Swindon Factory **HG**	
14.3.63	*Aberystwyth*	
1.65	*Shrewsbury*	
6.11.65	**Withdrawn**	
	Sold as scrap to Woodhams, but later purchased by Severn Valley Ry	
1.73	Arrived at Bridgnorth	
9.77	Returned to steam	

N.B: Loco was LM Region book stock from 30.12.62 until withdrawal

The usual Canton cleanliness somewhat dimmed, No.7820 DINMORE MANOR on 5 March 1961. PHOTOGRAPH: JOHN HODGE

						Boilers and mileages:		
24.11.43	Swindon Stock	8.12.45	Oswestry (wait)	4.47	Oswestry	First	6419	
26.11.43	Oswestry	29.12.45	Swindon Factory **I**	5.47	Whitchurch LMS	2.9.41	..	(98,091)
5.44	Whitchurch LMS	28.1.46	Oswestry	8.47	Oswestry	24.11.43	6414	(177,279)
6.44	Oswestry	6.46	Whitchurch LMS	9.47	Whitchurch LMS	28.1.46	6408	(263,939)
3.45	Whitchurch LMS	7.46	Oswestry	15.10.47	Oswestry (wait)	28.11.47	..	(329,906)
4.45	Oswestry	9.46	Aberystwyth	29.10.47	Swindon Factory **I**	8.2.50	6413	(412,476)
2.5.45	Oswestry **R**	10.46	Whitchurch LMS	12.47	Whitchurch LMS	3.6.52	6421	(508,816)
17.5.45	Oswestry	11.46	Oswestry	1.48	Oswestry	21.2.55	6419	(612,639)
23.8.45	Oswestry Shops **L**	12.46	Whitchurch LMS	30.5.49	Oswestry Shops **LC**	18.4.57	..	(691,000)
24.8.45	Oswestry	1.47	Oswestry	8.6.49	Oswestry	9.2.60	6432	(779,026)
26.9.45	Oswestry **R**	2.47	Moat Lane	9.1.50	Swindon Factory **HG**	14.3.63	6425	(897,944)
24.10.45	Oswestry	3.47	Whitchurch LMS	8.2.50	Oswestry			

Waiting to depart from Birmingham (Snow Hill) on 16 August 1958, No.7821 DITCHEAT MANOR heads the 11am for Pwllheli. A nice atmospheric picture, but presumably the photographer - full of youthful enthusiasm in those days - overlooked the dangers of 'carriage window' shots. PHOTOGRAPH: BRIAN MORRISON

28.12.63	..	(925,050)

Tenders:

First	1871
2.9.41	1762
24.11.43	1844
28.4.47	1683
8.6.49	2074
3.6.52	1793
9.10.54	2363
21.2.55	1794
20.4.57	1970
9.2.60	1921
11.61	2226
14.3.63	2073

..............ooo..............

7820 DINMORE MANOR
To stock: 20 November 1950
Summary of sheds:

First	Oswestry
8.52	Aberystwyth
10.52	Oswestry
12.53	Chester
12.54	Laira
22.9.59	Truro
16.6.60	St.Blazey
16.9.60	Canton
7.9.62	Cardiff East Dock
29.4.63	Shrewsbury
10.64	*Oxley*
9.65	*Shrewsbury*

Engine history:

11.50	Oswestry
8.52	Aberystwyth
10.52	Oswestry
18.3.53	Oswestry (wait)
23.3.53	Stafford Road F'cty **HI**
1.5.53	Oswestry
12.53	Chester
4.9.54	Chester Shops **U**
18.9.54	Chester
12.54	Laira
9.3.55	Laira Shops **U**
25.3.55	Laira
18.10.55	Swindon Factory **HG**
17.11.55	Laira
5.5.58	Laira (wait)
12.5.58	Swindon Factory **HI**
27.6.58	Laira
22.9.59	Truro
16.6.60	St.Blazey
16.9.60	Canton
3.1.61	Swindon Factory **HG**
14.2.61	Canton
9.2.62	Laira Shops **U** (failed?)
11.3.62	Canton
10.6.62	Westbury Shops **U** (failed?)
18.7.62	Canton
7.9.62	Cardiff East Dock
29.4.63	Shrewsbury
7.11.63	Swindon Factory **HG**
13.1.64	Shrewsbury
10.64	*Oxley*
9.65	*Shrewsbury*
6.11.65	**Withdrawn**
	Sold as scrap to Woodhams, of Barry, but later purchased by Gwili Railway
9.79	Arrived at Gwili Railway
3.85	Moved to West Somerset Rlwy for restoration

N.B: Loco was LM Region book stock from 19.5.63 until withdrawal

Boilers and mileages:

First	6422	
1.5.53	..	(102,893)

17.11.55	6413	(192,135)
27.6.58	..	(266,409)
14.2.61	6421	(343,946)
13.1.64	6417	(421,268)

Tenders:

First	1750
23.2.57	1856
16.5.53	1979
22.5.54	1696
28.8.54	1784
10.8.57	1866
27.6.58	1761

..............ooo..............

7821 DITCHEAT MANOR
To stock: 27 November 1950
Summary of sheds:

First	Oswestry
11.53	Shrewsbury
12.53	Tyseley
18.6.59	Newton Abbot
1.9.59	Shrewsbury
10.61	Croes Newydd
3.63	Aberystwyth
11.64	*Oxley*
10.65	*Shrewsbury*

Engine history:

11.50	Oswestry
19.2.53	Stafford Road F'cty **HI**
26.3.53	Oswestry
11.53	Shrewsbury
12.53	Tyseley
22.10.54	Southall Shops **U** (failed?)
5.11.54	Tyseley
14.2.55	Southall Shops **U** (failed?)
28.2.55	Tyseley
18.6.55	Swindon Factory **HG**
8.8.55	Tyseley
16.8.57	Tyseley Shops **R**
30.8.57	Tyseley

30.10.57	Tyseley (wait)
7.11.57	Swindon Factory **HI**
17.12.57	Tyseley
18.6.59	Newton Abbot
1.9.59	Shrewsbury
5.11.59	Shrewsbury (wait)
18.11.59	Swindon Factory **HG**
7.1.60	Shrewsbury
10.61	Croes Newydd
15.10.62	Croes Newydd (wait)
22.10.62	Swindon Factory **HI**
8.1.63	Croes Newydd
3.63	Aberystwyth
10.64	*Oxley*
10.65	*Shrewsbury*
6.11.65	**Withdrawn**
	Sold as scrap to Woodham Bros Re-sold to Gloucestershire & Warwickshire Ry
6.81	Arrived at Toddington
6.89	Moved to Llangollen for restoration

N.B: Loco was LM Region book stock from 30.12.62 until withdrawal

Boilers and mileages:

First	6423	
26.3.53	..	(97,466)
8.8.55	6405	(173,827)
17.12.57	..	(247,378)
7.1.60	6403	(306,545)
8.1.63	6401	(403,483)
28.12.63	..	(434,726)

Tenders:

First	1784
21.8.54	2383 *
17.12.57	1749
7.1.60	1981
1.63	2056

* 2383 was 'intermediate pattern' (see text)

..............ooo..............

7822 FOXCOTE MANOR
To stock: 1 December 1950
Summary of sheds:

First	Oswestry
4.54	Chester
26.8.58	Oswestry
28.12.63	*Machynlleth*
1.65	*Shrewsbury*

Engine history:

12.50	Oswestry
24.4.53	Oswestry (wait)
4.5.53	Stafford Road F'cty **HI**
24.6.53	Oswestry
4.54	Chester
18.10.55	Chester (wait)
24.10.55	Swindon Factory **HG**
12.12.55	Chester
7.8.57	Chester Shops **U**
20.8.57	Chester
2.9.57	Chester Shops **U**
10.9.57	Chester
5.10.57	Swindon Factory **HI**
13.12.57	Chester
2.5.58	Stafford Road F'cty **U**
12.5.58	Chester
26.8.58	Oswestry
18.8.59	Oswestry **U**
3.9.59	Oswestry
6.5.60	Oswestry (wait)
21.5.60	Swindon Factory **HG**
1.7.60	Oswestry
29.1.63	Swindon Factory **HI** (start)
21.3.63	Oswestry
15.4.63	Oswestry (wait)
29.4.63	Swindon Factory **HI** (finish)
2.7.63	Oswestry
28.12.63	*Machynlleth*
1.65	*Shrewsbury*
11.65	**Withdrawn**

At an unspecified date in the late 1950s - when station nameboards were still truly informative - No.7822 FOXCOTE MANOR pulls into Ellesmere station, on the old Cambrian line between Oswestry and Whitchurch. PHOTOGRAPH: T. MIDDLEMASS/PAUL CHANCELLOR COLLECTION

Having returned to the South-west after its brief period at Neath, No.7823 HOOK NORTON MANOR stands at Laira shed. The date is 15 July 1956. PHOTOGRAPH: R.C. RILEY

12.4.56	Truro
6.56	Neath
7.56	Truro
10.9.58	Truro Shops **U**
26.9.58	Truro
14.10.58	Caerphilly Shops **HI**
20.11.58	Truro
29.11.58	Truro (in store)
3.4.59	Truro
16.4.59	Aberystwyth
6.11.60	Shrewsbury Shops **U**
15.12.61	Swindon Factory **HG**
15.2.62	Aberystwyth
12.11.62	Tyseley
4.6.63	Tyseley Shops **U**
20.6.63	Tyseley
7.64	**Withdrawn**
14.9.64	Sold as scrap to J.Cashmore of Great Bridge

N.B: Loco was LM Region stock from 30.12.62 until withdrawal

Boilers and mileages:
First	6425	
26.6.53	..	(99,812)
12.4.56	6426	(194,737)
20.11.58	..	(276,844)
15.2.62	6410	(365,656)
28.12.63	..	(422,360)

Tenders:
First	1838
26.6.53	1933
12.4.56	1656
13.8.60	1699
15.2.62	1921
25.1.64	1792

...............ooo...............

7824 IFORD MANOR
To stock: 12 December 1950
Summary of sheds (parent sheds only):
| First | Gloucester * |
| 22.8.52 | Laira |

	Sold as scrap to Woodham Bros.			26.8.51	Croes Newydd
	Re-sold to Foxcote Manor Society		First	Chester	28.7.52	Tyseley Shops **U**
1.75	Arrived at Oswestry for restoration	26.8.51	Croes Newydd	21.8.52	Croes Newydd
		12.55	St.Blazey	1.5.53	Croes Newydd (wait)
		1.56	Truro	8.5.53	Swindon Factory **HI**
11.85	To Llangollen for completion of restoration	6.56	Neath	26.6.53	Croes Newydd
		7.56	Truro	16.3.55	Croes Newydd Shops **U**
4.88	Commenced work on Llangollen Ry	16.4.59	Aberystwyth	27.3.55	Croes Newydd
		12.11.62	Tyseley	30.3.55	Tyseley Shops **U**
				21.4.55	Croes Newydd

N.B: Loco was LM Region book stock from 23.2.58 to 6.9.59 and from 30.12.62 until withdrawal

Engine history:
12.50	Chester	12.55	St.Blazey
10.8.51	Chester Shops **U**	1.56	Truro
		3.3.56	Swindon Factory **HG**

Boilers and mileages:
First	6424	
24.6.53	..	(107,415)
12.12.55	6408	(195,767)
13.11.57	6400	(261,128)
1.7.60	6407	(356,618)
21.3.63	6419	(462,621)
28.12.63	..	(482,693)

Tenders:
First	2022
12.12.55	2010
13.11.57	2146
1.11.58	1879
5.9.59	2072
1.7.60	2079
?.62	2073
21.3.63	2347
18.5.63	2368
2.7.63	1560 *
7.63	2347

N.B: Also tenders - 2228 (when in works 20.10.55 to 12.12.55) 2382 * (when in works 21.5.60 to 1.7.60) * 1560 and 2382 - Churchward 4,000 gallon tender (see text)

............ooo............

7823 HOOK NORTON MANOR
To stock: 6 December 1950
Summary of sheds:

The *other* Swindon station - Swindon Town - was ignored by most photographers, 9 June 1951, and lined black No.7824 IFORD MANOR takes on water prior to continuing with a Cheltenham-Southampton train. PHOTOGRAPH: R.C. RILEY

**Lined black No.7825 LECHLADE MANOR, with a modest loading, heads north across Barmouth Bridge on 15 May 1952.
PHOTOGRAPH: P.J. LYNCH**

7.54	Newton Abbot
1.55	Laira
10.55	Shrewsbury
30.11.56	Penzance
7.57	Carmarthen
18.6.59	Newton Abbot
9.59	Tyseley
8.2.61	Stourbridge
8.62	Oxley

* Initial allocation to sub-shed (see text)

Engine history:

12.50	Cheltenham
30.7.52	Laira Shops **U**
22.8.52	Laira
17.9.52	Laira Shops **U**
7.10.52	Laira
24.6.53	Swindon Factory **HG**
11.8.53	Laira
7.54	Newton Abbot
1.55	Laira
15.4.55	Laira Shops **U**
10.5.55	Laira
10.55	Shrewsbury
15.11.56	Shrewsbury Shops **U**
30.11.56	Penzance
7.57	Carmarthen
24.3.58	Swindon Factory **HG**
1.5.58	Carmarthen
18.6.59	Newton Abbot
9.59	Tyseley
23.12.60	Swindon Factory **HI**
8.2.61	Stourbridge
15.3.62	Stourbridge (wait)
21.3.62	Stourbridge Shops **U**
14.4.62	Stourbridge
8.62	Oxley
24.9.62	Oxley (wait)
22.11.62	Stafford Road F'cty **HC**
4.1.63	Stafford Road Stock
14.1.63	Oxley
12.9.63	Stourbridge Shops **U**
7.10.63	Oxley
11.64	**Withdrawn**

Sold as scrap to
J.Cashmore
of Great Bridge
N.B: Loco was LM Region book stock
from 30.12.62 until withdrawal

Boilers and mileages:

First	6426	
11.8.53	6410	(104,427)
23.2.56	..	(183,338)
1.5.58	6412	(257,176)
8.2.61	6417	(345,217)
4.1.63	6427	(378,214)
28.12.63	..	(430,677)

Tenders:

First	2378 *
11.8.53	2001
18.6.55	1698
25.2.56	2220
1.5.58	2380 *
8.2.61	2373

* 2378 and 2380 were 'intermediate
pattern' (see text)......

............ooo............

7825 LECHLADE MANOR
To stock: 15 December 1950
Summary of sheds (parent sheds only):

First	Croes Newydd
2.53	Carmarthen
10.61	Neyland *
12.63	Reading

* Initial allocation to sub-shed (see text)

Engine history:

12.50	Croes Newydd
29.11.51	Tyseley Shops **U**
15.12.51	Croes Newydd
18.11.52	Tyseley Shops **U**
19.12.52	Croes Newydd
2.53	Carmarthen

30.6.53	Stafford Road F'cty **HI**
26.8.53	Carmarthen
12.2.55	Aberystwyth Shops **U**
24.3.55	Carmarthen
2.4.56	Swindon Factory **HG**
30.4.56	Carmarthen
18.9.58	Swindon Factory **HI**
23.10.58	Carmarthen
22.2.60	Carmarthen Shops **U**
7.3.60	Carmarthen
10.1.61	Carmarthen Shops **U**
24.1.61	Carmarthen
31.7.61	Carmarthen (wait)
10.8.61	Swindon Factory **HI**
29.9.61	Carmarthen
24.10.61	Whitland
18.9.62	Carmarthen Shops **U**
9.10.62	Whitland
1.63	Neyland
9.7.63	Carmarthen Shops **U**
25.7.63	Neyland
9.9.63	In store (Llanelly ??)
12.63	Reading
11.5.64	**Withdrawn**
18.8.64	Sold as scrap to Birds of Swansea; cut up at Risca

Boilers and mileages:

First	6427	
26.8.53	..	(91,771)
30.4.56	6428	(171,435)
23.10.58	6402	(267,378)
29.9.61	6409	(365,709)
28.12.63	..	(425,024)

Tenders:

First	1849
30.4.56	2317
23.10.58	1950
29.9.61	2340
6.64	1831

...............ooo...............

7826 LONGWORTH MANOR
To stock: 21 December 1950

Summary of sheds:

First	Croes Newydd
2.53	Carmarthen
17.1.64	Llanelly
2.65	*Cardiff East Dock*

Engine history:

21.12.50	Croes Newydd
1.51	Swindon Factory **?**
1.51	Croes Newydd
7.8.51	Croes Newydd Shops **U**
13.8.51	Croes Newydd
19.11.51	Tyseley Shops **U**
13.12.51	Croes Newydd
2.53	Carmarthen
23.2.53	Carmarthen Shops **U**
12.3.53	Carmarthen
22.5.53	Swindon Factory **HI**
2.7.53	Carmarthen
31.12.55	Swindon Factory **HG**
30.1.56	Carmarthen
25.9.58	Swindon Factory **HG**
12.11.58	Carmarthen
3.6.61	Swindon Factory **HG**
2.8.61	Carmarthen
3.11.63	Swindon Factory **HG**
17.1.64	Llanelly
2.65	*Cardiff East Dock*
4.65	**Withdrawn**

Sold as scrap to Birds of
Swansea; cut up at Bynea

Boilers and mileages:

First	6428	
2.7.53	..	(96,965)
30.1.56	6422	(179,960)
12.11.58	6409	(281,215)
2.8.61	6420	(364,958)
17.1.64	6414	(436,894)

Tenders:

First	1933
2.7.53	2135
2.8.61	2316
17.1.64	1638

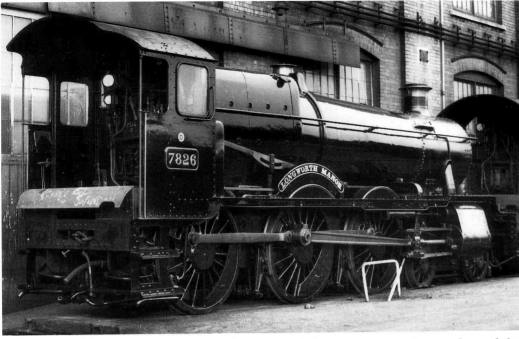

No.7826 LONGWORTH MANOR was, perhaps, one of the more camera-shy members of the class. This picture was taken outside Swindon Works in January 1956, shortly after the engine had been repainted in unlined black. PHOTOGRAPH: BRYAN WILSON COLLECTION

31.10.62	6430	(419,549)
28.12.63	..	(468,993)

Tenders:

First	2176
2.7.53	1715
1.5.54	2383 *
16.8.55	1715
29.5.57	1781
23.9.59	1973
5.62	2028
31.10.62	1901

* 1781 was 'intermediate pattern' (see text)

...............ooo..............

7828 ODNEY MANOR
To stock: 28 December 1950
Summary of sheds:

First	Neath
11.52	Shrewsbury
5.61	Croes Newydd
3.63	Aberystwyth
1.65	*Shrewsbury*

Engine history:

12.50	Swindon (in store)
18.2.51	Swindon Stock
22.2.51	Neath
23.1.52	Pontypool Road Shps **U**
14.2.52	Neath
11.52	Shrewsbury
12.11.53	Stafford Road F'cty **HI**
18.12.53	Shrewsbury
23.8.54	Shrewsbury Shops **U**
8.9.54	Shrewsbury
2.6.56	Swindon Factory **HG**
30.7.56	Shrewsbury
21.12.56	Shrewsbury (wait)
28.12.56	Shrewsbury Shops **U**
8.1.57	Shrewsbury
4.10.57	Stafford Road F'cty **U**
10.10.57	Shrewsbury
18.1.58	Shrewsbury Shops **U**
29.1.58	Shrewsbury
17.6.59	Shrewsbury (wait)
5.8.59	Swindon Factory **HI**

...............ooo..............

7827 LYDHAM MANOR
To stock: 22 December 1950
Summary of sheds:

First	Chester
28.8.58	Oswestry
28.12.63	*Machynlleth*
1.65	*Shrewsbury*

Engine history:

12.50	Chester
28.11.52	Chester (wait)
11.12.52	Swindon Factory **HG**
20.1.53	Chester
16.6.53	Chester Shops **U**
2.7.53	Chester
7.4.54	Chester Shops **U**
1.5.54	Chester
13.7.55	Swindon Factory **HI**
18.8.55	Chester
15.4.57	Chester (wait)
24.4.57	Swindon Factory **HG**
29.5.57	Chester
23.8.58	Oswestry Shops **LC**
28.8.58	Oswestry
24.1.59	Oswestry Shops **U**
10.2.59	Oswestry
27.2.59	Oswestry Shops **LC**
6.3.59	Oswestry
8.7.59	Oswestry (wait)
11.8.59	Swindon Factory **HI**
23.9.59	Oswestry
5.3.60	Oswestry (wait)
14.3.60	Stafford Road F'cty **HI**
11.4.60	Oswestry
18.6.60	Shrewsbury Shops **U**
7.7.60	Oswestry
1.1.62	Stafford Road **U**
24.1.62	Oswestry
28.7.62	Oswestry (wait)
23.8.62	Swindon Factory **HG**
31.10.62	Oswestry
28.12.63	*Machynlleth*

1.65	*Shrewsbury*	
2.10.65	**Withdrawn**	
	Sold as scrap to	
	Woodhams of Barry	
6.70	To Newton Abbot for	
	restoration	
30.3.73	To Torbay Steam	
	Railway	

N.B: Loco was LM Region book stock

from 23.2.58 to 6.9.59 and from 31.12.62 until withdrawal

Boilers and mileages:

First	6429	
20.1.53	6413	(75,112)
16.8.55	6417	(170,480)
29.5.57	6415	(225,591)
23.9.59	6425	(311,717)

The climb to Talerddig Summit, on the Cambrian main line between Shrewsbury and Aberystwyth, required hard work on the part of the engine. Here, even a modest three-coach loading is clearly not a doddle for No.7827 LYDHAM MANOR. The date is 3 June 1964. PHOTOGRAPH: DEREK CROSS

17.9.59	Shrewsbury
3.5.60	Shrewsbury Shops **U**
18.5.60	Shrewsbury
28.8.60	Shrewsbury Shops **U**
12.9.60	Shrewsbury
24.12.60	Shrewsbury (wait)
6.2.61	Stafford Road F'cty **LC**
20.4.61	Shrewsbury
5.61	Croes Newydd
16.12.61	Croes Newydd Shops **U**
7.1.62	Croes Newydd
13.6.62	Croes Newydd (wait)
18.7.62	Swindon Factory **HG**
28.9.62	Croes Newydd
3.63	Aberystwyth
1.65	*Shrewsbury*
2.10.65	**Withdrawn**
	Sold as scrap to Woodhams
6.81	Re-sold to Glos & Warwickshire Ry and taken to Toddington for restoration
5.88	Returned to steam on Gwili Ry

N.B: Loco was LM Region book stock from 30.12.62 until withdrawal

Boilers and mileages:

First	6430	
18.12.53	..	(92,364)
30.7.56	6425	(173,686)
17.9.59	6427	(271,051)
28.9.62	6416	(355,645)
28.12.63	..	(402,613)

Tenders:

First	2379 *
7.53	1992
24.9.55	2333
30.7.56	2382 *
12.7.58	2128
14.7.62	1723
28.9.62	1864

* 2379 and 2382 were 'intermediate pattern' (see text)

...............ooo...............

7829 RAMSBURY MANOR
To stock: 29 December 1950
Summary of sheds:

First	Neath
11.52	Shrewsbury
3.53	Carmarthen
4.64	Llanelly
5.64	Reading
8.64	Swindon
11.64	Didcot
7.65	*Gloucester*

Engine history:

12.50	Swindon (in store)
18.2.51	Swindon Stock
22.2.51	Neath
11.52	Shrewsbury
15.1.53	Shrewsbury Shops **U**
6.2.53	Shrewsbury
3.53	Carmarthen
6.10.53	Swindon Factory **HI**
10.11.53	Carmarthen
27.6.56	Carmarthen (wait)
18.10.56	Swindon Factory **HG**
19.11.56	Carmarthen
15.6.59	Carmarthen (wait)
24.6.59	Swindon Factory **HG**
16.9.59	Carmarthen
23.1.61	Carmarthen Shops **U**
9.2.61	Carmarthen
5.2.62	Carmarthen (wait)
22.3.62	Swindon Factory **HG**
31.5.62	Carmarthen
4.64	Llanelly
5.64	Reading

Shrewsbury station on 11 June 1965. The engine is No.7828 (minus its ODNEY MANOR nameplates) with the up 'Cambrian Coast'. PHOTOGRAPH: DEREK CROSS

8.64	Swindon
11.64	Didcot
7.65	*Gloucester*
31.12.65	**Withdrawn**
	Sold as scrap to J.Cashmore of Newport

Boilers and mileages:

First	6431	
10.11.53	..	(83,014)
19.11.56	6427	(176,418)
16.9.59	6404	(274,806)
21.5.62	6431	(352,886)
28.12.63	..	(394,695)

Tenders:

29.12.50	1827
10.11.53	1921
19.11.56	1973
16.9.59	1781
5.61	2027
31.5.62	1831
6.64	2340

Carmarthen's No.7829 RAMSBURY MANOR enters Haverfordwest with 12.5pm Milford Haven-Paddington on 24 August 1962. PHOTOGRAPH: E. THOMAS

PETO'S REGISTER - Volume One:
The Kings Addenda and Corrigenda

Volume One of this series, which dealt with the Kings, took a considerable time to research and prepare, and the final text was subjected to several checking stages. Unfortunately, though, a few errors slipped through and were not spotted until after the book had been published. For this, we apologise sincerely. On a more positive note, since the publication of that book we have had considerable feedback from readers and, as a result, not only have certain 'grey areas' been clarified, but some additional information has also come to light. We are very grateful to all those who have shared their knowledge with us.

Happily, as *Peto's Register* is an ongoing series it is possible to include the necessary corrections and additional information in subsequent volumes. We therefore take this opportunity of including the relevant details for Volume One (The Kings).

N.B: *The sources of the following corrections and additions are as follows: Mr.Ashley Butlin, Mr.Eric Bruton, Mr.Paul Chancellor, Mr.John Hodge, Mr.Michael Hale, Mr.Gerry Parkins, Mr.R.C.Riley, Mr.Eric Youldon. Sincere thanks to you all.*

P.4, photo caption: Add: "Note the lever on the left-hand side of the bell - it was dispensed with circa 1935."

It has also been suggested that the lever was probably removed during one of the engine's three visits to Swindon Works in 1935 - probably at the same time as the lowering of the top lamp iron.

P.5, photo caption: Delete the second sentence which refers to the lever on the bell. Add: "It can be seen that the centre lamp iron, being displaced from its normal position by the bell, is now on the buffer beam."

P.6, col.3, line 3: After "…..6ft 6in" insert: "To try this out, between December 1926 and March 1928 a Castle class engine - believed to be No.5001 - had been fitted with 6ft 6in coupled wheels."

P.9, photo caption: Add "The engine has an experimental speedometer, the connection for which can be seen in the conventional position near the centre of the rear wheel."

P.11, col.2, para.2, line 7: Delete "96 tons" and substitute "81 tons 10cwt".

P.11, col.3, line 5: Delete "…an 89-ton load" and substitute "…an 81.5-ton load…"

P.15, top photo caption: The boxes on the running plate contained valve spindles, presumably for a loco requiring repair at Old Oak shed. The spindles had probably been carried in the luggage van of an ordinary train from Swindon to Paddington, and carried from Paddington station to Old Oak shed on the running plate of No.6009. This was a common method of transporting small items between a station and a running shed.

P.16, top photo caption: Add: "A little way below the cabside numberplate is the prefix letter 'W' - No.6000 was one of only four Kings to carry the early post-Nationalisation prefix. In the case of No.6000, the prefix letter could not be sited above the numberplate as that space was occupied by the B&O medallions, nor could the prefix be sited immediately below the numberplate as that space was occupied by the 'Double Red' route availability discs."

P.17, col.1, para.2: A suggestion we have received is that the slot in the front of the bogie was to help cool the bearings of the leading bogie axle. We emphasise that no information was provided to substantiate or to explain that suggestion.

What now for *Peto's Register*? A last, stirring sight of a King, a Wolverhampton engine on a stopover at Ranelagh Bridge, outside Paddington. A reminder that humbler fare - the myriad GWR tanks - await too, their place in the series. What to put in Volume 3? - feel free to write with suggestions....

P.17, col.3, 'Springing': The penultimate line of the paragraph should read: "Nos.6020-6029 were built *without* equalising beams."

P.17/18 - 'Inside Valve Casing': Second and third lines should read: "....most of the first twenty engines....".

P.18, bottom photo caption: Loco is No.6021 KING RICHARD II, not No.6023 as stated.

P.19, col.3, 'Speedometers': With reference to the last paragraph - there *is* photographic evidence that No.6028 (at least) was fitted with an experimental speedometer. See page 9.

P.20, lower photo caption: Second line - ".....valve covers on most of Nos.6000-6019....".

P.22, top photo: Incorrect photo used. Caption refers to the 'correct' one, not the one in the book.

P.24, photo captions: Our original wording could possibly be taken to imply that a locomotive's superheater can be seen externally. At the risk of stating the obvious, what can be seen externally is actually the casing.

P.26, lower photo caption: Add: "Note the narrow window on this side of the cab - the window on the other side was standard, as can be seen in the picture above."

P.29, col.3, para.1, last sentence: Mr.Gerry Parkins, a former footplateman who worked with the Kings, disputes that a single chimney King would have had to be steamed very hard to reach 100mph. Mr.Parkins states that 100mph was obtained many times with a single chimney King on downhill roads, particularly on the section between Savernake and Crookwood Signal Box (between Patney and Lavington) when a few minutes of lost time had to be regained. "I have personally seen the speedometer on 100mph after dipping down beyond Patney with a single chimney King", he writes.

P.30, photo caption: The date of the photograph has been confirmed as 18 November 1956.

P.35, col.3, last para, lines 3, 4, 5: It has been suggested to us that No.6014 was taken off the Cardiff train at Filton - i.e. it did not actually work through to Cardiff. Feasible, perhaps, as the Kings were not officially permitted into Cardiff at that time - this was principally because the bridge over the Rhymney River west St.Mellons was not up to strength. Nevertheless, the apparently under-strength bridge didn't prevent No.6007 working through to Canton shed in April 1943 (see page 40, para.2).

P.35, photo caption: Where else but Teignmouth? The answer is Dawlish!

P.36, upper photo caption: Loco name should read KING RICHARD II.

P.37, col.3, last para: With reference to the first sentence - it has been suggested that the 'Drawing Office Tests' undertaken by No.6005 in 1931 (see p.18,

last para) included a trip (or trips) via Reading West Curve, hence No.6018's use of the curve on 9 June 1937 might not have been the first time a King had used the curve.

P.39, col.2, line 4: Should read: "....before No.6028 derailed virtually alongside its path."

P.44, col.3, last para, lines 5/6: Should read ".....where such a practice was officially permitted at that time."

P.45, col.1, line 5: After "....Devon Banks", insert: "This engine change obviated a stop for changing at Plymouth, the train therefore running non-stop from Newton Abbot to Truro."

P.47, photo caption: Add: "Note the GWR's vintage dynamometer behind the engine."

P.48, photo caption: Add: "The cover of the left-hand (the far side, as we are looking) inside steam chest is incomplete."

P.48, col.2, para.2: Mr.Paul Chancellor, the author of 'Western Change' (RCTS 1995) has kindly provided a few additional details from his own researches..... on 11 and 18 August 1962, No.6026 worked excursion trains from Paddington to Weston-Super-Mare and return, a similar duty being undertaken by No.6000 on 1 September and by No.6018 on 8 September.

P.49, col.2, para.2, line 6: Delete sentence beginning "One year later...." and substitute: "A year or so later, Nos.6010 and 6024 were similarly transferred".

Further information has been supplied by Mr.John Hodge about Kings at Canton. He writes: "Four of the Kings allocated to Canton for mid-September arrived in advance of the 'official' transfer dates, Nos.6003/6004 apparently arriving double-heading the 1.55pm ex-Paddington on 9 September 1960. (This negates the unqualified statement elsewhere in the book that Kings worked double-headed only between Newton Abbot and Plymouth - *Ed*) It was one of the other pair, No.6023, which appears to have been the first to work from Canton; it arrived on ECS on 9 September (1960) and worked the 8am to Paddington on 10 September. No.6004 worked the 7.10am to Cardiff on 11 September, and on 15 September it failed at Bristol with a bogie defect - its duties that day were the 8.55am Cardiff-Shrewsbury and the 2.24pm Shrewsbury-Bristol. On 16 September - bogie problem presumably sorted - No.6004 worked to Paddington and returned with the 5.55pm. Two of the Kings allocated to Canton in mid-September 1960 didn't actually arrive until well after the 'official' transfer dates. No.6019 was at Swindon Works on 'transfer day' (19 September) and appears not to have arrived until 5 October, working the 12.45am newspaper train. No.6018 eventually turned up on 23 October, heading a VIP special." Mr.Hodge also remarks that No.6024, which was transferred to Can-

ton in 1961, was regarded by local crews as 'an old tub - not a patch on 6023'.

P.55, photo caption: Add: "This engine was the only member of the class to have twin inspection covers in the smokebox saddle - compare this picture with the 'single cover' No.6003 on page 47."

P.60, photo caption: Incorrect caption details. The engine is No.6015 KING RICHARD III and the train is the 10.20am ex-Plymouth - i.e. an *UP* working; the photograph was taken at 1.43pm on Sunday 22 July on the Westbury cut-off just past Fairwood troughs (note the wet roof on the leading carriage).

P.70, photo caption: Doubt has been cast about this being an ordinary 'Riviera' working. The grounds for doubt are that the train is on the relief line and that there are no roof label boards on the first two carriages.

P.73, photo caption: Add: "Another legacy of the engine's streamlined days was the stud on the centre oil box (above the inside steamchests) - this protruded through the apron and was used to carry the train reporting number. The reporting number was still occasionally carried in this position in 'post-streamlined' days."

P.89, photo caption: Add: "The engine's right hand steamchest cover is incomplete."

P.96 - col.2, section in italics: Delete: "The dates quoted above..." and substitute: "The dates quoted below...".

P.96, summary table: No.6009 - first BR blue livery - date should read 5/48.

Registers:

Explanatory notes - p.53: Although unlikely to be relevant to the Kings, we have been informed that locomotives under the jurisdiction of 'Swindon Pool' were occasionally returned temporarily to traffic.

6005: Cut up at Great Bridge, not Newport

6007: Withdrawal date should read 7.9.62 (alternatively quoted as 21.9.62).

6009: Cut up at Newport 5.63.

6010: Loco transferred to Canton 10.61, and remained allocated to Canton for the rest of its life. Subsequent references to Old Oak Common are therefore incorrect. This also affects the 'summary of sheds' for this loco on p.67.

6018: Tender change of 19.3.63 might not have been just for book-keeping purposes - the engine was still in working order at the time (see photo p.79).

6022: It seems that the entry showing a move to Newton Abbot on 27.9.48 might be an error. We have no irrefutable proof, but a number of secondary sources indicate that when the engine left Swindon Works on 27.9.48 it went back to Laira. If a correction is required, it would affect the 'summary of sheds' for this loco on p.82.